Romana Sălăgeanu
Regional Participation within European Multi-Level Governance

Romana Sălăgeanu

Regional Participation within European Multi-Level Governance
Saxony-Anhalt: Regional Parliament, Regional Government, Stakeholders

Budrich UniPress Ltd.
Opladen • Berlin • Toronto 2017

All rights reserved. No part of this publication may be reproduced, stored in or introduced into a retrieval system, or transmitted, in any form, or by any means (electronic, mechanical, photocopying, recording or otherwise) without the prior written permission of Barbara Budrich Publishers. Any person who does any unauthorized act in relation to this publication may be liable to criminal prosecution and civil claims for damages.
You must not circulate this book in any other binding or cover and you must impose this same condition on any acquirer.

This publication has been submitted as a PhD thesis at the Otto-von-Guericke University, Magdeburg and the Babeş-Bolyai University, Cluj-Napoca. The defence took place on the 29.09.2015.

A CIP catalogue record for this book is available from
Die Deutsche Bibliothek (The German Library)

© 2017   by Budrich UniPress Ltd. Opladen, Berlin & Toronto
www.budrich-unipress.eu
 ISBN   978-3-86388-741-4
 eISBN   978-3-86388-302-7

Das Werk einschließlich aller seiner Teile ist urheberrechtlich geschützt. Jede Verwertung außerhalb der engen Grenzen des Urheberrechtsgesetzes ist ohne Zustimmung des Verlages unzulässig und strafbar. Das gilt insbesondere für Vervielfältigungen, Übersetzungen, Mikroverfilmungen und die Einspeicherung und Verarbeitung in elektronischen Systemen.
Die Deutsche Bibliothek – CIP-Einheitsaufnahme
Ein Titeldatensatz für die Publikation ist bei Der Deutschen Bibliothek erhältlich.

Budrich UniPress Ltd.
Stauffenbergstr. 7. D-51379 Leverkusen Opladen, Germany

86 Delma Drive. Toronto, ON M8W 4P6 Canada
www.budrich-unipress.eu

Jacket illustration by Bettina Lehfeldt, Kleinmachnow – www.lehfeldtgraphic.de
Editing: Alison Romer, Lancaster, UK
Technical Editing: Anja Borkam, Jena – kontakt@lektorat-borkam.de
Printed in Europe on acid-free paper by Books on Demand GmbH, Norderstedt, Germany

Acknowledgements

I am thankful to my scientific tutors Prof. Dr. Wolfgang Renzsch and Ass. iur. Maître en Droit Karen Schlüter, from the Otto-von-Guericke University, Magdeburg. They were a great source of inspiration and they motivated me to constantly improve my research. I am deeply grateful for their thoroughness and useful guidance during the last decade.

I am grateful to the actors of Saxony-Anhalt and the staff of the representation of Saxony-Anhalt to the European Union for their insightful contribution to my research and to my professional development. I appreciate the financial assistance I was awarded from the German Academic Exchange Service (DAAD) and the European Social Fund for completing my research.

Finally, I wish to thank my family for the significant support and encouragement during all the research stages, without which I would not have completed this book.

Table of contents

List of abbreviations 11

Abstract 13

1 Introduction 15
1.1 Research scope 17
1.2 Structure of the book 18

2 Theoretical framework for regional participation within European Multi-Level Governance 21
2.1 Region 21
2.2 Regionalism 22
2.3 Regionalisation 24
2.4 Subnational mobilisation 26
2.5 Regional participation 28
2.6 European Multi-Level Governance from theoretical perspective 30
2.7 The Multi-Level Governance Type I and Type II 33
2.8 European Multi-Level Governance from the European institutional perspective 34
2.9 European Multi-Level Governance implementation at European level and within Member States 38
2.10 Regional participation within European Multi-Level Governance – bottom-up analysis model 41
    2.10.1 The region and European Multi-Level Governance 41
    2.10.2 Research questions 43
    2.10.3 Methodology 44

3 The Europeanisation of Saxony-Anhalt 49
3.1 Introductory history of Saxony-Anhalt 49
3.2 The industrialisation 51
3.3 The establishment of Saxony-Anhalt after 1945 54
3.4 The re-establishment of Saxony-Anhalt 1989-90 56

4 Saxony-Anhalt in the European Union – the bottom-up dimension 61
4.1 Instrastate institutional changes after 1989 62
4.2 The *Landtag* of Saxony-Anhalt 66
4.3 The *Landesregierung* of Saxony-Anhalt 69
4.4 Stakeholders in Saxony-Anhalt 73

5 Political guidelines of Saxony-Anhalt's participation within European Multi-Level Governance 77
5.1 The 4th legislative period: 2002-2006 79
    5.1.1 Social and political background of the election 79
    5.1.2 Political goals and resources of Saxony-Anhalt 80
    5.1.3 Participation processes of Saxony-Anhalt within EMLG 83
    5.1.4 The actors' functions and the policy content connection 86
5.2 The 5th legislative period: 2006-2011 88
    5.2.1 Social and political background of the election 88
    5.2.2 Political goals and resources of Saxony-Anhalt 89
    5.2.3 Participation processes of Saxony-Anhalt within EMLG 93
    5.2.4 The actors' functions and the policy content connection 97
5.3 The 6th legislative period: 2011-2016 98
    5.3.1 Social and political background of the election 98
    5.3.2 Political goals and resources of Saxony-Anhalt 99
    5.3.3 Participation processes of Saxony-Anhalt within EMLG 103
    5.3.4 The actors' functions and the policy content connection 104

6 Regional participation of Saxony-Anhalt within European Multi-Level Governance: the complement of the European Regional Policy 109
6.1 The European Regional Policy 110
6.2 Political goals of Saxony-Anhalt regarding the European Regional Policy 114
6.3 Resources of Saxony-Anhalt and their functions regarding the European Regional Policy 115
6.4 The participation processes of Saxony-Anhalt regarding the European Regional Policy 117

6.5 Findings 120

7 Regional participation of Saxony-Anhalt within European Multi-Level Governance: the complement of the European Chemicals Policy 123

7.1 European dimension of the chemicals industry 123

7.2 The chemicals industry in Saxony-Anhalt and its role for the participation within European Multi-Level Governance 127

7.3 The European Chemical Regions Network 130

7.4 The European Chemical Regions Network and its functions within EMLG.. 137

7.5 The High Level Group for the Competitiveness of the European Chemicals Industry 141

7.6 Spill-over of the European Chemical Regions Network within EMLG: ChemLog and ChemClust 147

7.7 Findings 152

8 The regional participation pattern of Saxony-Anhalt within European Multi-Level Governance 157

9 Conclusions 167

10 Bibliography 173

Appendix 1: Extracts from the European Commission's White Paper on European Governance (2001)... 199

Appendix 2: Extracts from the European Parliament's Resolution on governance and partnership at a national, regional and project basis in the field of regional policy (2008) 203

Appendix 3: Extracts from the Committee of the Regions' White Paper on Multilevel Governance (2009)................................. 205

Appendix 4: Extracts from the Committee of the Regions' Scoreboard Table with MLG best-practices and recommendations (2013) 209

Appendix 5: Extracts from the Europe 2020 Strategy (2010) 211

Appendix 6: Article 5 Common Provisions Regulation (2013) 215

Appendix 7: Key recommendations for regional authorities in chemical regions (2012) 217

Index 219

List of abbreviations

CDU: *Christlich Demokratische Union Deutschlands*/ Christian Democratic Union of Germany
CEFIC: The European Chemical Industry Council
CF: Cohesion Fund
ChemLog: Chemical Logistics Cooperation in Central and Eastern Europe
ChemClust: Chemical Cluster Development in European Regions
COM: European Commission
CoR: Committee of the Regions
Council: Council of the European Union (Council of Ministers)
DG: Directorate-General within the European Commission
EAFRD: European Agricultural Fund for Rural Development
ECRN: European Chemical Regions Network
EMLG: European Multi-Level Governance
EP: European Parliament
EMFF: European Maritime and Fisheries Fund
EMK: *Europaministerkonferenz* (Europe-ministers' conference)
EPP: European People's Party
ERDF: European Regional Development Fund
ESF: European Social Fund
ESI: European Structural and Investment Funds
EU: European Union
FDP: *Freie Demokratische Partei*/ Free Democratic Party
FDR: Federal Republic of Germany
GDR: German Democratic Republic
GG: *Grundgesetz*/ German Basic Law
HLG: High Level Group
KPD: *Kommunistische Partei Deutschlands*/ Communist Party of Germany
LRAs: Local and regional authorities
MEP: Member of the European Parliament
MFF: Multi-annual Financial Framework
MLG: Multi-Level Governance
MPK: *Ministerpräsidentenkonferenz* (minister-presidents' conference)
MS: Member States
NUTS: Nomenclature of Units for Territorial Statistics
OP: Operational Programme
PA: Partnership Agreement
SED: *Sozialistische Einheitspartei Deutschlands*/ Socialist Unity Party of Germany
SME: Small and Medium Enterprise

SPD: *Sozialdemokratische Partei Deutschlands*/ Social Democratic Party of Germany
TEN-T: Trans-European Transport Network
VCI: *Verband der Chemischen Industrie*/ The German Chemical Industry Association
WP: White Paper

Abstract

The book provides an account of the European Multi-Level Governance (EMLG) characteristics and of the regional participation within it, by describing the EMLG and by identifying the topics and categories of meaning for regional participation within it. It establishes the mechanisms responsible for regional participation, highlighting patterns that emerge from it. The book does not offer the entire EMLG picture with all the processes involved in it, but it offers a perspective of the regional dimension of this phenomenon.

The main research question is: Why does the regional participation of Saxony-Anhalt within EMLG occur? The purpose of the qualitative analysis is to explain the process of regional participation in EMLG, taking into account Saxony-Anhalt. The analysed data is based mainly on literature concerning the EMLG and the regional participation, but also on documents from the supranational, national and subnational levels.

Multi-Level Governance (MLG) was a highly debated topic within the European integration literature in the 1990s, with regard to the European Regional Policy. Initially, it was merely understood as an approach to the way the EU functions. Since then, it has been further developed and it is currently part of the institutional understanding of EU governance at European level.

The case study, Saxony-Anhalt, was chosen because it offers a model of regional participation within EMLG. This model can be followed by both Western and Eastern European regions within the EU; only if their actors understand what the EU governance comprises and only if they mobilise and engage actively within EU governance processes.

The purpose of this book is to provide a framework of regional participation that can be considered "best-practice". This study is valuable for actors from the new EU Member States, where regional participation can or still needs to be built up and strengthened. The empirical contribution of this research is relevant for the literature on subnational participation within EMLG, since research on Multi-Level Governance can focus more on Central and Eastern Europe.

1 Introduction

The complexity of the European Union functioning system is based on the initial economic integration, meant to improve the economies of its Member States (MS). Competencies have been transferred towards the European level, making the European apparatus grow, becoming a "cryptic monster" (Enzensberger 2011) for actors within the MS. European integration has increased influence-driven activities towards political mobilisation for participation in European policy-making processes. This mobilisation has touched on the subnational level of the MS. Regions have been looking for their access and active participation within the EU governance processes as well (Marks/Hooghe 2001: 126).

The *Governance* concept has been a major subject for research in the field of EU studies, focusing on the characteristics, levels of jurisdiction and the impact of European policy-making. This term brings together policy making activities (preparation, consultation, formulation, implementation, transposition, and compliance), actors and institutions situated at different levels of policy-making, administration and implementation: the European, the national, the subnational and the local (see Tömmel/Verdun 2009: 1-2). One of the 1990s favourite topics was the connection between regions and governance and the representation of interests within European Multi-Level Governance (Kohler-Koch/Rittberger 2009).

Governance draws attention to the systems of regulation and the interdependent interactions of private and public actors, change of administrative behaviour, and increased openness for collaboration with private actors. Governance is understood as a mix of institutionalised ways of coordination, its outcome being the adoption and implementation of collectively binding decisions (Mayntz/Scharpf 1995; Mayntz 2004). This mix implies both structures (institutions and constellations of actors) and processes. From this perspective, the scope of this book is narrowed to the subnational level and looks into the structures and processes of regional participation within European Multi-Level Governance.

The common market's emergence within the EU triggered transfers of competencies and treaty changes (e.g. SEA; Maastricht, Amsterdam, Nice and Lisbon). These processes brought significant changes in the Member States, especially for the German *Länder*. They saw their autonomy and state quality endangered. This is why actors of the German subnational level struggled to maintain the importance of their role within the EU. One of their achievements is the emergence of the Committee of the Regions (CoR), an actor that represents the interests of the regional and local level within the European policy-making processes.

The foreign policy status of European integration has changed since the deepening of the integration process. In Germany, European affairs are no longer dealt under the umbrella of the foreign policy competence, which belongs solely to the federal government. Most of the implementation processes take place at regional and local level. These are levels that internalise European policies and that have to bear the costs of their implementation. Hence, regional authorities have begun to act and mobilise on their own in order to represent their interests in EMLG processes (Börzel 2002).

Regions have been subject of research since the 1990s, when the reform of the European Regional Policy[1] emphasised the regions' importance as handling actors of European governance. The research focused its attention firstly on the emerging regionalism processes and then on the mobilisation activities that regions were implementing (Keating 1998). Therefore, the regions have been emerging as active actors in the EU arena, enriching the palette of different interests that are taken into consideration within the European policy-making processes.

The book understands EMLG as the way of the EU functioning. This functioning day-to-day process comprises the following formal elements: the involved actors and institutions, the establishment of policy objectives, the preparation of decisions, decision-making processes at the European level, the implementation of rules decided upon and the assessment of European policies. These processes involve the EU territorial levels, the European, the national, the subnational and the local. The actors responsible for regional participation in the EU require understanding of EMLG processes in order to strategise their involvement. But EMLG comprises informal elements that shape the formal processes, e.g., the constant communication and information exchange that takes place on a regularly basis between involved actors.

---

[1] Many quoted authors and actors used the term "Cohesion Policy" because of the economic, social and territorial cohesion goal pursued by the policy. But the book uses the term "European Regional Policy" because it comprises all elements for which DG Regio is responsible. The "Cohesion Policy" addresses the three main European funds: ERDF, ESF and CF, but the European Regional Policy manages also the EMFF and the EAFRD. The last two funds are eligible for the maritime and fisheries, and the agricultural rural development area of the policy. The term "European Regional Policy" is used as the umbrella for the funds regulations. These regulations and the composition of the funds change from one funding period to another. That is why the book mainly uses the general policy term. Nevertheless, when the term "Cohesion Policy" is used, it can be understood as part of the European Regional Policy. For more details on this policy see European Commission 2016d.

1.1 Research scope

Governance is a compilation of mechanisms and strategies of coordination adopted in conditions of "complex reciprocal interdependence among operationally autonomous actors, organisations, and functional systems" (Jessop 2004: 52). EMLG involves state actors that cooperate and negotiate as partners in a "complex network, pooling their sovereign authority and other distinctive capacities to help realise collectively agreed aims and objectives on behalf of the network as a whole" (Jessop 2004: 57).

The book understands regional participation within EMLG as the applied strategy of a subnational entity. Saxony-Anhalt embodies the motto of the EU, *Unity in Diversity and Diversity in Unity*, and sustains the lack of a unified European model of how regions should function and act in the EU. The case study shows a high possibility for developing bottom-up mobilisation processes. The envisioned regional strategy relies on the main idea of combining elements that a region has at its disposal (resources, access channels, economy, interests, and priorities) to achieve its goals as a European entity.

The regional participation's empirical analysis is based on the European Regional Policy because it offers grounds for establishing the political and economic goals that influence the relation of the regional authorities with other European actors and policies that are important for the region. The analysis of regional participation relies on the premise:

> The regional participation within European Multi-Level Governance starts in the region itself, and it develops within the institutions responsible for carrying it out and through the interaction with other actors. This institutional structure depends on the type of region (administrative, development region or a federation state). However, the impulse of becoming powerful bursts from within. The later action is stimulated and facilitated by other actors engaged at several other political levels.

The book firstly provides an overview of the literature on regions and regionalism, and how the European Commission and the Committee of the Regions conceive European governance. The second part of the book presents regional participation's patterns of Saxony-Anhalt within EMLG. Most of the policy content analysed is related to the European Regional Policy and its spillovers.

Research has been done on the subnational interest representation at European level (Tatham 2016; Beyers/Donas 2013). The current book deals with the pattern of regional participation within EMLG of Saxony-Anhalt during specific legislative periods. This pattern starts with the definition of interests and policy goals. The analysis looks into how those goals were pursued by actors of the subnational entity. Thus, an inquiry made from a bottom-up perspective is present. The inquiry emphasises the possibilities that subnational authorities have to assert themselves within the European Multi-Level Governance. The book reaches for an exploratory agenda to identify explanations from the literature and to provide an action pattern from the case study, Saxony-Anhalt.

1.2 Structure of the book

Chapter 2 presents the concepts: region, regionalism, regionalisation, subnational mobilisation and regional participation. The next part summarises the literature on the concept of Multi-Level Governance, comprising both the scientific discourse and the practical comprehension of European institutions. The book first develops a rough description of EMLG's characteristics and of regional participation within it, in order to identify the topics and meaning that are relevant for regions. The last part of the chapter presents the research questions and the methodology.

Chapter 3 summarises the history of Saxony-Anhalt that offers the context for the qualitative analysis. Chapter 4 describes the institutional framework and the stakeholders as premises for the regional participation's analysis. Chapter 5 presents the political goals of Saxony-Anhalt during the three analysed legislative periods and their prioritisation.

Chapter 6 presents the regional participation's analysis based on the European Regional Policy. Chapter 7 illustrates the regional participation's analysis based on the European Chemicals Policy. These are two priorities set by Saxony-Anhalt and analysed in this book. Chapter 8 states the pattern involved in shaping the process of Saxony-Anhalt's regional participation in EMLG.

The appendices 1-6 provide an insight into how EMLG is conceived by the European Commission, the European Parliament and the Committee of the Regions. The European Commission provides a profile of Saxony-Anhalt in the innovation monitoring process. This profile can be found on the internet presence of the European Commission (2016a). It states the features of governance, the economic situation, and the innovation strategy of Saxony-Anhalt. Appendix 7 provides a list of key recommendations for regional authorities in chemical regions based on a study that regarded the contribution of Saxony-Anhalt for the chemical regions of the EU.

There are some conceptual remarks that need to be underlined. Even though the title consists of English terms, due to specific terminology of the German federalism, some German concepts are used in the research. Other terms will be mentioned either in English or German at the beginning of each chapter, but mostly their German form will be used. This is the case for terms such as *Land, Länder, Landtag, Landesregierung, Bundestag, Bundesrat, Bundesregierung* and the abreviations of the political parties, such as *CDU, SPD* and the others. The terms *regional* and *subnational* are considered synonyms and both are used in this research. The use of these two terms makes the difference between European and national level. Due to the high differences between subnational entities in the EU, the book does not wish to undermine the state-quality of Saxony-Anhalt.

2 Theoretical framework for regional participation within European Multi-Level Governance

Theoretical research of the European integration is constantly looking into processes at European level and within the MS. It strongly focuses on the triangle European Commission – Council – European Parliament, with a focus on the national interests that shape European politics. The scope of the European competencies is very broad. There are policy fields in which the influence of national governments over the content of European policies are complemented by European and regional interests, such as the case of the European Regional Policy, in which the European Commission and even the European Parliament are often considered allies of the regions (Hooghe 1996).

The concept of Europeanisation has a series of definitions and explanations in the European studies literature, such as the political unification that comprises external and internal aspects of European dynamics. It can also be used as an attention-directing device that provides the starting point for exploration (Olsen 2002: 943). Europeanisation mainly facilitates the research of domestic changes that have been triggered by the development of the EU (see Bulmer/Radaelli 2004; Börzel/Risse 2003). Hence, such studies look into how polity, institutions, politics, public discourse or identity, and policies change within the MS (Börzel/Risse 2006: 485).

Domestic changes occur within the EMLG system that is guiding the empirical research in this book. Its characteristics have been analysed in contrast to well-known theories on European integration (see Marks/Hooghe/Blank 1996; Kohler-Koch 1998; Bomberg/Peterson 1998; Bache 2004; Piattoni 2010). The European integration and regionalisation are complementary processes in which authority is dispersed from national level either towards the EU or downwards to the subnational level (Marks/Hooghe 2001: 19). With regard to these processes, the chapter firstly presents the definitions and working guidelines of the concepts that define regional participation within EMLG. In the second part, the emergence of EMLG as the EU functioning style is tackled.

2.1 Region

The concept of region is being broadly used because of the many European regions' particular characteristics. The broadness of the term relies on the common element used by the European Commission for delimiting and acknowledging the regions of the Member States, namely the NUTS[2] classification, used for the implementation of the European Regional Policy. Regions have both common and different elements. The common feature is the territorial space within specific borders of the region (Bickerton/Gagnon 2011: 276). The different characteristics of regions are: ethnic, cultural, religious elements and the language within the region, the history and the economic development of the region (Bango 2003: 215). In these terms, EU's regions are units that mobilise and cooperate. Through their mobilisation, they strive for their development.

The EU membership caused the displacement of arenas of policy-making, increase in the number of relevant decision-makers from outside the nation-state, and unpredictability of policy outcomes. Regions have been either strengthening their existence or they have been emerging as actors leading to regionalism movements (Sălăgeanu 2016: 56).

Tatham uses the concept of sub-state entities and defines these as "the level of government and /or administration immediately beneath the state" (2016: 1). According to him, these entities belong to a third category of players in the European Union, next to supranational and national players in the EU policy-making. However, the relevance or impact of these entities as policy players is still not clear (Tatham 2016: 1). Hence, the analysis based on Saxony-Anhalt seeks to find the relevance of its regional participation within EMLG.

2.2 Regionalism

The body of the literature talks about "regionalism" and "new regionalism". Regionalism was originally a national phenomenon that was re-oriented in the 1980s towards economic developments that were triggered by globalisation, impelling a functional pressure. The erosion of the state, the local and regional political mobilisation and the development of market and society were the elements that contributed to an economic and social meaning of the territory (Keating 1998: 72-9).

Regionalism is perceived as the aspiration of the regions to acquire more decision-making competencies, in order to deal with challenges posed by the EU increasing interdependencies (Sodupe 1999: 74). New regionalism is, on

---

[2] Nomenclature of territorial units for statistics. The NUTS 2 category is considered for the EU funds' allocation. Saxony-Anhalt is a NUTS 2 region for the 2014-2020 funding period.

the other hand, understood as the consequence of the evolution processes at state level, civic society and market. This evolution has been favoured by the globalisation process and by the adaptation of the subnational level to globalisation (Sagan/Halkier 2005: 9-10).

Regionalism establishes itself where the same space can bring together the coexistence of elements such as: geography, economic cohesion, administrative structures, territorial mobilisation, and cultural and popular identity (Keating 1998: 9-10). The triggering elements of developing a regional awareness for regions of the MS were stronger either at a regional or at a national level, depending on the pursued goals of regional actors – regional autonomy or European compliance. The Eastern MS have been dealing with an emerging regional level especially as a consequence of European integration.

Keating defines two key features of territory that are relevant for regionalism: the political and the normative. Territory features an effective unit that provides opportunity for political mobilisation. The normative characteristic of the territory is its framework, in which a democratic and accountable government structure can work. This structure can provide inclusively and non-discriminatory implementation of participation rights (Keating 1998: 109).

Therefore, regionalism is a complex phenomenon inspired by political and economic developments. National policies influence its top-down form. Its bottom-up dimension is based on the political and economic regional mobilisation. Regarding the territorial dimension, the political character is a key element. Europe provides a new context for old political demands such as separatism and autonomy, but no unitary model. This shortage facilitates the emergence of different types of regionalism (Keating 1995).

Regionalism as a bottom-up movement looking for enhancing the powers of a specific territory has created new challenges for nation-states. This led to the recognition and importance of the territorial dimension within the European political processes. The salience of territory is due to European development policies such as the European Regional Policy. These policies contribute to the re-evaluation of the territorial politics forms (Keating 1998: 46-9).

One can speak of regionalism, if the region that is considered to be the action space is created by those actors that depict themselves as regional and operate in the regional space they created. The creation of the regional space is mainly a result of a top-down process, such as decentralisation and institution building at regional level. Precisely for this type of top-down process, the term of regionalisation is used in the new Member States. On the other hand, the fulfilment of a regional plan and the emergence of the region as a collective actor are considered to be vital goals for regional actors (Schmitt-Egner, 2005: 31).

Considering the top-down and bottom-up approaches and looking at the subnational level within old and new MS there is a differentiation to make between regionalism, as bottom-up political movements that arise in the regions, and regionalisation, a top-down approach from central government to regions (Loughlin 2011: 209). Next to these two approaches, there are also different processes of decentralisation. Decentralisation can be political, administrative and fiscal (Loughlin 2011: 209). The decentralisation type defines what the actors of the decentralised institutions and level may do.

There is a stronger regionalism trend within older MS, understood as political mobilisation of individuals, who have specific interests and who pursue them at one or several levels simultaneously (Bickerton/Gagnon 2011: 277). The regionalism movements are based on historical developments within the territory. Within the newer MS, the trend is towards regionalisation based on the Europeanisation rationale. This trend is countering a highly centralised mentality and state-structure, perceived and implemented as a top-down adaptation process to the misfit of the European integration, towards administrative or development regions.

Rowe points out that there is "a new fault line" between EU15 regions and the ones of the new MS, which "do not constitute historic or linguistic regions where national governments sought consciously to cut across inter-ethnic, religious and linguistic divides in the territorial restructuring programmes of the 1990s" (2011: 9). Therefore, not all regions of the EU MS have the same framework for participation in EMLG.

2.3 Regionalisation

History influences the Member States' political systems. The EU consists of a heterogeneous system of subnational levels of the MS. Some national governments had to establish a subnational layer in their political system, e.g. Poland, Romania, or Greece. Other MS already had it, such as the federal states Germany and Austria. Another group of MS strived towards federalisation, e.g. Belgium, or Spain where an asymmetric system governs, the UK sought out the devolution and Italy implemented a hybrid regionalisation (Magone 2011: 311).

In the first case, the regional level emerged as an adaptation to the misfit created by the European integration. However, the emergence of the regional layer triggered different outcomes in the MS. For other countries, which had some goodness of fit, the process of regionalisation created a window of opportunity for the empowerment of their subnational actors to gain more influence on the European processes. Goodness of fit can be found where a regionalist tradition was developed (Sagan/Halkier 2005: 267).

Regionalisation can be understood as "a three-fold process of structuration" that creates independent arenas of negotiation, intensifies communication and stimulates learning (Benz/Eberlein 1999: 333). This process pursues the improvement of cooperation and of effective problem solving. Thus, if a regional level emerges, its institutions and actors must comprehend its purpose in order to adequately establish its functioning framework and tools. Nevertheless, such institutions depend on the purpose the government assigns them and that shapes processes at the regional level (Benz/Eberlein 1999: 335).

Regionalisation within European states, a top-down assisted reform, was triggered by movements within the territory and reforms at national level. The German *Länder* were among the driving forces that empowered the discourse on the role of the regional level within the EU. Making use of their veto power within the Federal Republic of Germany, the *Länder* achieved constitutional rights to have a say in European policy-making by arguing that the European affairs were no longer foreign affairs of the federal government (Börzel 2002).

The European Commission defines regionalisation as:

> the process which creates a capacity for independent action aimed at developing a specific area (sub-national but supra-local) through the mobilisation of its economic fabric and, where appropriate, of features of local and regional identity, and through the development of its potential. This process can occur on the basis of existing institutions, or can give rise to a new territorial organisation which will better fulfil these aims. It is always conditioned by the constraints imposed by the political and institutional framework, which in turn can be influenced by other factors (2000: 23).

From the perspective of the European Commission, regionalisation stresses that intermediate-level territorial institutions must take on board interests related to their enhancement of competencies (2000: 24). These institutions need to include a socio-economic perspective of these interests, and a cultural and political one, when appropriate. Therefore, from a European institutional perspective, there are five types of regionalisation:

- Administrative regionalisation, according to which the states create authorities subordinated to the government, with the purpose of promoting regional economic development (e.g. Greece, England, Sweden, Bulgaria, Estonia, Hungary, Lithuania, Slovakia, Slovenia).

- Regionalisation through existing local authorities, which take on functions related to regionalisation (e.g. Finland, Denmark, Ireland).
- Regional decentralisation through new emerging territorial authorities between the national level and the existing administrative levels (e.g. France, Poland, Czech Republic).
- Political regionalisation or institutional regionalism. This type is legally different from regional decentralisation because it grants legislative powers to a regional assembly. There is also a constitution that defines and guarantees such characteristics of a regional government (e.g. Spain, Italy, Belgium).
- Regionalisation through the authorities of the *Länder* (European Commission 2000: 24-8).

Regions continue to receive much attention in the research field because they are characterised as "knowledge and innovation hubs". Theses 'hubs' are perceived as the "most desirable spatial scale" that can provide sustainable growth (De Propis/Hamdouch 2013: 997). Hence, regions play an innovation and development role within EMLG.

High heterogeneity of the regionalisation processes across Europe has resulted in many different changes of how regional authorities were established, abolished or suffered no changes. However, there is a trend of strengthening regional authorities, which must not necessarily be part of a federal system (see Marks/Hooghe/Schakel 2008; Hooghe et al. 2016). This is connected with their active participation in the EMLG processes.

Fitjar argues that there is a causal relationship between prosperity and regionalism, according to which the relationship between economic development and regionalism also depends on the bottom-up perspective of elites and masses (2010). They mobilise at a regional level bringing forward the specificities of their region. Regional participation within EMLG is analysed from this bottom-up perspective. It explores the interaction of Saxony-Anhalt with other territorial levels within the EU.

2.4 Subnational mobilisation

Subnational mobilisation is a "multi-dimensional phenomenon" that comprises all the subnational activity of a region (Rowe 2011: 3). The process of European integration triggered the regionalisation processes, increasing the active participation of regions within EMLG. The European Commission's openness for subnational actors' input increased their role and stimulated their enhanced interest to the EMLG processes.

Subnational mobilisation is "the growing engagement of subnational governmental actors with the institutions and processes of EU policy-making" (Jeffery 2000: 1). The developments within the European Union that indicate subnational mobilisation are: the established formal involvement mechanisms for subnational actors within their state, the regional information and liaison offices in Brussels, the interregional cooperation within EU programmes, the treaty changes that introduced the possibility of subnational input into the Council of the EU, the creation of the Committee of the Regions and the establishment of the subsidiarity principle (Jeffery 2000: 2).

The principle of subsidiarity implies that decisions should be taken as close to the citizens as possible. When the lower level cannot perform specific functions, the decisions should be taken by the higher level. However, the Maastricht Treaty's definition of subsidiarity is interpreted as "devolving functions back to the national governments but not in its original meaning of devolving them to sub-national levels of government" (Loughlin 2011: 203). Next to the activity at the EU level, subnational mobilisation can be seen as an instrument that challenges the state power and that supports supranational authority (Hooghe 1995: 177; see Marks 1996). Hence, the devolution towards the national level can be interpreted as a coping mechanism for the transfer of competencies towards the EU.

Jeffery criticised the fact that Multi-Level Governance, as initially developed, was focused mainly on the EU Structural Policy and, that the approach maintained a top-down perspective focusing on the national state towards the European level (2000: 7-8). On the other hand, Jeffery stressed intrastate channels as the complements for the influence driven activities of regional actors (2000: 3). Factors that frame the mobilisation activity are: the constitution regulations, intergovernmental relations, entrepreneurship, legitimacy and social capital (Jeffery 2000: 12-17). Constitutional regulations strongly influence subnational mobilisation because they regulate the operation framework of the subnational institutions. Nevertheless, strong constitutional rights do not induce a strong influence of regional institutions directly, because mobilisation has to be wanted, legitimate and appropriate, depending on the situation of each specific regional government.

Existing policy resources – expertise, information, legitimacy – affect intergovernmental relations that contribute to a stronger formulation of interests. Regarding the entrepreneurship, the effective internal administration adaptation, the leadership and the coalition-building strategies are relevant for the subnational mobilisation. Legitimacy and social capital depend on their availability in each region (Jeffery 2000: 12-17). Therefore, there is a strong connection between institutional structures, rules and informal procedures that take place; such as the learning processes through networking and the representation of shared goals and interests. All these are part of the active regional participation within EMLG as understood in this book.

Subnational mobilisation seeks to gain access to the EU policy-making processes. However, having access does not guarantee that influence will be exerted on those who have the decision power. This book uses the bottom-up perspective of subnational mobilisation and understands European affairs as part of the domestic policy. The qualitative analysis looks for areas in which the subnational actors of Saxony-Anhalt mobilise and seek access to shape the European policies.

2.5 Regional participation

The European Regional Policy development and its specific features triggered a need for enhanced regional input to establish the appropriate content of European policies. The European level empowered the regional input and placed incentives at the disposal of regional authorities. But, the capacity of those authorities depended much on the intrastate frameworks and the willingness of local, regional and national governments to allow a strong representation of regional interests and input from the regional authorities (see Jones/Keating 1995; Bullmann 2001).

European, national and subnational actors are connected and interdependent because they fulfil different tasks within the EU multi-level structure in order to achieve common goals (Crieckemans/Duran 2010; see Magone 2011). In this context, regions matter because they provide the "key level in functional transformation" (Keating 1998: 185). Regions offer the "arena for negotiation and territorial systems of action, in economics, society and politics" (Keating 1998: 185). Political heterogeneity and institutional and constitutional features of subnational actors allow the active participation within EMLG. Their activity depends on their characteristics, interests, and policies that affect the region significantly.

As research shows, regions have been examined as elements of the EU politics processes. Keating regarded regions as political arenas that are part of the decision-making system (1998: 78). Moreover, regions are considered as a space for politics because they are acknowledged as subjects of the European integration (Carter/Pasquier 2010: 296). This awareness of third level actors (Jeffery 2001) stimulates interaction among subnational actors and the actors that have already been active at European level. Therefore, European politics make room for the emergence of the regional dimension (see Sălăgeanu 2014b).

The actions of regions in the "Brussels Game" have been analysed as an interaction between regions and their national governments. The strategies adopted by regions were to engage in cooperation with the national government or to reject such cooperation, in other words, to engage in "bypassing or co-operative diplomacy" (Tatham 2010; 2016). Tatham pointed out the complexity of the subnational mobilisation. His analysis of the two types of "paradiplomacy" was guided by the level of devolution of the subnational actors, the position of the government parties at national and subnational levels, the resources and experience of subnational actors with the European integration (Tatham 2010: 78-81).

The patterns of cooperation between the subnational level and national governments have been described also as "ring-fencing" or "circumventing the central state" (Bauer/Börzel 2010: 257; Börzel 2002). The strategy of gaining direct access at EU level is the one circumventing the national level. It involves representing regional interests at European level during the drafting process of European policies.

Subnational actors need to identify channels and possibilities available for their engagement within the EMLG. The specific actors, their competencies and strategic use of these elements need to be part of the mobilisation process. They should be aware and pursue their motivation, interests and goals (economic, cultural or administrative). Mobilisation could change the situation of a subnational entity, if its actors pursue a well-defined strategy. Resources are not the only relevant element for the participation of a region. However, the way they are used is crucial. A main goal is to get heard by other actors at European level (see Sălăgeanu 2014b).

The conditions under which regions of the MS emerged influence the way these are represented at European level, how they understand and perceive their contribution and how they organise their activities of either implementation or influence-creating activities. Subnational actors rely on their connections with the European and national actors, and to their cooperation with other actors from different regions or Member States.

Regional participation within EMLG is understood in this book beyond the subnational mobilisation because the participation is conceptualised as the long-term engagement in the cooperation processes with the EU levels, with the national government at the EU level or at home, with the EU institutions and actors, and with other actors at different locations.

Regional participation within EMLG starts in the region. But the region does not act solely. It engages in cooperation, seeks allies for common development and economic purposes and participates in networks in order to enhance the outcomes of its endeavours. The region is a learning unit, which provides information and is capable of initiative when confronted with challenges. Economic disparities at subnational level enable the region to use financial instruments provided by the EU (see Keating 1998). European regulative policy-making can create difficulties (economic, structural or administrative) for its units and actors who need to implement European regulations. From this perspective, the connection between regional participation within EMLG and the openness of European institutions towards regional participation is complementary.

2.6 European Multi-Level Governance from theoretical perspective

Governance contains a normative dimension that involves rules on how procedures should be enforced, in addition to clarify how these procedures are being implemented. This concept offers relevant insights into the European integration process and into the capacity of the EU to fulfil the goals set by its leaders (Peters/Pierre 2009: 91).

Understandings of governance comprise the following elements: "the capacity of a society to develop some means of making and implementing collective choices" that provides "mechanisms for identifying common problems, deciding upon goals, and then designing and implementing the means to achieve those purposes" (Peters/Pierre 2009: 91-92); it involves both the public sector and non-state actors, and provides the environment for networks of different actors to contribute to steering actions performed by state-actors; "extremely complex process involving multiple actors pursuing a wide range of individual and organizational goals, as well as pursuing the collective goals of the society" (Peters/Pierre 2009: 92).

Multi-Level Governance is "a polity-creating process in which authority and policy-making influence are shared across multiple levels of government – sub-national, national and supranational" (Marks/Hooghe 2001: 2). The dispersion of authority has fostered the subnational level's emergence as political space, especially in countries with "little tradition of regional government" (Gamble 2004: v). Marks explains the emergence of MLG as consequence of the institutional creation and dispersion of the decision-making authority (1993: 392).

The MLG approach was informed by neo-functionalist insights and some of the neo-functionalist ideas are considered useful for the empirical analysis of Saxony-Anhalt. The neo-functionalist theory understands European integration as a dynamic process that is explained through the concept of spill-over[3] and through "change in expectations and activities on the part of participating actors" (Niemann/Schmitter 2009: 47). "It contests both that states are unified actors and that they are the only relevant actors"; the integration process is shaped by multiple, diverse, and changing actors and their interactions (Niemann/Schmitter 2009: 47). The neo-functionalist theory considered "the autonomous influence of supranational institutions and the emerging role of organized interests" with a regional focus to be important (Niemann/Schmitter 2009: 46).

The European integration's polity-creating process comprised two power narratives: decentralisation and centralisation of power. The first narrative was based on the premise that the European Commission promoted the emergence of the mobilisation processes of the subnational level through the European Regional Policy. The second narrative asserted that decision-making competencies were transferred to the European level. The transfer reduced the access to European decision-making processes for some regional entities, such as the German *Länder*. Thus, governments located at different territorial levels "enmeshed in territorially overarching policy networks" creating the MLG framework (Marks 1993: 401).

The Maastricht Treaty and its Protocol on Economic and Social Cohesion enlarged the scope for autonomous decision-making of the European Commission. It increased the Commission's competencies for structural intervention and rates of Community assistance, putting greater emphasis on Community initiative programmes, and simplifying the planning process (Marks 1993: 395-396). Even though the authority and decision-making competencies have shifted, the EU and its MS can be considered as the same jurisdiction. The sovereignty drift towards the EU is a "political process of dividing and sharing of competencies" (Benz/Zimmer 2010: 18). This common jurisdiction is in search of solutions for interdependent tasks that go beyond national governments (Benz/Zimmer 2010: 18-19).

The subjects in the quest for common European solutions were no longer just states or institutions understood as "set of rules" (Marks/Hooghe/Blank 1996: 348). They became actors, individuals or groups that act within the institutions (Marks/Hooghe/Blank 1996: 348). These actors engaged in informal negotiations, information exchanges and know-how transfers. Such liberties make the difference between government and governance. The involvement of such actors from all territorial levels and all sectors makes the

---

[3] The concept of spill-over refers to the implication that the "integration in a particular sector leads to relevant interest groups to move part of their activity to a higher level of aggregation and therefore gradually shift their focus on expectations to European institutions" (Niemann/Schmitter 2009: 49).

EU governance multi-level and multi-dimensional, empowering the EMLG patterns.

Moreover, common jurisdiction gives for territorial levels the possibility of their interpretation of governance. But European Governance can be more than MLG. Kjær made the difference between MLG as the type of European Governance that involved the three levels – European, national and regional – and that included policy and negotiation networks within policy-making processes (2010). Then there was the broader European Governance that embodied the orientation and coordination of the game's rules, regardless if the game involved networks, markets or hierarchy. That way, European Governance allowed a window of opportunity for policy-making ways that did not require multi-level networks or elements (Kjær 2010: 111-116).

European decision-making processes are divided into four categories: the policy initiation (agenda setting), the decision-making, the implementation and the adjudication processes (Knodt/Große Hüttmann 2006: 223-225). Within these processes, regions have a high interest to have their political goals represented. EMLG did not emerge with the goal to federalise the European Union. The participation of regional actors was considered an instrument for improvement of the European Regional Policy's implementation. The increased potential of regional actors to influence European policies developed in time, because they were considered "crucial partners in producing more meaningful regional development plans than those drawn up by remote Member State bureaucracies" (Conzelmann 2009: 15).

Piattoni developed the concept of MLG to a conceptual space with three MLG axes: a. between the centre and the periphery, b. between the domestic and the international, and c. between the state and the society (2010: 27). The first axis followed the logic of regionalism and decentralisation or devolution movements. The domestic-international axis followed the logic of intergovernmentalism and understood international cooperation and regulation as the reduction of state's autonomy. The third axis followed the logic of functionalism and emphasised the involvement of NGOs and civil-society organisations within the EU governance processes (Piattoni 2010: 27-29).

Piattoni argued that the subnational dynamism had "pok[ed] holes in the fences of autonomous sovereign states", the European Commission being aware of the subnational actors' power (2010: 60). Moreover, the Commission had lured "subnational authorities to the other side of the national fence by offering them the instruments with which they can face the global challenge" (Piattoni 2010: 60).

2.7 The Multi-Level Governance Type I and Type II[4]

The Multi-Level Governance concept embodies contrasting visions of the collective European decision-making. Subnational authorities are mostly implementing the enforcement of the EU binding legislative acts. Hooghe and Marks differentiate between two MLG types (2010). In some cases, the subnational actors manage to be part of the decision-making process, which they will later implement. Their participation is based on the promotion of the involved actors' prepared and established interests. The area of interests represented by regional actors determines the type of MLG that they would get involved into (see Sălăgeanu 2016).

Federalism is considered to be the intellectual foundation of Type I. Similar to federalism, the characteristics embodied by Type I are: shared power among the governments that operate at different territorial levels; the bundled functions of governments; the levels' non-intersecting jurisdiction membership and the broad system framework (Hooghe/Marks 2010). The EU pushed forward MLG Type I through simultaneous empowerment of supranational and subnational institutions. Type I fits the processes of political deliberation, in which the relevant questions are who gets what, when and how (Hooghe/Marks 2010: 18).

On the other hand, MLG Type II fits the processes of problem solving, where efficiency is of essence. Some salient features of EU architecture are consistent with this type, such as: task-specific jurisdictions, intersecting membership of governments to different jurisdictional levels and flexible governance design (Hooghe/Marks 2010: 19). The empirical analysis of the regional participation of Saxony-Anhalt within EMLG considers the differentiation of two types and tackles the participation of Saxony-Anhalt in both MLG types.

The main benefit of MLG lies in its flexibility. It allows jurisdictions to be custom-designed in response to externalities, economies of scale, ecological niches and preferences. Following the logic of the empirical analysis in this book, type I and II are complementary. Both types can be applied for one policy (European Regional policy) that expands its output to other policies, such as industry, environment, transport or others.

---

[4] The "MLG" concept is used when the authors that developed it are cited. Otherwise, the usage of the "EMLG" concept is preferred because it embodies the different MLG systems within the EU, such as the Federal Republic of Germany, and the EU itself as well.

2.8 European Multi-Level Governance from the European institutional perspective

The European governance system was not always effective from the perspective of the European Commission, which released in 2001 a White Paper (WP) on European Governance. The goal of the WP was to open up the process of EU policy-making and to increase its accountability. The WP set the principles of European Governance: openness, participation, accountability, effectiveness and coherence (Official Journal of the European Communities 2001: 7).

Openness referred to the work of European institutions that were accountable for the EU's decisions and operations. The wide participation throughout the policy-making chain delivered "quality, relevance and effectiveness of EU policies" (Official Journal of the European Communities 2001: 8). Accountability brought transparency to the processes that took place within the European institutions. The principle of effectiveness relied on the provision of adequate regulations and measures that were based on the impact evaluations. In many cases, the impact evaluation required specific know-how (Official Journal of the European Communities 2001: 8).

The cooperation between European actors who created policies and actors who delivered the expertise played a major role in the policy-shaping phase. The steady cooperation brought coherence of European integration, which required "political leadership and a strong responsibility on the part of the Institutions to ensure a consistent approach within a complex system" (Official Journal of the European Communities 2001: 8).

The WP projected its improvements of European Governance to the multi-level aspect through the inclusion of the regional territorial dimension among its proposed measures, e.g.:

- To establish a systematic dialogue with representatives of regional and local governments at early policy-making stages,
- To take into account the regional and local level conditions by allowing flexibility of the legislation,
- To enhance the consultation and partnership arrangements of European policies (Official Journal of the European Communities 2001: 10).

The European Commission cannot acquire the local and regional input without having to rely on the cooperation and openness of subnational actors. The establishment of a mechanism for their involvement requires input from within the territory as well. This kind of cooperation requires active participation of both affected parts. Therefore, EMLG is no longer a concept developed from the European Regional Policy, but it is becoming a political practice within the EU, driven by certain actors who are aware of the outcome potential of the participation in EMLG. That is why the channels for the regional and local involvement in European governance are used and contribute to the enhancement of the subnational mobilisation.

The European Commission acknowledged the potential of the Committee of the Regions to connect the governance levels. The region was the new space for self-contained economic, social and political operations. The regionalisation of policies meant their implementation at regional level, identifying the development chances based on the adequate resources' allocation (Schlangen 2010: 47). The CoR contributed to the encouragement of an evolving EMLG practice and prepared a White Paper that defined Multi-Level Governance. The WP proposed the improvement and strengthening of regional participation within the processes of European governance. The CoR understood MLG as the instrument that could accomplish the political goals of the EU and defined it as the:

> coordinated action by the European Union, the Member States and local and regional authorities, based on partnership and aimed at drawing up and implementing EU policies. It leads to responsibility being shared between the different tiers of government concerned and is underpinned by all sources of democratic legitimacy and the representative nature of the different players involved (Committee of the Regions 2009: 3).

The Cohesion Policy regulations referred to the partnership principle, in connection to the information and experience exchange functions that were best implemented through the presence of regions in Brussels. The discussions organised by regions in Brussels were visited by COM officials, who presented European policies and gathered information about the different problems and challenges the regions were faced with. That is how the COM officials could learn directly from the concerned actors (Ahner 2012: 145).

The CoR's White Paper stressed the importance of the governance model, the institutional organisation and the contribution of all players. Local and regional actors were considered part of the players if they were indeed regarded as "genuine partners rather than mere intermediaries" (Committee of the Regions 2009: 4). The CoR defined partnership beyond the participation and consultation, involving the responsibility of players. On the other side, MLG was challenged by the need to ensure an equal balance between the institutional and the partnership-based governance (Committee of the Regions 2009: 5; see Appendix 3).

Multi-Level Governance was regarded as a valuable tool for regions, particularly when the EU affected through its policy without having the explicit competence to do so. The CoR emphasised the intense cooperation with the European Commission and the European Parliament. Another instrument that implemented this cooperation is the organisation of the yearly Open Days: European Week of Regions and Cities activities. This event is core evidence of the bundled actors, who are eager to participate and get in contact with European actors. The participation of officials, such as presidents of the institutions, at the works of the CoR further indicates the close inter-institutional cooperation.

The Committee of the Regions advocated the collaboration with the relevant networks at local and regional level to promote the interconnection and interaction within the European society between political, economic, associative and cultural domains (2009). Furthermore, it proposed tools aimed at bridging the communication gap and encouraged innovative and partnership-based methods of governance to put MLG into practice. For that purpose, the CoR emphasised the role of the authorities' mobilisation and their involvement in the operational mechanisms of territorial cooperation through instruments of networks, organisations or associations (2009). Participation was about the contribution to more efficient policy at early stages and not about "institutionalising protest" (Official Journal of the European Communities 2001: 11). This is what regional participation within EMLG is all about.

The demand of the German *Länder* to have an actor representing the regions at European level was achieved with the creation of the Committee of the Regions. The solution was "remedying the treaty's blindness to the regions" (Clement 1996: 14). The Committee of the Regions has been struggling ever since to enforce its demands for more consideration during its existence. It has been promoting the role of regional and local authorities as part of EMLG. In its White Paper on MLG, the Committee of the Regions highlighted the importance of the Treaty of Lisbon, because it represented the institutional recognition of EMLG. It also stressed the indisputable democratic legitimacy of local and regional authorities (Committee of the Regions 2009: 9).

Piattoni appreciated the CoR's WP on MLG as a "major achievement" that contributed to the development of Europe through partnership (2009: 67). She assessed the document as a step towards mobilising the members of the CoR for more legitimate participation within the EU, especially for improving European legislation by bringing in ideas and solutions. Through such participation, the territorial dimension of European policies was emphasised.

The CoR managed to bring in a different interpretation of subsidiarity, according to which all "levels and actors should be simultaneously involved"; that involvement was established as "a de facto correspondence between subsidiarity and partnership" (Piattoni 2009: 69). Member States still need to internalise and practice domestic MLG in order to implement it at European level. The European project still needs a better communication with its citizens. The critical points of the CoR's WP are that it did not develop enough the aspects of governance and it ignored the difficulties the regional and local authorities have during implementation processes (Piattoni 2009: 73).

The CoR's work is based on the principles of subsidiarity, partnership and closeness to citizens to make the voice of local and regional authorities heard. Those principles correspond to the ones defined by the COM's White Paper on European Governance (2001).

The 2009 CoR's WP initiated the drawing of an EU Charter on MLG, which was adopted in May 2014 by the CoR. The Charter committed its signatories to "explain and promote the principle of multilevel governance" (Committee of the Regions 2014: 1). The purpose of the Charter was to "connect regions and cities across Europe, whilst promoting MULTI-ACTORSHIP with societal actors such as the social partners, universities, NGOs and representative civil society groupings" (Committee of the Regions 2014: 3). The Charter stated that MLG contributed to the learning processes and innovative policy solutions through best-practice exchange and participatory democracy. The promoted principles of the MLG process were: transparent, open and inclusive policy-making, participation and partnership, policy efficiency and coherence, budget synergies, subsidiarity and proportionality and protection of the fundamental rights. The CoR committed itself to the MLG implementation through promotion of the citizens' participation in policy-making processes, cooperation, fostering a European mind-set, strengthening institutional capacity building and creating networks (Committee of the Regions 2014: 3-4).

Next to the CoR's work on MLG, the EP has been looking into the functioning of MLG in the MS as well. This reflects its awareness of MLG as a way of European governance and the importance of the partnership principle implementation. A study requested by the EP revealed that governance and partnership were treated merely as "formal requirements" and these were respected by MS only during the consultations phase. During the programme implementation, these requirements were considered "as major administrative burdens", especially due to the lack of resources and administrative capacity (European Parliament 2008a: ix). According to the study, a successful approach to governance and partnership required a social and political culture of the state, previous experience with structural funds and openness towards the participatory processes.

2.9 European Multi-Level Governance implementation at European level and within the Member States

The CoR understands MLG as the core concept of the EU functioning system. That is why it developed an instrument for the MLG measurement. The first results of the instrument stated that there was no "mainstreamed culture of MLG in the preparatory phases of policies, meaning that there is often a lack of MLG administrative routine" (Committee of the Regions 2013: 1). The scoreboard emphasised that a better practice of MLG took place in the area of processes, during consultations, stakeholders' involvement, but the content of policies or the innovative measures dismissed the MLG objectives. The results showed that the political process for the Europe 2020 strategy had the highest score. For this field, practices related better to MLG than to the content (Committee of the Regions 2013: 10).

The CoR's Scoreboard presented scores and identified best-practices and proposed improvements (Committee of the Regions 2013: 23-4). The categories of the scoreboard analysis comprised the dimension of procedures (information and consultation; stakeholders' involvement and responsiveness) and the dimension of EU policies' content (territorial/integrated/place-based policy; smart regulation mechanisms; innovative instruments for implementation) (Committee of the Regions 2012a: 20).

The second Scoreboard results confirmed the trend of better respect of MLG objectives within the procedures than regarding the content of the policies (Committee of the Regions 2013: 23-26; see Appendix 4). It analysed among others the Structural Funds regulation. The general result was that is better scored at the procedures than at the policy content. The information process for structural funds showed a "sound institutional routine with respect to multilevel information and consultation" because of its openness and transparency. Local and regional authorities (LRAs) were also interested in taking in the information and participate in the debates (Committee of the Regions 2012a: 6). The CoR recommended to local and regional authorities to increase their efforts to influence the process by establishing a permanent dialogue through routines and adequate resources.

The CoR suggested to the LRAs to intensify their work on understanding MLG in order to counteract further disagreements, because the LRAs were capable of launching ideas that were taken on board, such as the category of transition regions, which was one of the CoR's proposals. The idea of transition regions was also heavily promoted by Saxony-Anhalt through its Brussels office but also through its CoR member, Michael Schneider, in particular through his work as CoR rapporteur for the Cohesion Policy. This particular topic is tackled in chapter 6.

Schneider defined the use of MLG as "a model of government that reflect[ed] these different voices and focuse[d] heavily on the need for European policy to be rooted locally in the regions and with the public" (Schneider 2009: 38). The CoR emphasised the high responsiveness of the EP-REGI committee to LRAs' positions (Committee of the Regions 2012a: 7). Therefore, institutional cooperation was part of EMLG implementation.

Among the recommendations meant to close gaps discovered during the Scoreboard analysis, the CoR stressed that the legislators (the Council and the European Parliament) needed to "make sure that despite Europe 2020 earmarking, the fund regulations will be flexible enough in order to respect territorial needs" (Committee of the Regions 2013: 18). A broader MLG debate should bring in the LRAs' positions during the ongoing negotiations in order to avoid the COM withholding funds based on other reasons than the LRAs performance within the implementation processes. The CoR considered the fact that the Commission and the Council should take into consideration that the LRAs envisaged themselves different from other stakeholders. Meanwhile, the CoR welcomed the "most relevant innovation with respect to strategic planning" in the form of partnership agreements between the Commission and the Member States (Committee of the Regions 2012a: 7-8; see Appendix 6).

In 2012, the CoR adopted another opinion regarding MLG at the plenary session in February, promoting "building a genuine European culture of multilevel governance" (Committee of the Regions 2012b: 2). The emergence of such a culture relied on: consolidation of the basis and principles of MLG within the European and national institutions and political frameworks; MLG implementation through relevant mechanisms and instruments; and financial independence of local and regional authorities to pool resources efficiently due to a fair distribution of public funds (Committee of the Regions 2012b: 2-3).

Regarding partnership-building as fundamental principle for the programming and implementation of the European Regional Policy, the study ordered by the EP noted that the impact was so far limited and that it was also often seen as time-consuming, requiring extensive effort without achievement of its added value. Regarding the involvement of local and regional authorities, their participation was influenced by the centralisation or decentralisation of the political-administrative system, the functioning of the fiscal equalisation systems and the financial and economic significance of EU funds for each state (European Parliament 2012: 9).

In the context of European Regional Policy, MLG mainly relies on the implementation of the partnership principle (European Parliament 2014: 10). On the other hand, the uneven practice of this implementation principle indicated a significant improvement scope. The challenges identified by the EP study corresponded with those determined by previous scientific research, namely: lack of tradition and resources, shifts in allocation, priorities of the EU-MS relations, high administrative costs of MLG and the democratic deficit (European Parliament 2014: 11).

The EP emphasised that the pre-existing institutional system of territorial governance determined the extent of MLG in the process of programming and management of Operational Programmes (OPs) because it determined the involved actors and their participation's capacity. The EP welcomed the flexibility of the Cohesion Policy that provided the Member States to make its own arrangements depending on the specific institutional and administrative context and its historical background (European Parliament 2014: 66-67).

The study confirmed empirically both the MLG's advantages and the problems that were tackled by literature. The established benefits were: increased legitimacy of policies and better–informed policy-making through enhanced participation of different actors; enhanced commitment and ownership; increased transparency of decision-making and effectiveness of the OP's development. The named difficulties were the complexity of the process, the blurred responsibility and the trap of joint decision-making. Moreover, the study assessed the implementation of the partnership principle in Poland and Slovenia in a better light than the literature did (European Parliament 2014: 68).

The study revealed that a top-down perspective of decision-making pertained. It recommended that the EP encouraged the Commission to offer more technical support to the authorities in charge with the OPs in order to improve the partnership and to better acknowledge and understand the difficulties present in the territory. The study encouraged all European institutions to increase transparency of how partnerships functioned. It further recommended that the evaluation of MLG's implementation and the effectiveness and efficiency of the partnership as part of the OPs' implementation should be assessed by the MS as well (European Parliament 2014: 71-74).

The Commission (2009-2014) continued the investigation path opened by the CoR. Commissioner Hahn[5] requested a report on the MLG situation and the partnership. The report was prepared by Luc Van den Brande, who was also one of the initiators and co-rapporteurs for the CoR's White Paper on MLG. He contributed to the development of the MLG Scoreboards. Van den Brande stated that MLG could become a binding principle only if the European legislation would entail this principle, which was achieved in Article 5

---

[5] Johannes Hahn was the European Commissioner for Regional Policy from 2010 until 2014.

of Regulation 1303/2013, namely the Regulation providing common provisions for European funds during the funding period 2014-2020 (2014; see Appendix 6). The article provides the base for the elaboration of the code of conduct that the European Commission prepared for the funding period 2014-2020 (Van den Brande 2014: 2).

The Van den Brande Report argued that MLG helped the communication of the EU policies, objectives, and results, enforcing the process of information, which was analysed by the CoR Scoreboard. It pointed out the need to abandon the hierarchical approach that placed the EU above the MS and the MS above the regions (2014). The report emphasised that partnership could bring these entities closer to the citizens. His proposal was that progress would be the possibility for "RLAs to conclude direct communication partnerships with the European Commission" (Van den Brande 2014: 9).

Van den Brande welcomed the "double paradigm shift" of the 2014-2020 Cohesion Policy that could improve its effect and promote "greater ownership of cohesion spending" through the anchoring of MLG in the common provision regulation and partnerships with the relevant socio-economic and societal actors (Van den Brande 2014: 11). He considered that the MLG was a precondition for the achievement of territorial cohesion and that decentralised mechanisms were its key elements (Van den Brande 2014: 6). Even more, the report recommended that RLAs should be "co-authors" and "co-signatories" of the Partnership Agreements (PAs) in order to be involved in the drafting process of the PAs, as the Fifth Cohesion Report considered necessary (Van den Brande 2014: 12-13).

So far, the acknowledgement of EMLG has been attested. Besides, the reports and studies performed by European institutions confirmed the importance of intrastate structures and frameworks that the regions have. Regional participation has been strongly supported by the European Parliament and the Committee of the Regions as presented in the last pages.

2.10 Regional participation within European Multi-Level Governance – bottom-up analysis model

2.10.1 The region and European Multi-Level Governance

The concept of European Multi-Level Governance applied in this book comprises the levels of parliament, government and administration within the EU and its MS. These levels are intertwined and they play an active role in the process of formulation, deliberation and implementation of European policies. This interlocking brings together political and administrative actors where each has a specific function. The involved actors need to know how the EU works to make use of the access channels they have at their disposal. The book describes and explains how EMLG works and under which conditions Saxony-Anhalt participates in it.

The region is a territorial entity at the subnational level of an EU Member State. This entity is a political and/or administrative construct that operates within European Multi-Level Governance, as defined in the previous section. The region is interdependent with the European, national and local level in the EU. The mobilisation of the region's actors is facilitated by EU's financial incentives and by European policies that affect the functioning and development of the region. The specific characteristics of the region are influenced by its political, cultural, economic and historical development. These elements shape the region's strategy of participation within EMLG.

The new institutionalism "reasserted the view that institutions matter" and extended the understanding of institutions by adding to the formal organisation the "informal patterns of structured interaction between groups as institutions themselves", as these would constrain or shape group behaviour (Bache/George 2006: 24). The new institutionalism de-constructs the behavioural argument of the institution as a neutral arena where different societal groups struggle for influence, arguing that formal institutions were no neutral arenas since their structures and rules "biased access to the political process in favour of some societal groups or others" and that institutions could become autonomous political actors in their own right (Bache/George 2006: 24).

Rational Choice Institutionalism focuses on the constraints imposed on actors by formal institutions. It points out how the behaviour – in this case, mobilisation – of actors is oriented by the frameworks they need or wish to act within. In this sense, there are elements to be taken into consideration when analysing the participation in political processes, but from two perspectives: of interest groups who try to influence legislative processes and, of involved and responsible parties for the legislative process (initiative and decision-making institutions and actors, COM, EP, national governments). Therefore, according to rational choice institutionalism, the following elements are taken into consideration, by interest groups: the access points to political processes of institutions; the previous relations between interests groups and legislators and the procedures that prevailed for the passage of the legislation affecting groups. The responsible parties for legislative processes take into consideration: the relative openness to interests groups (national or supranational); the extent of intergovernmental issues and the increasing role of institutions, such as the EP (Bache/George 2006: 24).

The undertaken analysis considers the mobilisation of regional actors and their activity where access points (COM, EP, CoR, Minister Council – via intrastate interest mediation) allow it as part of their participation strategy in the EMLG processes. The strategy and pattern of regional participation are the focus of the analysis on Saxony-Anhalt. The documents' analysis looks into the mobilisation of Saxony-Anhalt during the last three legislative periods (2002-2006; 2006-2011; 2011-2016).

2.10.2 Research questions

The main research question is: *Why does regional participation of Saxony-Anhalt within European Multi-Level Governance system occur?* In order to answer this question, following questions are pursued in the book:

- What is the European Multi-Level Governance system?
- What is regional participation?
- What are the access channels available for EMLG?
- What sets the mobilisation of Saxony-Anhalt?
- Who does what within Saxony-Anhalt and within EMLG?
- What are the strategies implemented by Saxony-Anhalt?
- What does Saxony-Anhalt offer as best-practice?
- What can other regions learn from Saxony-Anhalt?

The purpose of this qualitative analysis is to explain regional participation within the EMLG process, looking at Saxony-Anhalt for the last three legislative periods. The data is based mainly on documents from different governance levels (European, federal and subnational). The analysis took into consideration the theoretical and practical features of EMLG.

EMLG highlights the interconnectivity between European incentives and the ongoing mobilisation at regional level. Less developed regions have at their disposal different instruments that could improve their economic situation. The interconnectivity relies on the interdependence of the EU levels, the role and influence of political, economic and administrative entities within the EU, the two-way pressure (bottom-up and top-down) and its influence on emerging processes among regional actors. Mobilisation could change the situation of a subnational entity, if its actors pursue a well-defined strategy. Therefore, the pattern of mobilisation and the use of instruments is what regional participation within EMLG is about.

2.10.3 Methodology

An empirical qualitative data analysis method was implemented, based on the case study Saxony-Anhalt. The research is situated in the post-positivism methodology, searching for patterns and relationships within the analysed content. This approach was used in order to reduce the data and to describe specific categories and their meaning. The analysis systematically looked for patterns of regional participation within the EU.

The undertaken steps are: the literature analysis as basis for the modelling of the regional participation's framework within EMLG, followed by exploration of the participation processes of Saxony-Anhalt based on the documents' analysis. The practical EMLG elements, presented by European institutions (see Appenices 1-4), eased the analysis, because they serve as predefined themes in the document analysis. The research sets off from the idea that European policies are part of the MS' domestic policy. Therefore, the division domestic-international is not applied.

The analysis explores the co-occurrence of activities that describe regional participation within EMLG of Saxony-Anhalt. The chapters on the empirical analysis provide also a context of the occurred participation in order to explain why actors were active. The empirical document analysis starts with the coalition agreements of each legislative period. These coalition agreements are considered as primary goal setters for each of the analysed period. The analysis looks further in public documents that attest the activities of Saxony-Anhalt's actors and their interaction with the EU institutions, national institutions and actors from other regions.

The qualitative analysis followed six variables that are relevant to regional participation within EMLG. The first two, the historical background and the institutional and legal framework, are considered independent. The "historical specificity of regions" and the institutional design can strengthen or weaken territorial politics and regional identities (Bickerton/Gagnon 2011: 279). The literature analysis on the history and institutional framework of Saxony-Anhalt provides guidelines for the empirical analysis of the documents.

The document analysis on Saxony-Anhalt looks for patterns of action that revolve around the variables: political goals and principles; use of resources such as actors, financial means, institutions; functions performed by actors and participation processes. Among the resources for political actors, the history of regions can be as well accounted for (Bickerton/Gagnon 2011: 278). Patterns are relevant for the explanation of how regional participation within EMLG works and they also validate the following hypotheses:

1. The history of a territory can define its current development through the use of its specificities for further development.

2. The institutional and legal framework of a territory empowers and triggers the mobilisation activities of the region in the context of the acknowledged European Multi-Level Governance.
3. The regional political prioritisation process is influenced by European policies and guides the strategy of mobilisation activities.[6]
4. The top-down EU incentives, for regions, contribute to the subnational mobilisation of Saxony-Anhalt's actors. The mobilisation allows Saxony-Anhalt to become part of a European stakeholder such as the European Chemical Regions Network.

The participation processes comprise the intrastate access and processes in which actors of Saxony-Anhalt are involved. The processes involve several steps, and different governance levels. The multi-dimensional-character of the representation of interests as part of the process of participation is increasingly considered crucial, yet not always used in all analyses (Knodt/Corcaci 2012: 184).

These processes are based firstly on the information principle and secondly, in the case of Germany, on the participation principle via the *Bundesrat* in cases of competencies transfer upwards to the EU. The intrastate participation via the *Bundesrat* gives access to negotiations with the *Bund*. Direct representation via the Brussels office ensures a direct contact with European institutions. The CoR allows direct participation for members from the region's functioning structures.

Political goals and principles are used for the analysis of mobilisation's activities. The goals show the interconnection with documents prepared by the EU. The correlation of principles shows the way same values interrelate and guide activities and actors into the governance affairs of the EU as a whole.

Resources comprise actors, financial means and institutions. Resources also comprise the available information for the involved actors: the *Landtag*, the *Landesregierung*, and the representations of Saxony-Anhalt in Berlin and Brussels. Further resources are the information put at disposal by the authorities of Saxony-Anhalt, such as the ones used for the analysis: the newsletters of the Brussels office and of the government, (the one from the Brussels office functions as a diary of Saxony-Anhalt's activities at the European level), and the government's declarations and press releases.

---

[6] The mobilisation depends on the political programme of the actors and on their engagement in pursuing their goals. The interaction between the political goals and the cooperation among actors and institutions and the levels depends on the clear choice of priorities. The European Union provides incentives for engagement in both European policy-making processes (the example of transition regions) and European policy implementation (the example of ECRN).

The actors' functions affect the processes mentioned above, and these have been taken into consideration by the region when a strategy of participation within the EU was developed. The following functions are considered during the pattern analysis:

- To gather and filter relevant information on EU affairs that is relevant for the regions' actors,
- To represent the interests of the region,
- To maintain contact with EU officials and partners,
- To participate in the early warning mechanism (European Parliament 2016[7]),
- To develop partnerships,
- To promote the image of the region at the EU level and that of the EU within the region (Rowe 2011: 83-4; Knodt/Corcaci 2012).

The function of information gathering is an essential one because the strategy pursued by the region depends on such information from the European level. A direct contact with important officials and decision-makers in the European Commission is a crucial part of the participation process within EMLG. Actors within the Commission and the EP are interested in the information the regions or different actors have to offer. Representations of regions in Brussels managed to create the communication and access channels between the EU actors and those in the region.

The early warning mechanism also offers the regions the chance to protect themselves from the negative impacts of European regulations. This function is closely connected to the need for information and the time factor which enables intervention, where the regions' representations can contribute substantially. This is how resources are connected to their functions and the processes they are involved in. Partnerships imply creating connections between political and economic actors in the region and political and economic representatives at European level.

These functions have been evaluated as functions of the information offices in Brussels. The information, filter, early warning and contacts maintenance with EU actors have been assessed as the most important ones, whereas functions of consultation, visiting groups, partnerships and public relations

---

[7] These mechanisms refer to the powers given by the Treaty of Lisbon to the national parliaments to review the EU legislative proposals. If the national parliaments feel that the EU legislative proposals do not comply with the subsidiarity principle, they are allowed to issue opinions. The subsidiarity compliance control can be performed by the German regional parliaments as well and they can voice their concerns to the national parliament. Thus this function is also considered in the analysis.

and image campaigns seem to be secondary. However, the filter function and the maintenance of contacts with EU officials have been increasingly important in the policy-making cycle (Knodt/Corcaci 2012).

The empirical analysis of this research regards these functions as depending on the strategy applied by the region and the principles engaged in the action of their institutions and actors. The analysis strives to present the capacity of the region to operationalise its regional participation within EMLG through the use of the resources that are deployed within the participation processes. Resources are used according to their functions. The involved actors pursue the determined goals and implement the principles that are connected to those goals.

The study focuses on the patterns of these variables during a specific period of time. Regional participation within EMLG is understood as a process that evolves, like the process of European integration. The time line is relevant because it offers a picture of the progress of Saxony-Anhalt's participation process within EMLG. Saxony-Anhalt is seen as an entity that socialises within EMLG and learns.

The interactions within EMLG are "positive-sum games" because they require time, trust, expertise and negotiation space (Niemann/Schmitter 2009: 48, 60). The categories of actions and the variables are a compilation of elements from the literature and from the analysed documents.

The next chapter presents the history of Saxony-Anhalt that provides the context for the political goals of the three analysed legislative periods. Chapter 4 presents the institutional framework of Saxony-Anhalt that provides the legitimacy of the bottom-up participation within EMLG. Chapter 5 presentes the analysed legislative periods and chapters 6 and 7 presend the analysed of the two policies. Chapter 8 sumarises the findings of the regional participation and it pattern.

3 The Europeanisation of Saxony-Anhalt

Europeanisation takes into consideration that the EU is a functional multi-level system. Early studies on Europeanisation pointed towards a fusion of the levels, a connection between decision-making processes and the administration of the Member States that merge in order to be able to function. From the central-state point of view, the fusion thesis regards the participation of national actors that take part in the European institutional framework. It describes the fusion of competencies and accountability, which can no longer be attributed to the national state and the European level separately (Marks/Hooghe/Blank 1996).

The Europeanised national governance comprises the management of interdependent relations that arise as a consequence of the joint use of instruments by different levels of the European governance (see Official Journal of the European Communities 2001). Even though the German multi-level governance system has extended to the European supranational level, the national level still plays a crucial role. The German *Länder* rely on the support of the *Bund* in achieving their goals.

At the beginning of the European integration research, European affairs were regarded as foreign affairs, being the sole competence of national governments. The European level provided both challenges and incentives for subnational actors to trigger their interests and mobilisation in the field of European policies, influencing their structure and strategies for participation in EMLG (Knodt 1998, 2000). However, over the course of European integration, the mobilisation of the subnational level in Germany increased leading to the re-interpretation of European affairs as domestic policy, therefore, involving the *Länder* in the European policy-making processes (Jeffery 2000; Börzel 2002).

Hence, by understanding Europeanisation as the EU's development, the Member States and their regions developed in parallel, contributing to the EU development. This chapter presents the history of Saxony-Anhalt and its role for Saxony-Anhalt as a region within the EU. This overview is relevant to the empirical analysis of the mobilisation and regional participation of Saxony-Anhalt within EMLG.

3.1 Introductory history of Saxony-Anhalt

The introductory history of Saxony-Anhalt provides a basis of the hypothesis that the history of a territory can define its current development making use of its specificities. The history of Saxony-Anhalt until 1989 is considered to be an independent variable (see Bickerton/Gagnon 2011). Its legacy is used by the political and economic actors in order to pursue the economic development of Saxony-Anhalt. A special focus is dedicated to the development of the region as an economic centre, especially through industrialisation.

The present Saxony-Anhalt territory has a history of more than one thousand years; meanwhile the *Land* Saxony-Anhalt has a short unitary historical tradition. Evidence of German population in the area of Saxony-Anhalt pointed towards 500 B.C. The connections with the Romans indicate the fact that the area was a political and economic centre in early times. The settlement and agricultural territories of the current Saxony-Anhalt played a particular role in Central Europe (Tullner 2008: 15).

In the 10th century, the Saxony Duke Heinrich became the first German King. This way, the territories around the central Elbe space became centre of the power and a main point of the German empire's history. These historical developments laid their fingerprints on the current identity of Saxony-Anhalt (Tullner 2008: 21). The son of Heinrich, Otto the First, was considered to be the most important ruler of medieval German history and the greatest son of the *mittelelbischen* homeland. Otto boosted the importance of the space and especially of Magdeburg. Magdeburg carries on as a significant trade centre and as an ecclesiastical metropolitan city (Tullner 2008: 22).

During the 12th century, the Magdeburg town law, *Stadtrecht*, was developed, one of the most important laws in Europe. The German and European law history was further influenced by the *Sachsenspiegel*, a book of law written by Eike von Repgow. The present territory of Saxony-Anhalt is well known as the homeland of the Reformation. The region comprises some of the most important sites related to the Reformation such as: Wittemberg, Eisleben (Martin Luther's birth place), Mansfeld and Magdeburg (Tullner 2008: 29). The topic of the reformation has been promoted by authorities of Saxony-Anhalt and the representation of Saxony-Anhalt to the European Union. Tourism has been advertised and in 2017, 500 years of reformation will be celebrated (Investment and Marketing Corporation Saxony-Anhalt 2016).

The positive development of the region was severely damaged during the thirty years war. After the conflicts, the area was one of the most desolated. It was no longer a political or economic nucleus in Central Europe, *Mitteleuropa*. The Westphalian peace caused the loss of political independence of the territory (Tullner 2008: 40).

The city of Magdeburg was seriously destroyed. The natural scientist Otto-von-Guericke was at the time mayor, who represented the city at the peace negotiations. The city came under the political power of Brandenburg, which was interested in having the connection to the Elbe-passage. Due to the economic importance of Magdeburg, the city was re-constructed but as part of the *Kurfürstentum* Brandenburg. Magdeburg became in the 18th century the strongest fortification of Prussia (Tullner 2008: 44).

The Leipzig battle from 1813 had a significant importance for the future of the Saxonian province. Until then, the king of Saxony was loyal to the French emperor Friedrich August. During the negotiations of the Vienna congress, the king had to give 57.5% of the territory to Prussia, an old enemy of Saxony. The Prussian government split the territory of Saxony and distributed it to the provinces of Silesia, Brandenburg and Saxony. The smallest part of Saxony together with other Prussian territories became the new Prussian Province Saxony (Barmuß/Kathe 1992: 140).

3.2 The industrialisation

Tullner argued that a main impulse for the industrial development of today Saxony-Anhalt was the agriculture, contributing to the development of an economic area (2005). Magdeburg was the centre of sugar beet, even though the first fabric was in Silesia.[8] The ban of Napoleon on imports triggered the development of factories, refineries and commercial stores around Magdeburg for the processing of sugar beet and sugar trade (Tullner 2005: 8). Due to the import ban imposed by Napoleon, innovation arose in Saxony-Anhalt through the processing of sugar from sugar beet. The processing required industry and machines. Therefore, a spill-over effect took place, from the need of machines and pieces to the development of factories and of the brown coal industry, in order to comply with the energy demand.

A network of enterprises arose around Weißenfels, Webau, Halle, fostering the delivery of brown coal, its processing (smouldering), and production of paraffin and of other products, setting the beginning of the chemical industry. Among these developments, the invention of the compactor, *Brikettpresse*, by Carl Exter – firstly tested in 1858 around Halle, contributed to the further development of the industry. Even if the sugar industry stopped for a while after the end of the Napoleon era, the economy measures and the Prussian tariff law, *Zollgeset,* revived the industry in the area, especially due to the access to the Elbe, a main transport opportunity. Agriculture fostered the research and, in 1863, the first chair of agronomy was opened at a German university, in Halle, today, a city in Saxony-Anhalt (Tullner 2005: 10-11).

---

[8] Build by Franz Carl Achad, the student of the chemist Andreas Sigismus Marggraf, who discovered that sugar could be produced out of beet (Tullner 2005: 6).

If at the beginning Magdeburg was the central location of industry, the factories that developed later were in other areas, such as the enterprise of Friedrich Zimmermann in Halle, of Wilhelm Siedersleben in Bernburg, and of Friedrich Dehne in Halberstadt. In Buckau, Rudolf Wolf developed the production of railroad locomotives for the first time in Germany, after they had been produced in England (Tullner 2005: 11-12). This was not the first experience with technological innovation from England. These industrial elements contribute to the use of the territory's specificities by Saxony-Anhalt's authorities in shaping the development's strategy.

In 1778, an English steam-engine was used close to Magdeburg for the lignite mining industry. The first steam-engine built by German technicians was built in 1785 in the Mansfelder industry, also part of the today Saxony-Anhalt (Tullner 2008: 48-50). Later, English firms set up offices and establishments in the area, for example, in 1861, John D. Garrett built a factory for agriculture machines, contributing to the mechanisation of agriculture. Further developments were carried out by John Fowler from Leeds (Tullner 2005: 12).

During the 19th century, the provinces Saxony and Anhalt developed under the command of Prussia. The well-developed traditional agriculture, the existing and extending railroad network, the development of the sugar beet cultivation and processing, and their central position within the empire, favoured the development of these provinces. Agriculture helped the development of machineries factories (around Magdeburg) that produced mechanical tools for agriculture. Brown coal production (around the area of Halle) was the source of energy for the processing of sugar (Tullner 2008: 66). Magdeburg became the centre of machine building whereas, between Halle and Bitterfeld, the chemical industry arose (Welz 2004: 274).

The production of tar, industrial oils, light lamps, paraffin and candles developed and the industry of potash evolved. At the beginning of the 20th century, the provinces Saxony and Anhalt became economic regions, with important industries such as the chemical industry and electrical energy production based on brown coal. Many factories for the chemical industry were built around Bitterfeld. The brown coal industry was meant to deliver electrical energy for Berlin. Before the First World War, the Hugo Junkers' industry of aircrafts building began in Dessau and the centres of the chemical industry were Bitterfeld, Halle, Staßburg/Bernburg, Piesteritz and Leuna (Tullner 2008).

The contributions of Walter Rathenau (1867-1922) to the development of the electrochemistry are also worth mentioning. In 1893, AEG was founded, followed by the film factory Agfa and the colour factory. Through these developments, Central Germany became the centre of the German energy-driven economy. The sugar beet industry remained a main driver of the economy in the area, establishing the trend of developing a modern market based on agriculture and large-scale firms (Tullner 2005: 16-17). Therefore, agriculture contributed significantly to the economic development of the area, and the 19th century witnessed a structural change in the capitalist agriculture.

Characteristic of that development was the close bond between agriculture and industry. The constructive way of thinking contributed to a positive reaction to the hunger crisis due to a demographic positive change. The economic boost was also stimulated by merchants that invested in the construction of sugar beet and chicory factories. Further contributions came through the Prussian reforms that removed legal barriers for entrepreneurial actions (Schaal 2005: 20-24).

Even though locomotives were built, the Railway was not yet developed. But the establishment of the Hermann Gruson machine building factory in Buckau contributed to the production of pieces for the Railway (Tullner 2005: 14-16). The Gruson factory contributed to the development of chilled casting that fostered the military technique. A further development was the potash industry in 1861, in Staßfurt. The chemist Adolph Frank (1834-1916) built the first potash factory. Germany monopolised this industry until 1914. The first electrical locomotive drove, in 1911, between Bitterfeld and Dessau on normal tracks, inaugurating the electric driven railway traffic in Germany (Tullner 2008: 67).

After the First World War, the developments in agriculture, chemical industry and aviation industry expanded. The industry provided energy for other German regions.[9] Since 1917, the Electricity factory Saxony-Anhalt *AG* (stock company) provided common electricity for the provinces Saxony and Anhalt (Tullner 2008: 74). But, Saxony and Anhalt offered more than the industry. They facilitated the cultural development by promoting and hosting the *Bauhaus* style, which was forbidden in Weimar for political reasons. The cities Magdeburg, Halle and Dessau (which are today also part of the Land Saxony-Anhalt) became modern big cities. These elements contributed to the development of the regional identity that fostered the mobilisation of actors to promote the specificities of the region.

During the Weimarer Republic, the issue of the territorial new arrangement failed. However, the trade association Central Germany – *Wirtschaftsverband Mitteldeutschland* – advocated the overcoming of territorial fragmentation that the big industries in the area were facing. The association's interest was the economic welfare through the elimination of small-

---

[9] 1919 began the first on site production of *Ganzmetall-Kabinenflugzeug* of the world. The fusion of Junkers *Luftverkehr AG* with the german Aero Floyd took place in 1926, emerging the *Lufthansa* company (Tullner 2008: 74).

state relations and the establishment of a unitary state and administration structure (Tullner 2008: 76). In the 1920s, the issue of the Central Germany question – *Mitteldeutschlandfrage* – was whether to create a German *Land* comprising more provinces or to unite Saxony and Anhalt. Due to the belonging of Saxony to Prussia, the resistance of Anhalt to that affiliation, and due to economic interests, the plan of uniting Saxony and Anhalt was not accomplished until 1933. According to several plans, different cities such as Magdeburg, Halle or Leipzig were proposed as capitals of a new *Land* (Tullner 2008: 79).

During the 1929 economic crisis, the strong industrialised region had a high rate of unemployment. Radical political movements caught the attention and were successful among the people. The *Freistaat* Anhalt, known for its enlightened rulers, was the first German *Land* to have a *NSDAP* government since 1932. The industry enlarged further. Factories that were producing armament such as the Magdeburger Krupp-Gruson *Werk*, Polte-*Werke* already existed. Other companies just changed their production over to the armament-oriented production (aviation industry, chemical industry, machineries industry in Magdeburg) while new factories were built, such as BUNA-*Werk* close to Halle (Tullner 2008: 80-82).

The transportation network was upgraded as well. Two of the most important German highways, from Berlin to Rheinland and to Nürnberg, were covering Saxony-Anhalt. The Railway offered, in 1934, a fully electric transport way from Leipzig to Bitterfeld, Dessau, Magdeburg, Halle and back to Leipzig, called the *mitteldeutsche Ring* (Tullner 2008: 83-84). Towards the end of the Second World War, the region was occupied and its further existence was ruled by other powers.

3.3 The establishment of Saxony-Anhalt after 1945

The retreat of the American army and the take-over by the Soviet army of territories of Eastern Germany in 1945 was not received well by the people in the area. Many tried to leave the region when the Americans retreated. The Soviet army introduced a "soviet military administration" in each *Land*. Saxony and Thuringia were "re-activated"; Mecklenburg was united with the province Pomerania, Western parts of the Prussian province Brandenburg formed the province Brandenburg (Tullner 2008; 2012).

The Prussian districts Magdeburg and Merseburg and the *Land* Anhalt remained un-allocated, but there had been a plan ever since 1929 for this specific territory to be established as the *Land* Saxony-Anhalt. One of its promoters was the Prussian governor of Saxony, Erhard Hübener, who was later appointed by the Soviet army as president of the territory of the remained provinces Saxony and Anhalt, which they called the province Saxony. Hübener's plan caught life. The Soviet choice for the territory under Hübener's rule, called Saxony, meant that there were two Saxonies, the other having the capital Dresden. Hübener established the districts Magdeburg, Merseburg and Dessau (Tullner 2008: 90-92).

The Social-Democrat Party (*SPD*) and the Communist Party of Germany (*KPD*) were forcefully united to the Socialist Unity Party of Germany (*SED*) in April 1946. Due to continuous confusion with the province Saxony, the new Saxony was renamed Saxony-Anhalt according to a decision of its parliament, the *Landtag*. However, the name began to be used only in 1947, after the formal dissolution of Prussia. Most of the industry plants were destroyed by the end of 1945, many industry constructions were dismantled and the headquarters of technology collapsed (Tullner 2008: 94-95).

In 1947 a democratic constitution for Saxony-Anhalt was formulated, creating the potential for a democratic and federal development. People hoped for a free German unitary state without Soviet occupation. Hope triggered initiatives for the reconstruction of the destroyed cities and communes and endorsed the enthusiasm for regional culture and identity. The retreat of Hübener was an expression of the failure of a federal evolution in Saxony-Anhalt.

The government was led next by Werner Bruschke, who helped the implementation of the central policies of *SED*. In that centralist system, in 1952 the *Länder* were dissolved. Within the German Democratic Republic, the districts Halle and Magdeburg were created. Many insurrections followed. The *SED* began to improve Halle's economy, which became the chemical district. The Halle-Leuna-Bitterfeld area remained important to the chemical industry, but their performed industrial activity was harmful to the environment (Tullner 2008: 95-98). The development of the chemical industry played an important role for the mobilisation possibilities of Saxony-Anhalt. The empirical analysis shows how Saxony-Anhalt shaped its participation within EMLG around this specific sector.

The unification of the historical provinces and the emergence of the *Land* Saxony-Anhalt lasted from 1947 until 1952 and it was re-established in 1990. The region was characterised by the fertility of its soil, the mineral resources, the mining industry (copper, lignite, and ore) until the end of the 20th century. Other cities were known for their salt production. The trade development included arterial roads around the river Elbe. The region became part of the trade activities of the Hanseatic League (Tullner 2008: 15). Therefore, the space of today Saxony-Anhalt offers a great foundation for the economic development of the *Land* as it is today.

3.4 The re-establishment of Saxony-Anhalt 1989-90

The evangelical church and the Anhalt regional church played a crucial role in restoring the identity characteristics of Saxony-Anhalt after 1989. The dilemma of choosing the capital was left to the *Landtag*, which later chose Magdeburg. The dispute for the capital shows the lack of a political, an economic and a cultural centre of Saxony-Anhalt that could be accepted by the majority. Lower-Saxony offered help to Saxony-Anhalt thanks to the traditional cooperation between Magdeburg and Braunschweig (Tullner 2008).

The federal foreign minister at the time, Hans-Dietrich Genscher, was from Halle. His position in the federal government contributed to the development of self-awareness in the new *Land* Saxony-Anhalt. His affiliation with the Free Democratic Party (*FDP*) played a role in the 1990 election results in Saxony-Anhalt. The *FDP* received more than 10% of the votes being able to build together with the *CDU* a coalition for 1990-1994. However, the coalition was not continued for the second term of the *Landtag*, because the *FDP* did not reach the hurdle for the *Landtag* (Tullner 2008: 108-9).

During the first years, the re-established Saxony-Anhalt was faced with political disturbances that were reflected on the economic recovery of the *Land*. The collapse of the Soviet market triggered the collapse of most industries in Saxony-Anhalt. Many old factories, such as Agfa in Wolfen, ceased. The economic decline was further burdened by the environmental damage produced by the chemical industry. However, there was a strong political will to preserve and modernise the traditional German industry – such as the chemical headquarters Bitterfeld, Leuna, Buna. Modernisation was supported by both the Federal Republic of Germany and by the European Union (Tullner 2008: 110-13).

The opposition measures against the Socialist Unity Party of Germany ruling in Leipzig were backed up onto Halle and Magdeburg. Protests rose in Dessau, Wittenberg, Stendal, and Halberstadt. The re-establishment of federal structures was influenced by television personalities, who were known among people in the GDR. They demanded the right to decide on the local resources and to maintain the homeland regional traditions (Tullner 2012).

The idea of re-building the *Länder* began to develop in the district councils[10] (Tullner 2012: 72).

Re-establishing the *Land* Saxony-Anhalt was also important for Magdeburg and Halle, as they could become the capital city. The processes for the re-establishment of the *Land* from the former *Land* Anhalt were important, especially due to the longer history and traditions of the area that survived the communist time better than the ones of the Saxony-Anhalt. The established regional church was the continuous visible representation of traditions in Anhalt, which ceased to exist as an entity in 1945. The preservation of old traditions made even clearer the deficiencies in the *SED* ruling (Tullner 2012: 72-73).

Dessau, the former capital of Anhalt, was in a neglected situation. It suffered severe damage during the Second World War and its importance sunk. Due to high awareness of the historical development and traditions, the demands of the 1989 autumn for re-establishing the federal structures encouraged voices in Anhalt to demand the re-establishment of the Freestate Anhalt. Even though such demands were not feasible, the over 800 years old Anhalt pointed out its strong state-existence traditions and federal development. The strength of these traditions and the interests of Anhalt contributed to the establishing of a *Land* in the area of the Elbe (Tullner 2012: 73-4).

Due to a loss of power of the GDR government and their control in the territory, the district councils gained importance and became a stability factor during the collapse of the GDR, since they were the only functioning structures. The president of the Magdeburg district council, Siegfried Grünwald, promoted a policy for re-establishing the *Land* Saxony-Anhalt, making use of his new freedom of action. He contacted the minister-president of Lower-Saxony, Ernst Albrecht, on the 14th November. They agreed upon opening the borders in Böckwitz (GDR) and Zicherie (Lower-Saxony), a double location separated by the wall. From that moment on, the council acted as a government, *Landesregierung*, and the cooperation among the council of Magdeburg and Lower Saxony became the cooperation among the two *Länder*.

A Lower-Saxony office was opened in Magdeburg, followed by an agreement for cooperation, in 1990, regarding the policies for health system, transportation, tourism, and environment protection. Siegfried Grünwald started promoting the idea of re-establishing Saxony-Anhalt with Magdeburg as its capital. Alfred Kolodniak, president of the Halle district council, had a different position. As *SED* secretary, he was reluctant to reforms. In January 1990, he was discharged from office (Tullner 2012: 74-78).

---

[10] The district councils were subordinated to the government and would carry out the policies of the government. These were controlled, instructed and depended on the *SED* conductorship, *Bezirksleitung der SED* (Tullner 2012: 74).

Holtmann and Boll emphasised the role of citizen movements and their contribution to the collapse of the *SED* regime (1997: 11-12). The movements emerged from the opposition groups of the '80s and contributed as spiritual and intellectual initiators of the non-violent revolution from 1989 autumn. They had the freedom to act due to the Perestroika policy of Gorbatchew that triggered the loss of the *SED* monopole power.

During the transition period between the collapse of the old regime and the regional election from March 1990, opposition representatives managed to occupy positions in the public administration and to organise themselves regionally. In December 1989, the structure of the round tables started to take action within the GDR districts. In Magdeburg, Grünwald cooperated with the round table. His cause and the "capital race" were supported by the round table due to his cooperation with the government of Lower-Saxony. Halle had a partnership with Karlsruhe, but Kolodniak opposed the establishment of the round table. Halle and Magdeburg continued their rivalry for the capital of re-established Saxony-Anhalt (Holtmann/Boll 1997: 14-16; Tullner 2012: 78-82).

The deficient tradition of Saxony-Anhalt as entity of a federal system contributed to the difficulty of establishing its structure as a state in the Federal Republic of Germany. The first regional association of the *CDU* Saxony-Anhalt was established in February 1990. Gerd Gies was chosen president of the association and he was a candidate of the Magdeburg constituency. The Magdeburg candidates had the advantage of being perceived as new and fresh ones. In august 1990, the *CDU* regional party organisation of Saxony-Anhalt was established (Tullner 2012: 83-89).

The cooperation among political parties, unions and commerce chambers, both from Magdeburg and Halle and at all levels, encouraged the two German governments to create cooperation frameworks between communes, counties and districts from the GDR and communes, counties and the *Länder* from the FRG. Through the practice of these cooperation relations, the establishment of regional committees emerged. Relevant figures, such as Hans-Dietrich Genscher, accounted as one of the architects of the German unification, and the former mayor of Naumburg, Kurt Becker, returned to Saxony-Anhalt. Their commitment to the homeland raised the awareness and self-esteem of the population in Saxony-Anhalt. There was a clear will to re-establish the *Land* Saxony-Anhalt that was encouraged by the district councils and the round tables (Tullner 2012: 90-91).

A debate about establishing Saxony-Anhalt took place among committees for re-establishing the federal structure of the GDR with four versus five *Länder*, including Saxony-Anhalt. The change of power in Lower-Saxony triggered two developments: firstly, the governmental support from Lower-

Saxony declined, even though the established contacts were maintained, and secondly, many of the former *CDU* and *FDP* elected members and office holders were deliberately directed towards Saxony-Anhalt by the government in Hanover, which triggered a political surplus for the *CDU* in Saxony-Anhalt (Tullner 2012: 99-104). In the end, the *Land* Saxony-Anhalt persisted with Magdeburg as its capital.

Jones argued that every state had its own historical development that provided incentives for the domestic mobilisation of its territorial actors (1995: 289). The specificities of the region, such as the fertile soil and the chemically specialised south part, provided for much of Saxony-Anhalt's economy. The awareness of *Mittteldeutschland's* region persists today and enforces the cooperation among the *Länder* and between public and private actors based on specific sector related interests. Therefore, the historical development of the territory still plays its part in the development strategy of the region.

Next to the history of Saxony-Anhalt, the EU membership started with the membership of the Federal Republic of Germany after the unification. The new membership provided additional financial means and additional administrative burdens and challenges for the implementation of the EU *acquis communautaire*. For coping with the EU membership, authorities of Saxony-Anhalt needed to learn how to deal with them and how to advantageously use the EU membership. That happened through the institutional framework that is presented in the next chapter.

4 Saxony-Anhalt in the European Union – the bottom-up dimension

This section presents the main institutional developments within Saxony-Anhalt that provide the framework for its institutions to act within the Federal Republic of Germany and within the EU. It presents the base for the empirical research based on the premise that: institutional and legal framework of a territory empowers and triggers mobilisation activities.

The German federalism is a particular version of cooperative federalism. The German constitution stipulates a vertical dimension of the separation of powers, which assigns the powerful regional governments to prevent the re-emergence of the centralised national state (Börzel 2002: 45). Although German national interests and identity remain close to the European ones, European integration created a misfit within Germany. This was produced by the "imbalances in the allocation of power among governmental authorities" reducing the legislative powers at national and subnational level in favour of governments (Schmidt 2003: 224).

Through "by-passing" the national state, the regions' actions at European level contribute to the national government's loss of control over their actions. However, working against the national government would not be of use to the regions because of the national government's weight within the Council of the EU. The region's participation strategy can encompass both the national and the European level as valuable access points for the interest representation. This argument is pursued along the analysis. Next to the access channels, a good intrastate relation between authorities of the national and subnational level can increase the region's chances of goals achievement.

The German *Länder* have been developing strategies to participate in the European decision-making processes since the beginning of the European integration process. In order to avoid a transformation into administrative units, the German *Länder* tried to affect the European policy formulation within and outside the borders of the German state, especially since the 1980s. Their behaviour can be classified in two strategies: "let us in" and "leave us alone" (Eppler 2008: 4). These strategies resemble the terms used by Tatham, "bypassing and co-operative diplomacy" (2008).

The "let us in" strategy relates to the direct articulation of interests of the German *Länder* within the European decision-making process. This is realised through the offices in Brussels, which represent the interest of the *Länder* (*Landesvertretung*) and through their representation in the Committee of the Regions. The use of access channels in Brussels is complemented by the

61

use of the intrastate channel of cooperation with the national government (Eppler 2008: 5).

The "leave us alone" strategy has been increasingly adopted since the middle of the 1990s. This strategy targets to improve the regions' autonomy especially through the implementation of the subsidiarity principle. The "leave us alone" strategy can be interpreted as the "bypassing paradiplomacy" term used by Tatham. However, the increase of autonomy without interacting with the national level might be difficult.

The German *Länder* are among the driving forces that empowered the discourse on the regional's level role within the EU. Making use of their veto power as entities with state quality within the Federal Republic of Germany, the *Länder* achieved constitutional rights to have a say in the European policy-making by arguing that European affairs are no longer foreign affairs of the federal government. The *Länder* helped setting the European regional agenda in two ways: a. through mechanisms of shaping European policy priorities within the Federal Republic of Germany by setting markers for subnational involvement in domestic processes of European policy formulation; b. through their driving force for delivering the input of subnational actors in European decision-making processes (Jeffery 2001; Börzel 2002). This occurs through their institutional framework.

4.1 Instrastate institutional changes after 1989

Until the beginning of 1980, the *Länder* had no European formal and binding participatory rights, although Europeanisation had changed significantly the territorial balance of power in favour of the federal government. Regional parliaments had also no binding competence to override regional governments. During the ratification of the Single European Act, attention was redirected towards the *Länder* participation. For this treaty reform, the federal government requested the *Bundesrat* to ratify the reforms. The *Länder* responded offensively because they were not consulted during the negotiations. They considered that the further competencies transfer due to the reforms of a single European market was a serious threat to their state quality (Börzel 2002: 60-65).

The law ratifying the Single European Act introduced the procedural involvement of the *Länder* through the *Bundesrat*, the *Bundesratsverfahren*. It was a formal procedure allowing intrastate participation of the *Länder* in European decision-making, organised exclusively through the *Bundesrat*. The law obliged the federal government to inform the *Bundesrat*. The *Bun-*

desrat gained the right to express formal recommendations to the federal government, exclusively regarding the jurisdiction or essential concerns of the *Länder* (Börzel 2002: 66).

At European level significant changes occurred as a result of the Maastricht Treaty that changed the way the German *Länder* engaged in Germany and in the EU. The demand for an institutional representation of the regional and local level at European level was addressed by the MS. This allowed the emergence of the concept of "Europe of the Regions".

The Treaty of Maastricht determined the emergence of the Committee of the Regions as a political advisory institution. It is being consulted by the European Commission, the European Parliament and the Council of Ministers whenever legislative proposals affect the regional and local level. Germany has 24 full members of the CoR. Each *Land* has a representative. Three representatives are guaranteed for Municipalities and for Associations of Municipalities. The other five seats are covered by extra members of the *Länder*. Their membership is based on a system of rotation (Panara 2011: 148).

The German *Länder* achieved their constitutional participation right at the negotiation process of the Maastricht Treaty. The right to appeal at the European Court of Justice and the direct access of regional representatives to the Council of Ministers, demanded by the German *Länder*, were seen as specific German claims and were not approved. The *Länder* demanded further constitutional co-determination rights in the formulation and representation of the German bargaining position in the European decision-making process (Börzel 2002).

In order to counteract the loss of competencies due to the European integration process, the Federal Republic of Germany introduced in 1992 the Europe Article – Article 23 – in its Basic Law, *Grundgesetz* (*GG*). The article defines the way the Federal Republic of Germany as well as its *Länder* compensate competencies-loss by stipulating the participation of the *Länder* in policy-making processes of the EU. The *Länder* can undertake additional measures in order to promote their specific interests at European level (Börzel 2002). This participation is part of the regional government's activities.

The "de-parliamentarisation" is an effect of the European integration. Goetz argued that European integration strengthened national governments and thus it abetted the process of de-parliamentarisation (2006: 473). He explained that national executive actors gained power while national and regional legislative actors kept on losing competencies. The power of the government lied in its direct participation in negotiation and bargaining processes at the supranational level (Goetz 2006: 473).

The literature delivers different interpretations of the de-parliamentarisation process. On the one hand, parliaments have lost considerable scope of their attributions. On the contrary, Benz contested the thesis that parliaments have turned into powerless institutions due to the Multi-Level Governance system of the EU (2004: 896). He argued that this devolvement offered parliaments the chance to carry out reforms in order to ensure their participation in European negotiations.

The literature pointed out the process of de-parliamentarisation that emphasised competencies' loss of parliaments in favour of their governments. The Article 23 *GG* allows regularly indirect participation and a restricted direct participation of the *Länder* in decision-making processes of the European Union. This article stipulates that the federal government informs the *Bundesrat* "in an exhaustive and timely way about all draft Union acts in which the *Länder* may have an interest" (Panara 2011: 142).

In order to cope with the immense information flow of the European legislative proposals and other European communications, the *Bundesrat* has among the specialised committees the committee for European Union's affairs. This committee operates on a regular schedule like the others and advises about European proposals based on recommendations of the other expert committees. The committee investigates whether the principles of subsidiarity and proportionality are respected. It does not adopt resolutions in the name of the *Bundesrat's* plenary, as the „*Europakammer*" can do (Bundesrat 2016).

The *Länder* are granted a say in the transfer of competencies because the transfer requires the consent of the *Bundesrat*. Changes of the treaties must be adopted by a majority of two-thirds, from the *Bundestag* and the *Bundesrat*. The federal government has to inform and take into consideration recommendations of the *Bundesrat* with regard to European issues. The *Bundesrat* has the final decision on the German bargaining position in the Council of Ministers when former administrative or legislative competencies of the *Länder* are involved. When exclusive *Länder* competencies are at stake, a minister of a *Land* can be head of the German delegation and represent Germany in the Council's negotiations (Börzel 2002).

The *Länder* did not manage to secure the regions' right to appeal to the European Court of Justice in the treaties. The German law on cooperation between the *Bund* and the *Länder* concerning the European affairs grants the *Bundesrat*, the right to request the federal government to appeal to the ECJ on behalf of the *Länder*, if the European institutions change the *Länder* competencies (Bundestag 2009; Börzel 2002: 71). The law provides legal basis for direct contact of the *Länder* with the European institutions. The *Länder* are permitted to establish official representations in Brussels that cannot have diplomatic status, because it would be incompatible with the monopoly of foreign policy of the *Bund* (Panara 2011: 47).

The *Länder* have also the right to participate in the working groups and committees of the Council and of the Commission. The Article 23 of the German basic law restored the territorial balance of power and compensated the *Länder* for the loss of their competencies. Moreover, the *Bundestag's* role increased, because the *Bundestag* and the *Bundesrat* gained co-determination rights in the European policy-making through Article 23 of the Basic Law.

Members of parliaments use their rights of participation in European affairs strategically (Benz 2004: 891). They generally respect the action scope in European negotiations. This is why they draft their resolutions in close cooperation with their governments in order to strengthen the position of their government in negotiations at European level. The same procedures find place at the subnational level in Germany. Resolutions of the *Landtage* mostly confirm the strategies of the regional government.

The *Landtage* depend on the information they obtain from their governments. The Committee of the Regions monitors whether the EU legislative proposals respect the principle of subsidiarity. The *Landtage* can consult recommendations and position papers of the CoR and make use of the work carried out by this institution. The *Länder* are represented in the *Bundesrat* by members of their governments. The *Bundesrat* can also adopt binding mandates for the government. But this is only available for policies that affect the legislative powers of the *Länder*. However, the *Landtage* have little influence on the bargaining processes in *Bundesrat*. They can only adopt their resolutions regarding the strategy of their government.

Parliaments of the German *Länder* have established special committees for European affairs, as the *Bundestag* and the *Bundesrat*. These are confronted with the rivalry between other specialised committees, which deal with EU-related matters falling in their portfolio. Subnational executives are obliged to submit an annual report "on how EU politics affect the *Land* and what the government has done" (Hrbek 2010: 148). These reports give the opportunity to parliaments to control what governments are doing. But the government is not the only source of information for the *Landtage*. As the analysis in the next chapter shows, members of the *Landtag* of Saxony-Anhalt started to personally connect with European actors by holding committee meetings in Brussels and engaging in direct communication with important actors from the European institutions.

The adoption of Article 23 can be called as a process of Europeanising the German Basic Law (Clement 1996: 13). The Treaty of Lisbon was examined by the German Federal Constitutional Court before its ratification. The Court ruled that the treaty would be compliant with the Basic Law if the *Bundestag* and the *Bundesrat* were given sufficient participatory rights in the decision-making of the EU. In 1993, four laws were adopted that were complementary to Article 23. These laws provided the *Bundestag* and the *Bundesrat* with extended rights in European affairs and determined the framework of responsibility of the *Bundestag* and the *Bundesrat* in the European integration. Accompanying the ratification of the Treaty of Lisbon was the amendment of these laws (Bundestag 2009).

The responsibility law for European integration stipulated that measures proposed at European level and the further extension of competencies required the passing of a law according to Article 23. Without such a law, the German representative in the Council had to vote against the measure or the extension. The rationale of the amendments was an expansion of the *Länder's* and of the *Bundestag's* involvement in the European decision-making process (Panara 2011: 134-139).

During the preparation of the Treaty of Lisbon, the German *Länder* developed their agenda stressing the strengthening of the regional level. Their wish list entailed the designation of competencies for the *Länder* (Eppler 2008: 6). The demand for an explicit reference to the existence and the role of regional authorities within the EU was fulfilled as mentioned in Article 4 of the Treaty of Lisbon and the Preamble of the Charter of the Fundamental Rights.

The demand of the German *Länder* to have a catalogue of EU competencies was not achieved, but the Treaty of Lisbon made clear the division between categories of decision-making competencies. The principle of subsidiarity was invoked in the Treaty of Lisbon and the procedure of controlling its implementation has been extended to the Committee of the Regions and to national parliaments. Regional parliaments were not mentioned in the "early warning mechanism" or in the implementation control of the principle of subsidiarity. However, the *Länder* were taken into consideration. Their participation in the procedure occurred through the *Bundesrat* (Eppler 2008).

4.2 The *Landtag* of Saxony-Anhalt

Through the unification treaty, the new *Länder* became automatically part of the Federal Republic of Germany. Saxony-Anhalt maintained the flag and coat of arms that were used in 1952. However, Saxony-Anhalt had a smaller population and a smaller territory after 1989.[11] The *Land* had no legislative,

---

[11] From 24.669 square km to 20.445 square km (Tullner 2012: 126).

executive and judicial structures and, together with other four *Länder*, the federal government led it.

District administrative authorities remained active and were accountable to the federal interior ministry. The institutions and structures involved in the preparation work for establishing the structures of the *Land* were: the *Clearingstelle* in Bonn, the Clearing-coordinator, the government delegation, the *Land* delegation, and the project and guidance group of the two administrative authorities (Tullner 2012: 128). The first re-established institution of Saxony-Anhalt was its parliament.

The *Landtag* of Saxony-Anhalt began the "modern history of Saxony-Anhalt" in October 1990 (Sachsen-Anhalt 2010: 10). The first assignment of the parliament was to elaborate a new constitution that was adopted on the 16th July 1992. The constitutive session of the newly democratic elected *Landtag* took place in Dessau, where-in 1848/49 one of the most democratic constitutions of modern German constitutional history was developed.

The location's choice for the *Landtag's* first session emphasised the contribution of Anhalt's interests in the constitution process of the new Saxony-Anhalt. The close vote for the capital was in favour of Magdeburg (Tullner 2012: 132). The election of Gerd Gies as minister-president of Saxony-Anhalt also occurred at the first parliament session. Gies established the government coalition between the *CDU* and the *FDP*. The administrative structure of Saxony-Anhalt was composed of the districts Magdeburg, Halle and Dessau. This structure was dissolved in 2001, as a unitary administration office of the *Land* was established in Halle (Tullner 2012: 131-133).

The *Landtag* practises the legislative process, the regulation of the budget, the election of the minister-president and the control of the government. The election of the minister-president is crucial because the regional government – likewise the federal government – has a major scope in dealing with European affairs and with the European institutions. Other decisions of the *Landtag* are justified by competitive competencies that the *Bund* and the *Länder* share (Article 74 Basic Law).

The *Landtag's* plenum is considered to be a place of communication, where decisions are made. The decisions are firstly prepared by experts committees. The work of these committees is being carried out by members of each political group, government officers and the legal service for legislation and advisory of the *Landtag* (Sachsen-Anhalt 2010: 72). The political parliamentary groups manage the consultation and decision-making process within the *Landtag* (Benz 1998:115).

In the 1990s, most German regional parliaments increased their interest in the European affairs. This was visible through their information requests to the regional government, their written opinion expressed through position papers, and the creation of Europe-committees. The involvement of the members of regional parliaments in European affairs occurred through personal contact with MEP, participation in trans- and interregional networks and parliamentary cooperation with other regional parliaments (Müller/Mauren 2002).

The *Landtag* of Saxony-Anhalt defined the stipulations for its participation in European affairs in the constitution, a law on the information of the parliament by the government from 2004 and an agreement between the *Landtag* and the *Landesregierung* on the information of the *Landtag* based on Article 62 of Saxony-Anhalt's constitution.

The first article of the Saxony-Anhalt constitution emphasises the affiliation of the region to both the Federal Republic of Germany and to the European Community. Reich noted that the expression of belonging to the EU stressed the sovereignty and the active participation of Saxony-Anhalt within the intrastate and European framework that is provided for the subnational level (2004: 47). Article 62 regulates the obligation of the government to inform the parliament.

The law on informing of parliament by the government stipulates that informing should take place in sufficient time, so that the parliament can prepare its position papers (Landesregierung Sachsen-Anhalt 2010b). The Rule of internal procedure of the *Landtag* contains specific procedures for the European affairs. According to these, the regional government is obliged to inform the *Landtag* of the government's intentions as well as of the legislative documents that are prepared by the European Union (Landtag Sachsen-Anhalt 2009: §54).

One of the specialised committees of the *Landtag* is the committee for federal and European affairs, and media. The committee's composition reflects the political groups' proportion of the *Landtag* and all the political groups that have at least one member of the committee, which prepares the advisement of the *Landtag's* decisions (Landtag Sachsen-Anhalt 2009: §14). This committee is always informed on European affairs. It has the right to forward drafts to other expert committees within the *Landtag* that prepare position papers (Wohland 2008).

Topics covered by the agreement between the *Landtag* and the *Landesregierung* of Saxony-Anhalt on the informing of the parliament by the government are:

- Consultation proceedings within the *Bundesrat* according to Article 23 Basic Law and regarding the early warning mechanism,
- Observations of the *Bundesrat* concerning violations of the principle of subsidiarity,
- Cooperation between *Bund* and *Länder* in European affairs,

- Works of the minister-presidents' conferences,
- Briefings about key aspects of the work of the Council of the EU and of the government's policies concerning the EU affairs (Landesregierung Sachsen-Anhalt 2010b: 4).

The contribution of the *Landtag* to Saxony-Anhalt's regional participation with EMLG is to elaborate position papers and vote resolutions. The government takes the resolutions of the *Landtag* into consideration. Resolutions and position papers are not binding for the government. The *Landtag* is also allowed to check whether the legislative initiatives of the Commission are not infringing upon the subsidiarity principle. The *Landtag* issues resolutions and opinions concerning European affairs, especially those that are of particular concern for the *Land*. The committee for federal and European affairs and media is allowed to make decisions about EU resolutions in the name of the plenum (Wohland 2008: 164).

The number of the *Landtag's* opinions concerning European affairs is low. The committee for federal and European affairs and media meets only once a month, which makes the process of opinions elaboration difficult. Since all political groups of the *Landtag* are represented in this committee, the committee's members need to achieve a consensus based on political bargaining in order to pass these resolutions (Landesregierung Sachsen-Anhalt 2010b).

The goverment's control has become one of the main tasks of the *Landtag* that supervises the position represented by the government in the *Bundesrat*. Members of the committee for federal and European affairs and media are responsible for the communication with members of the European Parliament or with the representation office in Brussels (Wohland 2008: 164).

4.3 The *Landesregierung* of Saxony-Anhalt

The *Landesregierung* is the executive institution of the *Land*. The constitution of Saxony-Anhalt provides the legal framework for the government's activity. The direct election of the minister-president by the *Landtag* provides him democratic legitimacy. The government rules by norms of the minister-president's guiding principle and of the ministries' resort autonomy. The government's resolutions are decided upon according to the cabinet's principle. In the case of a ruling coalition government, the coalition agreement settles the main rules and forms of the cooperation within the government. This agreement between the governing parties determines the political content of the government's policies (Putz 2006: 81, 84).

The first years of Saxony-Anhalt were not free of political conflicts among the governing parties of the government and the opposition ones (Böhmer/Schneider 2001). In 1990, the *CDU* and the *FPD* built the first government coalition. The first legislative period after the unification was unstable and the government was led by several minister-presidents. The social-democrat Reinhard Höppner was minister-president for the next two legislative periods, until 2002. The *SPD* and the *BÜNDNIS 90/DIE GRÜNEN* built a minority government in 1994 that was tolerated by the Party of Democratic Socialism (*PDS*). After the election of 1998 the social-democrats took over the government. They were again tolerated by the *PDS*.

In 2002 the election results changed the political balance. The *CDU* won 37% of votes. They built a new coalition with the *FDP* and the government was led by minister-president Wolfgang Böhmer. The government faced the challenge of the *Land's* budget and financial restructuration. The administration needed to be reformed and the creation of jobs was fundamental. From a highly industrial productive region (6% of the territory was needed to make 40% of the industrial production), the newly established *Land* inherited a highly ecological pollution (Welz 2004: 277). Most of the industries closed and about 20% of the jobs were lost.

Saxony-Anhalt's actors considered that the *Land* was integrated within the Federal Republic of Germany and within the European Community. The idea of the double belonging became the "credo" of Saxony-Anhalt's EU-policy. This was carried out through the establishment of the ministry for federal and European affairs in 1991. The ministry was more than a replica of the one in Lower-Saxony. It bundled the responsibilities for European affairs of the *Landesregierung* in order to compensate and to overcome the lacking expertise, and in this way, European affairs constantly gained importance (Wobben/Heinke 2006).

In 1991 the minister for federal and European affairs called on for the establishment of several institutions: a representation office in Brussels, a Euro-Info-Center within the Chamber of Crafts and a consultancy office in Halle. Offices in Saxony-Anhalt promoted the European funding programmes. The Brussels office gathered essential information from the European Commission, especially in the field of economy and environment (Wobben/Heinke 2006: 222).

In order to enhance the Europe-expertise, a Europe-department was created within the ministry for federal and European affairs. As part of the Europeanisation, the regional policy was to establish contacts with members from the European Commission and other European institutions. The regional interests' representation was extended to the intergovernmental level within Germany through the establishment of the conference of the Europe-ministers

(*Europaministerkonferenzen*, Schmuck 2009). Their mission was to coordinate the cooperation of the *Länder*. The consultancy processes during these conferences were mainly about the political strategy and institutional challenges the *Länder* were faced with (Wobben/Heinke 2006).

Rainer Robra has been in charge of the Saxony-Anhalt state-chancellery since 2002, which coordinates the activities of the *Landesregierung*. In this role, he has been also in charge of the „*Europapolitik*" of Saxony-Anhalt. As Europe-minister, Robra attended the Europe-minister-conferences (*EMK*) of the *Länder's* meetings. The Saxony-Anhalt representation in Berlin has a department that assists the work of the Europe-minister of Saxony-Anhalt, especially in the *EMK* case. Saxony-Anhalt's responsibilities concerning European affairs include the activities:

- Coordination of the main questions regarding the EU,
- Observation and analysis of the European political developments in order to inform the government about them so the *Land* policies could be shaped according to the subsidiarity principle,
- Representation of the *Land* at international conferences and international committees,
- Representation of the *Land's* interests during consultations of the *Bundesrat's* EU-committee,
- Representation of the *Land* in the *EMK*, in the CoR or in the Council of European Municipalities and Regions,
- Informing the *Landtag* about EU affairs and reporting to the *Landtag's* committee for federal and European affairs and media,
- Maintaining the contacts between the *Land* government and the EU officials and the MEPs,
- Presenting the *Land* in Brussels together with the Brussels representation,
- Providing information and consulting (Sachsen-Anhalt 2016c).

Saxony-Anhalt's representation to the *Bund*, in Berlin, is part of the state-chancellery in Magdeburg, which is led by the minister-president. The state-secretary Michael Schneider is director of the representation of Saxony-Anhalt to the *Bund*. He is also Saxony-Anhalt's authorised representative to the *Bund*. The representation in Berlin is the "hinge" between the government of Saxony-Anhalt, the *Bundesrat*, the *Bundestag* and the *Bundesregierung*. The members represent the *Land* within the committees of the *Bundesrat* and have the right to vote within the committees. Their staff in Berlin can participate at the *Bundesrat's* and *Bundestag's* committee meetings and plenary sessions. They maintain contacts with members of the federal ministries, other federal authorities and interest representatives. The representation public relations include events, many cultural ones, at which culture or economy, research and policies of the *Land* are presented to political and economic actors, and to the media and the society (Sachsen-Anhalt 2016a).

The state-secretary, Michael Schneider, began his political activity in Saxony-Anhalt in December 1990. He left the working group Education and Science of the *CDU/CSU Bundestag* political group to be the director of the Saxony-Anhalt *CDU Landtag's* political group. Minister-president Böhmer named him in May 2002 to be state-secretary for the federal and European affairs and the authorised representative of Saxony-Anhalt to the *Bund*. Since then, he has been the director of the representation in Berlin. He has also been representing Saxony-Anhalt in the Committee of the Regions since 2002 (Sachsen-Anhalt 2016b).

The representation of Saxony-Anhalt to the European Union, in Brussels, started its work in 1992 in order to facilitate a direct and effective contribution of Saxony-Anhalt to the European integration. At the time, it was called "the contact office of Saxony-Anhalt" and it was an outpost embedded in the ministry for federal and European affairs (Wobben/Busse 2012: 61). The representation has been under the jurisdiction of the state-chancellery since 1999. Its work guidelines are:

- To establish and to maintain close contacts with the European institutions, to the permanent representation of the Federal Republic of Germany to the EU, to the offices of the *Länder* and other regions and organisations represented in Brussels,
- To inform the *Landesregierung* and other public authorities in Saxony-Anhalt about the European political intentions, plans and programmes,
- To represent specific interests of the *Land* to the European Commission and other European institutions in early stages of decision-making processes,
- To facilitate the support and the guidance for other institutions or agencies of Saxony-Anhalt to reach the EU institutions,
- To present the region's long tradition at European level (Sachsen-Anhalt 2016d).

The horizontal cooperation among the 16 *Länder* is complemented by the work of the *Länderbeobachter*, the Observer of the *Länder*, and their common institution in Brussels. This institution supports the *Bundesrat* and informs the *Länder* about the EU related developments, especially within the Council of the EU. The staff of the Observer attends and reports on meetings of the Council. The information they provide to the *Länder* facilitates the federal government's control and whether this incorporated the *Bundesrat's* resolutions in the negotiations of the Council. The Observer works closely with the permanent representation of Germany as well (Der Beobachter der Länder bei der EU 2016).

4.4 Stakeholders in Saxony-Anhalt

Next to the regional parliament and government, there are stakeholders in Saxony-Anhalt interested in the participation of Saxony-Anhalt within EMLG. The historic development of the chemical and machine building industry in Saxony-Anhalt was faced with a massive process of deindustrialisation after the unification. Due to environmental damage, old industry sites needed to be demolished and new facilities were required so that the industrial sites could continue their work. Further existence of the chemical triangle Leuna-Schkopau-Böhlen was supported by Chancellor Kohl, in 1991, promising that it would be preserved (Wolf/Rannenberg 2000: 110).

There can be distinguished 3 development phases of Saxony-Anhalt in the EU: a. 1990-1996, b. 1996-2003, and c. 2003-2012. The first phase was shaped by many privatisation and restructuring processes performed by the *Treuhandanstalt*, federal and regional government. The EU kept a close record in order to ensure the implementation of the European laws regarding competitiveness policies and financing issues. Political and economic actors were committed to transform Saxony-Anhalt into a modern industrial region (Bratzke/Tobaben 2012).

The restructuring process involved actors from all levels, communes, *Länder* institutions, federal, and European level (Bratzke/Tobaben 2012: 186-7). A crucial question at that time was which companies should be rescued, in order to decrease the massive unemployment. The American DOW Chemical enterprise invested in the chemical industry location of Saxony-Anhalt. DOW accepted the challenge of re-emerging the local chemical industry together with a package of public subsidies of 4.5 billion *Deutsche Marken*. 95% of the investment was done by the end of 1999. An important factor for the decision of DOW to locate its investment in Germany was the need of stability. In addition, close vicinity to the market and low transport costs enhanced the attraction of Saxony-Anhalt as the location for new investment (Wolf/Rannenberg 2000: 110-113).

In 1991 Bayer invested, among the first corporations, in the Central German chemical triangle. It was one of the most advanced chemical infrastructures world-wide. The Bayer Chemical Park Bitterfeld-Wolfen implemented for the first time the "chemical park" concept, on a large scale becoming a model for other regions in Europe. Further investments came along from the American Dow Chemical Corporation in Schkopau, the French mineral oil producer Elf Aquitaine in Leuna and the Italian chemical corporation Radici Chimica in Zeitz. Investments led to the establishment of companies within those locations (Sachsen-Anhalt 2016e).

During the second phase, European funds were used for the development of the region, especially the area around Halle/Leipzig within the framework of the innovation policy. In 1996, the regional forum *Mitteldeutschland* emerged. Territories from several *Länder* built an industrial centre that triggered economic initiatives and led to the emergence of industrial networks, e.g. CeChemNet, the network of central German chemical parks, the network of central German waste disposal, and the network for plastics engineering (Bratzke/Tobaben 2000: 188-9).

In 1994, the establishment of a special European funding programme for the chemical industry in Bitterfeld was pursued (Wobben/Heinke 2006: 224). The use of the funding was for the environment's conservation and the future use of the property for recreation activities, because the damage of the GDR's chemical industry needed to be handled. Since then, the former chemical sites have been replaced by new chemical parks and Saxony-Anhalt developed into modern chemical headquarters. The chemical industry remained one of the most important sectors of the region's economy (Wobben 2007: 78-9).

In 2000, a consensus was established so structural funding would carry on after 2006. In 2001, the structural funds topic for Saxony-Anhalt after 2006 was a concern for Saxony-Anhalt's government that presented the progress made with the chemical industry to the European Commission and MEPs. Representatives of the European institutions welcomed the choice to preserve the chemical industry specific in Saxony-Anhalt and recognised its potential for future development. Saxony-Anhalt looked for new partners and established cooperation in the field of chemical industry with Polish Voivodeship Mazovia, which continues until today (Landesvertretung Sachsen-Anhalt bei der EU 2001, 2002).

Saxony-Anhalt provided a good environment for small and medium enterprises. The location and a connected market were the main aspects that the region offered to the new investing companies. These were elements that contributed to the involvement of Elf and DOW (Wolf/Rannenberg 2000: 110). The French enterprise Elf had also the choice at the beginning of the 1990s whether to leave Germany or to stay and invest. The location of the newly built refinery at Leuna was ideal for Elf and they invested in Saxony-Anhalt (Tricoire 2000; Tricoire/Wolf/Rannenberg 2000).

The third phase of development made it possible for Saxony-Anhalt, together with the developed clusters and networks, to represent its interests at European level. The chemical industry gave early signals expressing their wish to contribute to the regional partnerships and the interest representation process of Saxony-Anhalt (Bratzke/Tobaben 2012: 189).

The close cooperation between economy's actors and public authorities lead to the emergence of the European Chemical Regions Network, the

CeChemNet, and the Cluster *Chemie/Kunststoffe*. These cooperation and activities of Saxony-Anhalt are closely presented in the chapters 6 and 7 on the policy-oriented participation of Saxony-Anhalt in European Multi-Level Governance.

5 Political guidelines of Saxony-Anhalt's participation within European Multi-Level Governance

The book looks into the political preferences of Saxony-Anhalt's actors and how they made use of their institutional and strategic settings for their participation in EMLG. The new institutionalism names formal (structure, rules) and informal (values, norms) constraints for regional mobilisation, which have been comprised in the strategy design that a region should have. Mobilisation can have different meanings and different implementation methods. However, the declared motivation and will of subnational actors to be involved and to participate in EMLG, is a first step.

Participation was not solely a bottom-up desire due to loss of competencies and lack of political influence at European level. Participation of the subnational level's actors was increasingly desired and requested by European actors, as presented in the previous chapters. The Commission's White Paper on European Governance declared that participation was about shaping policies more efficiently through the use of consultation processes and experience of involved actors.

Detterbeck named the strategies that could be applied by small entities such as regions to determine their „*Europapolitik*" (2012: 170). Firstly, each entity needs to set its key interests and priorities, than a targeted search of partners becomes strategically crucial especially for back-up when cooperating with supranational institutions. Hence, this chapter presents Saxony-Anhalt's interests. Actors are no longer just states or the EU, according to the classic theories of international relations, but more and more they are collective actors such as governments, individual departments, parliaments or political parties. Through the German election system, the MEPs are strongly connected to the region's constituency (Renzsch 2012: 119). Hence, the actors' constellation of a region that mobilises has also become a multi-level one.

The chapter validates the hypothesis that the regional political prioritisation process is influenced by European policies. The political prioritisation guides the strategy of mobilisation activities. For this purpose, the chapter offers a chronological presentation of the EU's role for Saxony-Anhalt and the government's political guidelines. The period before 2002 shortly introduces the three analysed legislative periods that are presented separately.

At the beginning of the new political life of Saxony-Anhalt, there was hope that the promises of the *CDU* and the *FDP* would become a reality. The Saxony-Anhalt *CDU* association was the first one to be grounded in 1990 within the Eastern *Länder*. The *CDU-FDP* coalition governed from 1990 to 1994. The *CDU* had a primary role in the political development of Saxony-Anhalt, next to the *SPD* that was next to demonstrate how the situation could improve. *CDU* also had a strong position at the local level (Schnapp/Burchardt 2006: 187; Schieren 2000: 39).

The 1994 elections did not reveal a clear majority and the *SPD* formed together with the Greens a minority government coalition, led by minister-president Reinhard Höppner (*SPD*). Saxony-Anhalt had the highest unemployment and debt and the lowest investment rate among the Eastern German *Länder*. It was severely affected by the collapse of the machine building and chemical industry in the 1990s in comparison to other Eastern German *Länder* (Schieren 2000: 39).

The *SPD*, to whom Reinhard Höppner, minister-president from 1994 to 2002, belonged, lost the election for the 4th legislative period. People considered that the government's actions were bad for the economic development and contributed to the rise of the debt level, causing a massive emigration of the population (Detterbeck 2010: 362). As the next sections show, the topics of debt reduction and demographic situation continued to be among the main challenges of the government of Saxony-Anhalt.

In 1999 and 2000, Saxony-Anhalt received the most industry investments among the Eastern *Länder*, but the industry still needed further development, especially because of the high unemployment, which did not reflect the industry investments (Heimpold/Rosenfeld 2003: 29, 33). The government of the 4th legislative period did not start everything all over, but it relayed on work made by the previous governments, in particular regarding the field of the chemicals policy.

Minister-president Höppner established cooperation relations with Poland and the Czech Republic and set up crucial know-how transfers that Saxony-Anhalt could offer to the regions from the new Member States. Cooperation was the expression of the public relation and partnership function of the region within the EU. On this account, the instrument of interregional cooperation strengthened the subnational institutional structures. For this purpose, Saxony-Anhalt sent government experts to the PHARE/Institution Building programme and aimed to create a network of the European chemical regions, underpinning the official cooperation with Mazovia (Höppner 2002: 163).

Regarding the EU enlargement, minister-president Höppner considered it as an achievement of Europe's unification after 1989. He stated that the base of the future development in Saxony-Anhalt was to boost its economy by increasing labour division and cooperation with partners from Eastern Europe (Höppner 2002: 161). The 2004 EU-Enlargement was considered a chance for Saxony-Anhalt to become from "an accession area to a European connecting region" that could stimulate future investments (Thierse 2001: 59). As a connecting region, trans-European transport projects were of strategic importance for the government.

As part of the participation process of Saxony-Anhalt in EMLG, the region sent experts not only in the states that joined the EU in 2004, but also in Romania for support in the area of control of EU subsidies. Saxony-Anhalt was also involved in the reform of the European Regional Policy and the effects of the White Paper on Chemicals, which are addressed later on in the next chapters (Höppner 2002: 163). Therefore, its active participation within EMLG was considered significant for the development.

5.1 The 4th legislative period: 2002-2006

5.1.1 Social and political background of the election

In 2002, elections for both the *Landtag* and the *Bundestag* took place, in April and September. The voters' participation was greater in the *Bundestag* election, showing the increased importance of that vote. The results of both elections were surprising in Saxony-Anhalt. The *CDU* won at the *Land* level but did not win any direct mandates for the *Bundestag* (Renzsch 2003: 61). The political importance of the elections in 2002 was connected with the federal financial crisis, which was likewise related to the 2004 planned enlargement of the EU. The EU enlargement meant for Saxony-Anhalt 'a shorter piece of cake' from the European Funds after 2006. The federal financial instrument, *Solidarpakt Ost*, was as well shrinking and did not cover the support required for infrastructure development in Saxony-Anhalt.

The problem before the election was that a clear political message and clear guidelines for the government's actions were missing. The federal financial support had been generous until 1994. Still, there were no new structures established; only some models from Lower-Saxony were adopted. The revival of the industry did not record a significant success. It was a disappointment, because the big enterprises were no longer functioning.

Society problems in Saxony-Anhalt and in Germany were, in 1998, the jobs market and the low birth rate. The elections in 2002 became rather a protest, due to the increasing feeling of the Eastern German citizens as second class citizens (*** 2002: 42-3). Rannenberg and Wolf argued that the position of Saxony-Anhalt in 2002 was to follow the path of modernisation with the help of European funds, especially since the *Land* had little specificity, besides the chemical industry in Leuna and Schkeuditz, which could contribute to the development of Saxony-Anhalt (2002: 145-146).

Political goals and principles of Saxony-Anhalt were strongly related to the resources it had. Some of those resources were used in participation processes in the EU. The functions of actors pursued the content of European policies to develop the strategy that would meet their political goals. The awareness of European affairs as a crucial element of the *Land* policy has been enforced especially during the first analysed period, 2002-2006. Another important development at European level that influenced regional participation within EMLG was the EU enlargement. From this background, policy priorities of Saxony-Anhalt started to increasingly acknowledge the importance of participating in processes of shaping the EU policies.

5.1.2   Political goals and resources of Saxony-Anhalt

Wolfgang Böhmer (*CDU*) was elected minister-president after the *Landtag* election in 2002. During the election campaign, he defended the idea that Saxony-Anhalt needed a developing economic profile. He was aware that Saxony-Anhalt was facing interest rates payments amounting 1.5 billion *DM*, in 2003, and that a drop in the European funds was closing in, due to the EU enlargement from 2004. He expressed the will of the *CDU* to make youth-oriented policy and to make Saxony-Anhalt an attractive location for economic development. Böhmer emphasised the importance of research and science, and the innovation capacity, from which the competitiveness of the location depended on. Böhmer stressed the need to endorse cultural, historical and landscape specificities of Saxony-Anhalt as part of "Europe of the regions" (Böhmer 2002: 119-122).

The election led to a coalition between the *CDU* and *FDP*. Their primary support in the political cooperation was the coalition agreement (Landtag Sachsen-Anhalt 2002). Agreement that pointed out political goals for the legislative period 2002-2006. It made notice of the historical development of the region and what it used to be, namely a place for economy and competitiveness. At this point, the coalition agreement supports the first hypothesis of this research: that the history of a territory can contribute to the use of its specifics for the development of the region. Even more, this hypothesis is connected to ideas defended by the Commission in its 2000 WP on European Governance: that the territorial aspect must be part of the policy coherence, taking into account the local and regional conditions (see Appendix 1).

The importance of endorsing the specificities of Saxony-Anhalt was also part of the *SPD* election discourse (Fikentscher 2002: 125). On the other hand, the *FDP* emphasised the need to stabilise local industry through innovation and in particular through the chemical industry development (Pieper 2002: 141). The *FDP* political role was related to its partnership with the *CDU* within the government coalition from 1990 to 1994 and from 2002 to 2006 (Schnapp/Burchardt 2006: 187). The second government coalition between the *CDU* and the *FDP* continued with the same actors in the field of economy, agriculture, environment, construction and transport area, therefore configuring the government on established trust structures (Putz 2006: 87).

Building on the region's traditions, the political actors of the coalition decided to take on the responsibility and the task of restoring the financial power of the region, to provide opportunities for investments and future orientated activities. Key points of their political programme were to reinvent the region as an attractive and innovative economic place, where jobs could be offered. The objective took into consideration the goals of the Lisbon Strategy (see European Council 2000). Moreover, the actors noted the wish to make use of the geographical position of the region, namely in the centre of Europe. However, the situation of the budget posed a serious challenge (Landtag Sachsen-Anhalt 2002: 5). Key-words can be found in the political programme of Saxony-Anhalt, which are similar to the ones in the European documents, strategies or communications. The political program showed its European spirit.

The transportation topic was connected to the European policies. Transport networks needed to be connected not only to a region but with other regions as well. These were key elements for the industry success. The topics of transport and logistics were closely connected. These brought together many different regional actors that became projects partners. The political programme of Saxony-Anhalt highlighted that transport areas needed to be addressed and solved in order to increase the competitiveness of the region. The topic had been discussed by the European Commission as well and continued to be addressed by within the Commission's structures of the High Level Groups.

Minister-president Böhmer began his term with the purpose of making Saxony-Anhalt sustainable and to consolidate the budget by reducing staff members and costs and by implementing a strategy of deregulation. His aim was to create conditions for the development of Saxony-Anhalt's economy pursued by simplifying the laws for investment and by setting up the investment bank (Staatskanzlei Sachsen-Anhalt 2005: 1).

According to the Bertelsmann-foundation study on locations, Saxony-Anhalt managed to improve its success index in the years 2002-2004 and to get access to the dynamic economy of Germany. Industry-based economy managed to grow during those years (Staatskanzlei Sachsen-Anhalt 2005: 6). The industry growth was connected to the high investments in the settlements and locations that provided favourable conditions for companies to invest and to create jobs.

The main economy sectors in Saxony-Anhalt remained the food and the chemical industry. The chemical industry reached the second place in 2004 with a contribution of 16.8% of the processed industry, being the second larger employer and the biggest export sector (Staatskanzlei Sachsen-Anhalt 2005: 7-8). However, the industry faced the European legislative proposals that were about to enhance costs for companies. It was the case for the chemical sector due to the harmonisation intentions expressed in the 2001 European Commission's White Paper on the future of chemicals policy.

Next to the conditions for the economy, Saxony-Anhalt pushed forward the innovation strategy by promoting research in the areas of chemical and plastic materials, mechanical engineering, information and communication technology, life science and bio-technology, initiating the "biotechnology offensive". Furthermore, the sector of renewable resources, in the area of energy production through solar energy, started to develop (Staatskanzlei Sachsen-Anhalt 2005: 12-13). Therefore, economy increased its dynamics with the help of the infrastructure investments made by Saxony-Anhalt, building and restoring high-ways and roads.

The European Commission kept track of the EU funds implementation in Saxony-Anhalt through direct contact with Saxony-Anhalt's specific institution, the EU administrative authority (*EU-Verwaltungsbehörde*). A crucial contribution to infrastructure development of Saxony-Anhalt was the financial aid of European funds, especially the European Regional Development Fund (Staatskanzlei Sachsen-Anhalt 2005: 39-40). From the 3.4 billion € allocated for Saxony-Anhalt for 2000-2006, 2 billion € were invested in infrastructure and environment. Hence, much of the amount was used for creating the framework for economic development (Ministerium der Finanzen Sachsen-Anhalt 2005: 3).

In 2004, the Commission submitted the regulation proposals for the 2007-2013 European Regional Policy. Saxony-Anhalt again received a large amount (Ministerium der Finanzen Sachsen-Anhalt 2005: 4-5). From this amount, the European Regional Development Fund (ERDF) contribution of 1.9 billion € targeted the development of competitiveness of companies, the SMEs, infrastructure, industry and trade, and environment protection. The fund was used by companies to keep and create jobs. The European Social Fund (ESF) targeted the labour potential and the equality of opportunities while the EAFRD targeted the rural development (Ministerium der Finanzen Sachsen-Anhalt 2005: 13, 17, 20).

Next to the use of European funds, Saxony-Anhalt identified its challenges as a region in the European Union. It engaged in European policy-making processes by addressing actors from different levels and by promoting communication among regional and European actors, in particular in relation to the transition aid of the European Regional Policy, which was of great interest for Saxony-Anhalt from the early years of the 4th legislative period. The contribution of European funds decreased starting with 2007. The high administrative costs of Saxony-Anhalt were causing difficulties for its development. Saxony-Anhalt also needed to implement measures within its territory that could decrease the financial burden of a sudden drop in the EU funds income. Such actions required an administrative reform.

The *Landtag* decided on the administrative reform on several occasions. The first one was the county reform decided in 2005 that reduced the number of counties from 21 to 11 counties, starting with 2007. The county reform was connected with the administration reform, according to which Saxony-Anhalt decreased the number of administration communities. Such an administration community comprised at least 10.000 residents, doubling the number of residents and reducing the number of administration communities especially by fusing the existing ones.

The reform reduced the number of full administration units at the local level from 215 to 134. The reform was taken due to challenges that the administration faced regarding new tasks from the *Landesregierung*, in order to enhance closeness to the citizens. The newly established counties were more similar (statistically – number of authorities related to the number of inhabitants/surface) to other ones in the Federal Republic of Germany. The reform was very important for the budget of Saxony-Anhalt. The *Land* managed in 2006 to reduce costs with 5% in comparison to 2002 (Staatskanzlei 2005: 44-45).

Ideas addressed in the political programme of the 4th legislature period can be later seen again, such as the enforcement of the cooperation between science and economy – in the 6th legislature period. The fusion of economy and science competencies into one ministry showed that policies were interdependent and hence needed to be dealt as a joint policy.

5.1.3 Participation processes of Saxony-Anhalt within EMLG

This section presents the topics and categories of meaning for the participation of Saxony-Anhalt within EMLG. It offers an overview of the institution's activities for the legislative period 2002-2006 as part of their mobilisation strategy. The access channels to EMLG were presented in the previous chapters. The next pages illustrate processes that occurred in the region that allowed for further actions at other levels of EMLG.

Participation processes and functions performed by actors, such as interest representations, information, filter function and partnerships shape the political goals that would be set or may occur around the set goals. As already presented, the content of the coalition agreement was following a European spirit by taking into account the EU strategies and by adapting them to specific development needs of the *Land*.

The *Landtag* supported the work of the government through determined inter-institutional communication about developments at the European level and within the government. Among the identified crucial topics for the participation of Saxony-Anhalt within EMLG were: the future changes for the chemical sector according to regulation proposals of the European Commission and the future of the European Regional Policy after the EU enlargement (see Commission of the European Communities 2001). These two political priorities are closely analysed and presented in the next chapter. This section provides a short context for the future analysis.

The *Landtag* enforced its support for the work of the government related to maintenance of the Cohesion Policy's convergence goal for 2007-2013, in particular due to the statistical effect of the 2004 EU enlargement (Landtag Sachsen-Anhalt 2003: 1). The statistical effect of the EU enlargement meant that the increased number of regions that would be eligible for the European Regional Policy and their economic situation would change the statistical data that the policy based its funds allocation on.

Saxony-Anhalt was classified as a convergence region, the group of regions that received the higher percentage of the funds in order to increase the economy of the region. EU enlargement would change the classification for Saxony-Anhalt and other regions. There was the high possibility that these regions would receive fewer funds. Since Saxony-Anhalt depended on the financial support of European funds, the actors had an interest to maintain their funding classification. Hence, it was an important matter to be brought into the attention of the national and European institutions.

The *Landtag* appreciated the proposed financial support for the regions, affected by the statistical effect proposed by the *Landesregierung* (Landtag Sachsen-Anhalt 2004: 1-2) and the involvement of the *Landesregierung* in the debate and many discussions with different actors on the topic of the statistical effect. The matter was of importance also during the works of the minister-president conferences of the Eastern German *Länder* (Landtag Sachsen-Anhalt 2005a: 1). Even though the *Landtag* had no binding competence, the matter was debated and the finance minister, Karl-Heinz Paqué, informed the *Landtag* about developments related to the topic (Landtag Sachsen-Anhalt 2005b: 4367-8). Debates in the *Landtag* resulted in resolutions offered by the committee for federal and European affairs, based on information from the government regarding the proposals of the Commission, and the negotiations' state-of-play (Landtag Sachsen-Anhalt 2005b: 4369).

The Commission prepared proposals for a regulation package for the chemicals industry presented in its White Paper in 2001. The proposal was of importance especially for the private actors involved in the industry. Next to the challenge of new regulations, the chemical industry of Saxony-Anhalt faced a significant flood in 2002, which caused economic losses in Bitterfeld. Companies from the chemical park had to take security measures and to move commodities. Later, the enterprises, together with the government, needed to address the development of a flood prevention concept (Gabriel 2003: 225).

The flood increased the contact opportunity between actors from Saxony-Anhalt and European actors, due to the generous support from the European Commission, for flood damages. Members of the *FDP* and the *CDU* political groups in the *Landtag* met in Brussels with members of the European institutions to discuss the way European financial help for the flood could be used (Landesvertretung Sachsen-Anhalt bei der EU 2002(29, 30, 32)). The empirical analysis looked into how such events favoured the mobilisation of actors and what were the steps of regional participation in EMLG.

The first step was getting to be acknowledged at European level. For example, on the 28th November 2002, a panel discussion took place at the DOW factory in Schkopau (Saxony-Anhalt) on the topic of the EU enlargement and its effect on Saxony-Anhalt economic location (Landesvertretung Sachsen-Anhalt bei der Europäischen Union 2002). Representatives of the Commission and of the European Parliament in Germany, Manfred Maas, the state-secretary in the Saxony-Anhalt economy ministry, the Saxony-Anhalt member of the European Parliament Horst Schnellhardt, and representatives of the chemical companies in Saxony-Anhalt attended the panel discussion in November 2002.

These were the two main topics of the regional participation analysed in this book. From an early point of regional participation, these topics were related. Over the time and according to the principles and goals set by the European Commission, such as the Lisbon Strategy and the Europe 2020 Strategy, the EU policies and their goals became intertwined and interdependent.

A month later, an application for an INTERREG project was handed in. The goal of the project was to set up a network of chemical regions among the project participating regions, which could participate in EMLG. The project was successful and led to the emergence of the European Chemical Regions Network that is still active (Wobben 2007).

The EU Lisbon Strategy emphasised the need for Europe to become an attractive location for investments and jobs, especially through science and research (Krause-Heiber 2005: 22). The same need of improving their attractiveness applied for the regions. Norbert Heller, an official of the Saxony-Anhalt finance ministry, expressed the need to develop a long term strategy in order to quantify to EU Funds because a funding period affects nine years of Saxony-Anhalt's budget. He recommended that the managing authority of the European Structural funds of Saxony-Anhalt should be seen as a bank that provided financial means (Heller 2005: 29).

Thomas Große, from the representation of Saxony-Anhalt to the EU, stressed that Saxony-Anhalt needed to gather partners in Brussels, especially those who shared specific concerns (Ministerium für Wirtschaft und Arbeit des Landes Sachsen-Anhalt 2005: 35). Within the spirit of sharing knowledge and experience, Magdeburg hosted a seminar on best-practices in October 2005, where actors from different regions and actors from UK, regions from Sweden, and other actors from German *Länder*, Latvia, Lithuania, Austria and Denmark met (Managing Authority of European Structural Funds of Saxony-Anhalt 2005).

5.1.4 *The actors' functions and the policy content connection*

The participation processes presented above are implemented primarily through the actors of Saxony-Anhalt who are involved and are active within several structures. They perform their functions – gathering information, representation of interests, early warning, partnership and public relations – and they connect the content of the European policies and legislative proposals to the political goals of the region.

Most of the information gathered in Brussels, from the European level, was performed with the help of the representation of Saxony-Anhalt in the EU and through the personal contacts and representation of interests between political actors of Saxony-Anhalt and European officials. For clarification, Brussels gathers the different levels within EMLG. The European level comprises supranational institutions and their agencies and bodies.

The plenary of the Committee of the Regions evolved into a meeting place at which members of the EP and the COM participate, enforcing the communication process between the European institutions and the local and regional authorities' members (see Official Journal of the European Communities 2001). Saxony-Anhalt has been active in the CoR through its member, state-secretary Michael Schneider.

In December 2002, Schneider was appointed rapporteur for the second interim report on the economic and social cohesion that was presented by the

Commission in January 2003. That report was crucial for the 2007-2013 allocation of financial means, which affected the funds allocation for Eastern Germany (Landesvertretung Sachsen-Anhalt bei der Europäischen Union 2002(43): 6).

At the end of its first term, the government led by minister-president Böhmer presented its main achievements during the legislative period 2002-2006. The first year brought positive developments such as, the company Rosmann became active in 1994 in Saxony-Anhalt and opened in Landsberg a logistics centre. In October 2002, the minister-president of Saxony-Anhalt began his activity as president of the *Bundesrat*, according to the yearly rotation system. That particular role allowed him to pursue the specific interests of the Eastern German *Länder* within intrastate channels (Staatskanzlei Sachsen-Anhalt 2005: 2-3).

The Länder Thuringia, Saxony and Saxony-Anhalt established the „*Initiative Mitteldeutschland*" to develop the Central German region into a competitive and progressive region in the chemical industry. They agreed upon: a common concept for air traffic, fusion of their insurance institutions, agreements between the administrations for the cooperation in the sectors of food control and inspection, common use of the execution of justice decisions, and common use of training centres (Staatskanzlei Sachsen-Anhalt 2005: 48).

In 2004, Saxony-Anhalt undertook many initiatives. Commissioner Margot Wallström visited Saxony-Anhalt and minister-president Böhmer handed her the Hallenser Declaration, which comprised suggestions made by the chemical industry and the government for the new European chemicals regulation. Saxony-Anhalt made the partnership-agreement with the French region Centre, to tighten the German-French friendship and to promote the encounter between the two regions. The investment bank of Saxony-Anhalt began its work with the purpose of improving the financing chances for the middle class, by providing a faster and less bureaucratic access to subsidies. Regarding the economic development, Saxony-Anhalt welcomed in 2004 a new production facility of *Nice Pak Deutschland GmbH*, which created 90 long-term jobs (Staatskanzlei Sachsen-Anhalt 2005: 48).

In 2005, Saxony-Anhalt welcomed a new paper factory in Sperga that created 150 jobs and a new settlement in Halle, from the producer Dell, which created over 700 jobs. The *Land* also started its image campaign, "We rise earlier" („*Wir stehen früher auf*") in seven cities in Saxony-Anhalt and in Berlin. The campaign won the „*Politikaward*" in November 2005. The minister-president presented Saxony-Anhalt in St. Petersburg, where 18 companies from Saxony-Anhalt participated and made contacts with Russian companies. In December 2005, Saxony-Anhalt took over the presidency of the minister-presidents conference of the Eastern *Länder* for one year, according to the rotation principle (Staatskanzlei Sachsen-Anhalt 2005: 2-3).

The activities of Saxony-Anhalt regarding the EU comprised the establishment of an independent Europe-department within the state-chancellery. The department managed: to improve the strategic use of the contact office in Brussels, to establish a particular trainee programme for administration officials, to purchase and reconstruct the building in Brussels (the former GDR embassy) into the Centre of regions that hosts today the representation of Saxony-Anhalt to the EU and other representations to the EU or research offices, including the ECRN office (Staatskanzlei Sachsen-Anhalt 2005: 48).

From the EMLG framework presented in the first chapter, the activities of Saxony-Anhalt involving the use of resources based on political goals (defined generally by the coalition agreement and more specifically by the government) included the following: Saxony-Anhalt was involved in promoting the interregional cooperation within the EU and it pushed forward the idea of financing such interregional projects (Landesvertretung Sachsen-Anhalt bei der Europäischen Union 2002(18): 10-11). The initiative to bring chemical regions into a network was promoted by the Brussels office of Saxony-Anhalt since March 2000 (Landesvertretung Sachsen-Anhalt bei der Europäischen Union 2002 (22): 10).

Further cooperation among regions was promoted and taken up, such as the collaboration between Saxony-Anhalt and Asturia in the field of innovation and information technology policy. The need to continue the Brussels offices work emerged especially in the case of the task-oriented or policy-oriented working groups in Brussels (Landesvertretung Sachsen-Anhalt bei der Europäischen Union 2002(27): 11, 19-20). The emergence of the European Chemical Regions Network as a European stakeholder and the involvement in the policy-making process of Cohesion Policy after 2006 were major topics that guided the participation of Saxony-Anhalt within EMLG. The relevance of the European policies and their long-term effect occupied several governments of Saxony-Anhalt with those topics. That allowed for a continued cooperation from one government to another.

5.2 The 5th legislative period: 2006-2011

5.2.1 Social and political background of the election

The 2006 *Landtag* election was not in the shadow of the *Bundestag* election, like the one in 2002. The coalition between the *CDU* and the *SPD*, which ruled the government for the legislative period 2006-2011, was based on developments in the political landscape of the *Land* and not on the federal coalition development. The *CDU* had been the strongest power in the *Landtag* and especially at the local level. The 2002 election showed the discontent of the population with the results of the *SPD* government from 1998 until 2002, such as the negative economic development, the high unemployment, the emigration and the indebtedness (Detterbeck 2008: 178-180).

During the campaign for the 2006 election, Jens Bullerjahn and the incumbent *CDU* minister-president Böhmer were the main candidates for the minister-president position. Bullerjahn was the one who "promised more civil cuts, more 'concentration' of subsidies for economic reconstruction, and more spending cuts that the *CDU*" (Nagel 2007: 379).

The election of 2006 showed the citizens' assessment of the *CDU* being more competent, due to increased investments and development of specific growth poles, such as the chemical industry in the economy sector. Politically, the *CDU* had the upper-hand due to the establishment of a strong and responsible image as a „*Landesvater*" of minister-president Böhmer and through his activities as a spokesperson for the Eastern German interests (Detterbeck 2008: 185-187). Minister-president Böhmer played an important role in the re-orientation of the European structural funds and in the negotiations of the *Länder* with the *Bund* concerning the federal financial equalisation (Detterbeck 2010: 364). Detterbeck argued that the common political goals and lack of an alternative majority could lead to the governing of the great coalition between the *CDU* and the *SPD* for more than one legislative period (2008: 192). A coalition between the *CDU* and the *SPD* formed again after the 2011 *Landtag* election, presented in the next section.

5.2.2 Political goals and resources of Saxony-Anhalt

During the fifth legislative period of Saxony-Anhalt, the *Land* faced the beginning of the funding period 2007-2013, and the preparatory works of the policy-making process for the cohesion regulations for 2014-2020. One of the main difficulties appointed at the beginning of the coalition agreement was the regressing financial transfer both from the *Bund* and from the EU (Landtag Sachsen-Anhalt 2006: 6). The coalition agreement emphasised the presence of the European dimension in the region, stating the connection and the interdependence on the EU membership.

The European funds contribution for the development of Saxony-Anhalt was directly addressed in the coalition agreement; funds were an integrated part of the financial situation of the region. The programming process for the 2007-2013 European funding period was discussed in the coalition agreement because of its significance. The coalition agreement encouraged the commitment and the participation of Saxony-Anhalt in the processes of EMLG. The representation's work to the EU was appreciated due to the partnerships developed with many other regions and with actors from the European institutions (Landtag Sachsen-Anhalt 2006: 12, 41, 53; Sălăgeanu 2014c: 135).

The economic situation in Saxony-Anhalt, in 1990, was very difficult for achieving economic growth. That growth was achieved with the help of the European funds and with a crucial contribution of the *Solidarpakt*, the federal financial support for the Eastern German *Länder*, which stimulated in particular investments in the infrastructure (Sachsen-Anhalt 2005: II-IV). However, the loss of jobs in the industry from 1990 was not sufficiently counterbalanced. The 2006 formed government set its goal to reduce the debt by 2010 and to prepare a new administrative staff development concept for the purpose of financial consolidation (Sachsen-Anhalt 2005: 71-72).

In 2001, the federal chancellor and the minister-presidents agreed to update the financial aid for the Eastern *Länder* until 2019 in the amount of 206 billion *DM*. 100 billion were promised from the federal budget. Financial transfers decreased in time; Saxony-Anhalt was still weak in the area of infrastructure and had to relate to its Europe fitness in order to compensate for the federal funding with European funds (Renszch 2002: 177, 187). This meant that Saxony-Anhalt needed to be able to function on its own without the financial instruments and to reduce its high debt in the meantime. At the beginning of the 5th legislative period, the goal was still far from being achieved and the 2007 financial crisis hadn't started yet. For that purpose, Saxony-Anhalt continued its participation process within EMLG. The contacts with European officials were the main part of the policy-shaping of Saxony-Anhalt.

Further on the government's agenda was the territorial reform which begun in the 1990s and experienced several waves, in 1999 and 2005. After the 2002 election the laws for the reform were set aside, but in 2005 the topic was addressed again and a district reform took place (Kregel 2006: 136; see Kregel 2002). The territorial reform of municipalities and of administrative units strived for cost-efficient task achievement of high quality, closeness to citizens and compliance with the subsidiarity principle. The main elements were the financial support and the decreasing population. Due to the structural weakness of Saxony-Anhalt, many jobs needed to be reduced. The acceptance of the reform was higher among the population than among administrative staff and local politicians (Püchel 2002; Grünert/Popp 2009). The functioning of chemical parks and the cooperation in this field required that chemical parks were part of a single municipality in order to be able to increase their working framework. Hence, the territorial reform was complementary to the participation processes in EMLG.

In June 2010, the European Commission released its Europe 2020 strategy that guides the development of policies at European level and within the Member States until 2020. Strategy that set the goal of smart, sustainable and inclusive growth that should be achieved by 2020 through five objectives: employment, innovation, education, social inclusion and climate/energy (see Appendix 5). Saxony-Anhalt prepared a document – among its activities for the communication with the citizens – in which it expressed its own contribution to the implementation of the Europe 2020 strategy. Therefore, through the use of the rich tradition of the *Land*, Saxony-Anhalt would be strengthening its economic profile. The main goal, in doing so, was to maintain the originality and stability of the region (Staatskanzlei Sachsen-Anhalt 2010: 5; see Landesvertretung Sachsen-Anhalt bei der Europäischen Union: 2010(1): 7-8). The implementation of the Europe 2020 strategy was followed in Saxony-Anhalt according to six theses that the government laid down in its contribution to the Europe 2020 Strategy:

1. Consolidate, prevent, invest and modernise: the *Land* managed the budget 2008/09 without making new debts but the financial crisis overturned the same plan for 2010/11. However, the constitutional debt limit for Saxony-Anhalt entered into force in 2013 meaning that starting with 2012 the budget had to be balanced without taking new credit (Staatskanzlei Sachsen-Anhalt 2010: 7).
2. Education chances – from the beginning and for a life-time: education was conceived as the source of innovation within the economy and the society, therefore making the education policy one of the core policies of Saxony-Anhalt (Staatskanzlei Sachsen-Anhalt 2010: 11).
3. The Great arises from the Small: one of the core objectives of the government was to increase research, development and innovation possibilities in Saxony-Anhalt because there was a shortage of big enterprises and headquarters that could increase the export rate. Therefore, the foundation Future for advancement in research and innovation in the areas of economy, science and research was established, which awarded scholarships for students (Staatskanzlei Sachsen-Anhalt 2010: 15; Ministerium für Wirtschaft und Arbeit Sachsen-Anhalt 2010; see European Commission 2016a).
4. Life with new energy: Saxony-Anhalt has been already engaging in the area since it started to host the biggest European production line of photovoltaic cells and it became the centre of that type of activity in Germany. It also belonged to the main wind energy production. The „*Sollarvalley Mitteldeutschland*" was among the winners of the 2008 top cluster contest of the German federal government (Staatskanzlei Sachsen-Anhalt 2010: 20).
5. A strong community – cities and rural area: Saxony-Anhalt pursued the initiative of broadband development for the rural area, especially for the use of internet by the population providing the possibility of the e-government ini-

tiative to expand. In the meantime, authorities had to provide public services connected with high costs considering the efforts of the *Land* to balance its budget. Hence, Saxony-Anhalt needed to develop itself as a transport and logistic competent region (Staatskanzlei Sachsen-Anhalt 2010: 22).
6. Networking and Cooperation: Saxony-Anhalt pursued its further representation of interests towards the EU and the *Bund* in order to fulfil its goals. Due to the reducing funds available from the federal and European level, it made use, as much as possible, of opportunities provided by the INTERREG program (Staatskanzlei Sachsen-Anhalt 2010: 25).

In 2010, the government prepared an innovation programme for 2010/2011 that was communicated to the *Landtag* according to inter-institutional communication procedure. The strategy was based on a cluster potential analysis and it provided an open framework for the design of Saxony-Anhalt's innovation policy and its coordination with the financial instruments. The innovation program comprised two main pillars, the institutional development – targeting research institutions and science – and the innovation policy that gathered a system of measures that pursued the strengthening of the innovation capacity within the private enterprises developing the project dimension of the innovation strategy.

The innovation strategy aimed to develop clusters as core elements in the field of chemicals/plastics, machine building, automobile industry, biotechnology and pharmaceutical industry, renewable energy, and health economy. Core technologies with cross-sectional character were identified in the areas of virtual technologies, information and communication technology, microsystems technic, and nanotechnology. The development potential was identified in the field of food industry, creative economy and logistics (Landtag Sachsen-Anhalt 2010). These measures and the strategy complied with topics of the Europe 2020 Strategy for smart, sustainable and inclusive growth.

In March 2011, the strategy report concerning the half-time balance of the European structural funds in Saxony-Anhalt was published. The report identified the demographic development and the development of the public budget to be the main determinants of how Saxony-Anhalt would be developing in the future. These elements were crucial because they provided the necessary budget for the co-financing part of the EU funded projects (Landesregierung Sachsen-Anhalt 2010a: 11). The report made recommendations concerning the better supervision of projects and a realistic approach from the part of the departments responsible for different measures. Regarding the use of funds, the report emphasised the need to consider the demographic element for projects funded by the EFRD (Landesregierung Sachsen-Anhalt 2010a: 95).

In 2011, there was reason of joy for Saxony-Anhalt when the European Commission proposed a 2/3 volume of financial aid for the phasing-out regions (out from convergence goal into transition regions) in the regulations for the European Regional Policy 2014-2020 (Landesvertretung bei der Europäischen Union 2012(1): 1). The next chapter deals with the topic of the transition aid and the long-term involvement of Saxony-Anhalt at the EU and national level in pursuit of goal of transition regions.

5.2.3 Participation processes of Saxony-Anhalt within EMLG

The government's report for the *Landtag* regarding Europe-related activities for 2009 emphasised the attention to interregional cooperation with existing partner-regions and the continued interest representation at the federal and European level. Cooperation with regions across the EU contributed to the development of exports of Saxony-Anhalt and to developments in the area of research, technology and EU exchange programmes. One, on the main topic related to the EU in 2009 was, of course, the EP election. The EP election was the main focus of the EU-related public relations work of Saxony-Anhalt's authorities. For that purpose, Saxony-Anhalt organised a logo, internet presence, a government declaration, a Europe-award for citizen-media, a EU project day in schools, a EU-seminar for journalists, a Europe-roundtable and many information materials about the Lisbon Treaty and about Saxony-Anhalt's activities in the EU (Landesvertretung bei der Europäischen Union 2010 (1): 7-10).

The participation processes of Saxony-Anhalt in EMLG during the 5th legislative period emphasised the close cooperation that has been developing at European level among European institutions and actors from the subnational level. For example, the CoR's COTER and the EP's BUDG committees started to work closer together, especially regarding the funding issues for the Cohesion Policy 2007-2013 (Landesvertretung Sachsen-Anhalt 2007(1): 24-25). Saxony-Anhalt organised some of the government's cabinet meetings in Brussels, at which European commissioners attended. The *Landtag* also organised meetings of its committee for European and federal affairs in Brussels. Saxony-Anhalt organised events and participated actively in the Open Days events of the CoR.

In 2007, Germany held the presidency of the Council of the EU. On this occasion, Chancellor Angela Merkel proposed that one special meeting of the *Länder* minister-presidents conferences took place in Brussels. The meeting took place on the 7th March 2007. 11 minister-presidents accepted the invitation to Brussels and they discussed matters of the *Länder* with the vice-president of the Commission, Günter Verheugen, and with the Commissioner Viviane Reding. Such matters were: the social policy, the implementation of a common market, better legislative processes and media affairs. The minister-presidents participated at a high-level meeting with the president of the

European Commission, Manuel Barroso, and with Chancellor Merkel, where they tackled the energy policy. Such meetings offered the possibility for the *Länder* to present their concerns and interests related to European policies. Saxony-Anhalt held the presidency of the Europe-minister conferences and could coordinate the organisation of the meeting (Landesvertretung Sachsen-Anhalt bei der Europäischen Union 2008(1): 11-12).

In February 2009, minister Robra held a government declaration in front of the *Landtag* before the EP elections. He stated that through an active Europe-policy the government wished to solve the problems the *Land* was faced with. Among the treaty and policy changes at European level, minister Robra emphasised the role that the European funds played in the development of Saxony-Anhalt. Between 1991 and 2006, Saxony-Anhalt received more than 6 billion € which generated investments of over 20 billion €. The funds and investments that followed strengthened Saxony-Anhalt as an economic and science location. They facilitated the creation of jobs and the increase of competitiveness and innovation capability of the *Land* through the infrastructure and the taken environment protection measures, and the cities and rural areas developed.

Among the Europe-policy activities of Saxony-Anhalt, minister Robra mentioned the leading role of the *Land* as a *Bundesrat* rapporteur in the preparation of the *Bundesrat's* position paper concerning the 4th cohesion report, or the involvement in the preparation of common position papers of the *Bund* and the *Länder* regarding the financial system or the European Commission's Green Paper for territorial cohesion (Staatskanzlei Sachsen-Anhalt 2009: 10-12).

Brussels is a meeting point that offers the possibility for many actors to engage in common activities, emphasising the relevance of the regions in a continued strategic dialogue promoted by the European Commission in its White Paper of the European Governance. Such meetings gather the three territorial levels in a process of communication and information exchange proving that the European Multi-Level Governance system is a reality. The coordination among the German *Länder* is facilitated by their presence in Brussels.

Since 2003, the Committee of the Regions has been organising an annually "platform for political communication in relation to the development of the EU Cohesion Policy, raising awareness of decision-makers about the fact that regions matter in EU policy-making". The event is called the European Week of Regions and Cities (Open Days) and it offers the framework for exchange of good practices and know-how about regional and urban development between participants and officials of the European institutions. Participants include officials of the regional and urban administrations experts and members of scientific institutions (Committee of the Regions 2016a).

During the 2008 Open Days event, the CoR's COTER and EP's REGI committees held a joint meeting, at which Saxony-Anhalt's state-secretary, Michael Schneider, spoke in particular about the future financing method for transition regions. The topic regarding the regions' transition was tackled by Saxony-Anhalt's actors not only in Brussels, but also in Magdeburg where representatives of several European regions met in November 2008 to discuss the adaptation strategies of the phasing-in and phasing-out regions (Landesvertretung Sachsen-Anhalt bei der Europäischen Union 2009(1): 37-38, 60). The precise actions of Saxony-Anhalt with regard to this particular topic are presented in the next chapter. Another debated topic was the Commission's Green Paper on territorial cohesion.

A further topic discussed in Brussels was the European legislation for small and medium (SMEs) enterprises. The representation of Saxony-Anhalt to the European Union hosted a common meeting of the German Industry and Commerce Chamber, the Federal Association of the German Industry and the Federal Union of the German Employers' Associations, where challenges and chances for the SMEs, and the effects of the Small Business Act for SMEs and consumer protection were tackled (Landesvertretung Sachsen-Anhalt bei der Europäischen Union 2009(1): 65-66). Even though organising a meeting and debating specific topics does not mean influencing policy-making processes (Jeffery 2000), such events offer a great opportunity to learn from other actors and to share a position. This type of activities belongs to an increased communication process promoted by the European Commission.

In 2009, Saxony-Anhalt continued to apply for INTERREG projects with the proposal for the Interregional Partnership Platform (IPP). The goal of the project was to increase participation of partner regions to the financially sustained European programmes outside the structural funds. The project participating regions were: North Rhein-Westphalia, Asturia, Mazovia, Tartu, Cheshire, Novara, Limburg, Tee Vales and Schleswig-Holstein (Landesvertretung Sachsen-Anhalt bei der Europäischen Union 2010(1): 6).

Participation processes of Saxony-Anhalt within EMLG included the familiarisation of actors based in Saxony-Anhalt with processes and methods of EMLG. For example, the state-secretary of the ministry for rural development and transport, Andrè Schröder, participated in Brussels at a working meeting with Commissioner Danuta Hübner tackling the demographic problem (Landesvertretung Sachsen-Anhalt bei der Europäischen Union 2010(1): 20). The demographic development has been a great challenge for many areas in the EU and it influences fundamental policies, such as the education and the financial policies. Even though, the *Landtag* may have limited powers to contribute to European affairs, its members can gain valuable experience from tackling and debating EU affairs at European level. This way, they can build up the resources and the Europe-capability of Saxony-Anhalt.

Representatives of Saxony-Anhalt attended events organised by other stakeholders in Brussels. In 2009, the finance minister, Jens Bullerjahn, attended the yearly congress of the European taxpayers Confederation. On that occasion, minister Bullerjahn extended the cooperation scope between the institions of Saxony-Anhalt and the confederation. Saxony-Anhalt was represented also by the president of the Saxony-Anhalt Chamber of Tax Consultants. Minister Bullerjahn met with a member of the Commission's DG Economy and Financial affairs, in order to discuss the possible reactions to the crisis and the potential improvement for the competitiveness of the region's economy (Landesvertretung Sachsen-Anhalt bei der Europäischen Union 2010(1): 30-32).

The newsletter of the representation of Saxony-Anhalt to the European Union presented these activities, contributing to the transparency of the participation processes of Saxony-Anhalt within EMLG. Another challenge for the subnational actors is the choice of events to attend to because Brussels offers a wide variety of events in many languages and about many topics of interests for the EU interested actors. The choice is eased by the political prioritisation process of the subnational authorities. Prioritisation reveals who the potential partners can be and whom to address for tackling specific subjects.

In October 2009, minister-president Böhmer presented at the Konrad Adenauer Foundation a positive balance of the past 20 years since the unification of Germany. He stated that the big difference between Eastern Germany and Eastern Europe was that Eastern Germany was fully integrated into a functional Western national economy whereas Eastern Europe needed to transform its economy into a functional market economy. Eastern Germany had the opportunity to adopt the social standards of Western Germany (Landesvertretung Sachsen-Anhalt bei der Europäischen Union 2010(1): 62-3).

In 2010, further meetings concerning the Cohesion Policy and the future of territorial cooperation took place in Brussels. Saxony-Anhalt was invited to present its experience with the projects IPP and ChemClust, providing information on its networking activities and knowledge transfer (Landesvertretung Sachsen-Anhalt bei der Europäischen Union 2011(1): 19-20). In May 2010, the Saxony-Anhalt representation to the EU hosted the IQ-NET[12] con-

---

[12] The IQ-NET was grounded in 1996 by the European Policies Research Centre at the University of Strathclyde in Glasgow. The network of regional and national partners across the EU pursues to improve the quality of Structural Funds pro-

ference, where a paper about the future of the Cohesion Policy based on the input from the regions was presented (Landesvertretung Sachsen-Anhalt bei der Europäischen Union 2011(1): 209-30).

In January 2011, the committee for federal and European affairs and media of the *Landtag* of Saxony-Anhalt met again in Brussels. They organised discussions with the ambassadors of Germany to the EU, with commissioner Barnier, and with the director of the presentation of Valencia's to the EU about currency stability, the Cohesion Policy and common market (Landesvertretung Sachsen-Anhalt bei der Europäischen Union 2012(1): 3). In February 2011, a discussion forum about the 5th report on cohesion took place. Further dialogue related to the Cohesion Policy took place in the Council for General Affairs, and in May 2011, an informal council for regional policy debated the topic among the ministers responsible for this area (Landesvertretung Sachsen-Anhalt bei der Europäischen Union 2012(1): 6-8).

The chapter presents only a few of the activities of Saxony-Anhalt during the analysed legislative periods because the goal is to present elements that form the pattern of regional participation in EMLG. The presented policies and interests of Saxony-Anhalt are not exhausted but they present the interconnection between policies implemented by the subnational authorities and goals pursued by the European institution. These are interdependent and the strategic dialogue between the levels is required for an effective implementation of the Europe 2020 Strategy.

5.2.4 The actors' functions and the policy content connection

The Commission followed its recommendations from the White Paper on European Governance and enhanced its information exchange with the regional actors. A good example for this is the fact that in 2006, DG Industry invited representatives of the Member States, of the Commission and of the chemical industry, and of the ECRN to discuss the preparation of the High Level Group (HLG) on the Competitiveness of the European Chemicals Industry that began its work in 2007. The HLG began its work after the REACH regulation was adopted. The framework of the HLG was to bring together actors affected by the chemicals policy in order to improve its implementation and development.

The government of Saxony-Anhalt continued its information practices for the *Landtag* on the state-of-play of Operational Programmes and on the

> gramme management with help of experience exchange (IQ-NET 2016). Saxony-Anhalt joined the network in 2000 and had already hosted a conference in 2007, in Magdeburg (see Landesvertretung Sachsen-Anhalt bei der Europäischen Union 2008(1): 27-28).

Commission's communications about the energy policy. In that context, the minister for economy and labour and president of ECRN, Reiner Haseloff, met Commissioner Piebalgs in order to discuss issues of the energy policy. On that occasion, the minister presented the situation of Saxony-Anhalt in the field of renewable energy promised and enforced the support for research in the technological development of Saxony-Anhalt (Landesvertretung Sachsen-Anhalt bei der Europäischen Union 2008(1): 15).

At the end of its second term, minister-president Böhmer presented a review of the government's work and the main achievements of Saxony-Anhalt. Important for the economic development of Saxony-Anhalt were: the opening of the Dell-Service and distribution centre in Halle in 2007, the adoption of the staff development strategy for 2007-2020, the inauguration of the Neuro-scientific Innovation and Technology Centre in Magdeburg and of the second Euroglas-factory in Osterweddingen, the opening of the *Delipapier GmbH* in Arneburg and of the Multimedia centre in Halle, and the entry into force of the county reform.

In 2009, Dow Wolff Celluloses *GmbH* opened in Bitterfeld the worldwide biggest site for methyl cellulose. The former Henkel-factory in Genthin was taken over by investors and the location was maintained. In December 2009, the rank for the best economic development among the German *Bundesländer* for the years 2005-2009 of the journal „*Wirtschaftswoche*" was given to Saxony-Anhalt (Landesregierung Sachsen-Anhalt 2011: 65-67).

Therefore, the actors based in Saxony-Anhalt and those representing its interest at national and European level performed their functions, of information gathering and exchange, of contacts maintenance with the European actors and with the partners, and the representation of interests, using the common grounds of European policies and the region's own goals.

5.3 The 6th legislative period: 2011-2016

5.3.1 The social and political background of the election

The 2011 *Landtag* election was faced with the demographic element of a shrinking population and the decrease of voters' participation. The number of eligible voters in Saxony-Anhalt dropped from 2.2 million in 1990 to approximately 2 million in 2011. Participation to the election dropped from 65% in 1990 to 51% in 2011 (Statistisches Amt Sachsen-Anhalt 2016).

The results of the *Landtag* election were: 32.5% for the *CDU*, 23.7% for the Left party (*DIE LINKE*), 21.5% for the *SPD* and 7.1% for the Green party

(Statistisches Amt Sachsen-Anhalt 2016). Despite some loss of points in comparison to the 2006 results, the *CDU* won again the election. A coalition was formed between the *CDU* and the *SPD* political groups. A common element of the 4th, 5th and 6th legislative period is the leading role of the *CDU*.

The challenges for Saxony-Anhalt at the time of the election were the demographic development and the decrease in financial aid from the federal and European level. Saxony-Anhalt was still confronted with the highest degree of debt among the German *Länder*. The financial situation needed further consolidation.

At the same time, the European level was confronted with crucial topics for Saxony-Anhalt such as the Euro-zone crisis, the formulation of the European Regional Policy and the proposal for the multi-annual financial framework, which is the EU's budget for 2014-2020. The preparation and allocation of financial resources for the European Regional Policy were relevant for the contribution of European funds for regions, depending on the category of regions determined by the regulation package for the European Regional Policy.

5.3.2 Political goals and resources of Saxony-Anhalt

The coalition agreement's preamble stated the main political priorities of the coalition's political partners. The coalition agreement emphasised the need of a political labour market master plan that would lower the unemployment rates. The potential of the economic location of Saxony-Anhalt was used in order to strengthen the economic growth and the innovative sectors that provided new jobs. Strengthening families was another goal. That would be achieved by linking different offers for the education, advisory services, health, and sport sectors (Landtag Sachsen-Anhalt 2011a: 7). Nevertheless, the coalition partners trusted Saxony-Anhalt's contribution to the German unification success (Landtag Sachsen-Anhalt 2011a: 8, Sălăgeanu 2014c: 136).

Saxony-Anhalt, predominantly rural, needed a successful agriculture, forestry and food industry with sustainable structures. The *Land* was at a cross point of different European transportation axes. The coalition acknowledged the bridge function of Saxony-Anhalt between Western and Eastern Europe and supported the goal of a capable and effective transport infrastructure both for the *Land* interests as well as for the European interests (Landtag Sachsen-Anhalt 2011a: 8). Key points of the government's policies comprised creating qualitative and long-term jobs with the help of investments and due to the new companies' setting up in Saxony-Anhalt. The contribution of the 2007-2013 EU funds targeted the economic growth and employment (Landtag Sachsen-Anhalt 2011a).

Saxony-Anhalt's future laid in searching new technologies and developing new industry sectors. The government settled as focus the research of financial aid, namely for the chemical, machine and car supply building sectors. Next to these traditional sectors, financial support was allocated to the bio- and information technology (Landtag Sachsen-Anhalt 2011a). Due to the needed budget consolidation (see Renzsch 2017), the administration still had to shrink. The administration modernisation was pursued, including the transfers of duties and responsibilities towards the local level. The improvement of the cultural heritage remained among the key points of the government policy (Sachsen-Anhalt Online-Portal 2014).

The partners of the government coalition called for a strong Saxony-Anhalt. The region's strength was connected to the EU's contribution to the successful development of Saxony-Anhalt. The goal-setting of the government of Saxony-Anhalt was specific to each topic. Thus, each goal of the policies comprised a European component due to the large intervention of European laws and their effects on policies in the territories. Representation of the industrial policy goal-setting at European level was performed by the ECRN. This occurred through the following phases:

- Development of research initiatives,
- Active participation in discussions about the structural policy and implementation of the European industrial policy,
- Pursuit of European debates on handling industries that use intensively energy,
- Cooperation with associations of the chemical industry in Germany, concerning the HLG's recommendations' implementation for the chemical industry in Europe (Landesregierung Sachsen-Anhalt 2012: 2, 15).[13]

In 2012, minister-president Haseloff presented the first annual balance of the government's activity. The financial consolidation suffered some drawbacks due to the financial crisis of 2007-2008. Because Saxony-Anhalt was weak economically and financially in comparison to other *Länder*, the budget of Saxony-Anhalt was still highly dependent on the financial transfers from the federal and European level (Renszch 2017: 259-261). The government priorities were the financial consolidation, the confrontation of setbacks due to registered insolvencies, and the intertwined economy and science policies. The reduction of the public employees was among the measures needed to be taken (Staatskanzlei Sachsen-Anhalt 2012a).

---

[13] The innovation policy-based research pointed out the beacons of research in Saxony-Anhalt, namely the Chemical-Biotechnical Process Centre, the Centre for Silico-Photovoltaic, the Institute for mobility competence (Landesregierung Sachsen-Anhalt 2012.

Saxony-Anhalt registered a 2.8% economic growth, during the first year of minister-president Haseloff's mandate. But, the development of Saxony-Anhalt suffered another setback because of the 2013 floods. In spite of the government's efforts, to reduce the debt and to facilitate the economic development, the financial situation of Saxony-Anhalt depended on external factors, such as interest rates set by the European Central Bank, tax revenue or natural events, which challenged the government's course of action (Renzsch 2017: 264).

Whereas the goal for an economic development in Saxony-Anhalt in the 1990s was the quantitative result of creating jobs, a third phase of economic development required a qualitative stimulation of jobs creation based on innovation. According to the union of employers and economic associations from Saxony-Anhalt (*Arbeitgeber- und Wirtschaftsverbände Sachsen-Anhalt e.V.*), the companies-landscape in Saxony-Anhalt was dominated by small and medium enterprises and their investments in research and development were well below those of companies in Thuringia, Saxony or Baden-Württemberg (Arbeitgeber- und Wirtschaftsverbände Sachsen-Anhalt e.V. 2013: 6). 99.4% of the companies in Saxony-Anhalt are SMEs; therefore the industrial research is limited. Being able to bring forward innovation should achieve a reduction in the needed financial transfers (see European Commission 2016a).

The union identified in its position paper demands of the economic promotion: consolidation of small and medium enterprises, which was also a declared goal at European level, especially with help of European funds; the targeted settlement of funding in order to attract know-how and capital into the *Land*; and strengthening the innovation environment through an enhanced cooperation between science and economy (Arbeitgeber- und Wirtschaftsverbände Sachsen-Anhalt e.V. 2013: 7-8).

The position paper pointed out the crucial role of research, education and building facilities in matters of science policy, education policy, economic policy, regional and demographic policy, and financial policy. It also presented the strengths of Saxony-Anhalt such as the attractive offer of child care, affordable real estate possibilities and the efficient public sector. The union of employers and economic associations from Saxony-Anhalt expressed its support for the government's political goals, and emphasised the importance of the *Land's* financial consolidation and consistent public investment in innovation and value-added products (Arbeitgeber- und Wirtschaftsverbände Sachsen-Anhalt e.V. 2013: 21-2).

After the first half of the term, the government prepared a press release stating its achievements and further goals during the second half of the government period. According to minister-president Haseloff, investments in education and science achieved their objective and the family, education, and science policies goals for strengthening the industrial location Saxony-Anhalt continued to be the priorities of the government (Staatskanzlei Sachsen-Anhalt 2013a).

In February 2014, Saxony-Anhalt presented its regional innovation strategy (see Schlüter 2017). The strategy searched answers to several key questions: global challenges, location attractiveness for investors, endogenous potential for innovation and growth power, innovation repercussion for people and environment, internationalisation and Europeanisation of the innovation policy of Saxony-Anhalt. The analysis of those questions resulted in 12 guidelines. The guidelines named the top markets that needed to be an alignment to the innovation policy: the energy, the machine construction, the resource efficiency, the health and medicine, the mobility and logistics, the chemicals and bio-economy, and the food and agriculture sector (Ministerium für Wissenschaft und Wirtschaft Sachsen-Anhalt 2014: 5-6).

Further recommendations of the guidelines were: the use of the creative economy and the information and communication technologies as key enabling technologies in the mentioned areas. The need to use the endogenous potential of SMEs to innovate was emphasised. The dialogue between economy and science was considered a crucial element of the innovation system of Saxony-Anhalt. The following sectors would contribute to the innovation strategy implementation: infrastructure development, investments in the modernisation of production facilities, strengthening the enterprise culture, the insurance of qualified staff, the internationalisation and Europeanisation of the innovation strategy through the use of networks and knowledge-based economy, equal treatment of men and women, better use of financial instruments and resources, and implementation of the strategy through stable structures and transparent system of monitoring and evaluation establishment (Ministerium für Wissenschaft und Wirtschaft Sachsen-Anhalt 2014: 8-11).

The guidelines pointed to elements of the Europe 2020 strategy, marking the entanglement of the European goals and those of the region's policies, emphasising the strong dependency of Saxony-Anhalt to the federal and European policies (Schlüter 2017: 356). The ideas of the innovation strategy highlight an element that influences regional participation in EMLG. That is the need of the political and administrative actors to know very well the social and economic landscape of the region. The knowledge of the strengths and weaknesses allow the political prioritisation and the coordination of activities in EMLG. Activities do not have to take place only in Brussels but also on site, where companies need help or request the communication with the authorities.

5.3.3 Participation processes of Saxony-Anhalt within EMLG

Participation processes of Saxony-Anhalt during the 6th legislative period followed the set goals, such as to see if Saxony-Anhalt would receive as many European funds as possible in 2014-2020. The goal was that Halle would not be considered as a separate phasing-out region that would receive significant lower funds. The budget of Saxony-Anhalt was half covered by tax revenue, the rest depending on funds allocation from other sources. For example, in 2011, the contribution of structural funds of 538 million € allowed authorities to implement their policy without needing to resort to new debt (Staatskanzlei Sachsen-Anhalt 2011b: 5-6).

Since the financial consolidation was an important topic for the future development and policies of Saxony-Anhalt, a joint seminar together with Valencia was organised in February 2012 in Brussels. Among the conclusions of the seminar were the acknowledgements that an increased cooperation between the local and regional actors, and the European Commission was necessary in order to tackle development challenges. Furthermore, the regions' strategies needed to be adapted to the specificities (Landesvertretung Sachsen-Anhalt bei der Europäischen Union 2013(1): 9-10).

Among other developments in Saxony-Anhalt, the logistic element was a major topic for the chemical industry. On the topic of logistics, the investment and marketing society of Saxony-Anhalt organised a symposium in Brussels in 2012. Economic, political and scientific actors from Benelux and Saxony-Anhalt discussed the good logistic infrastructure of Saxony-Anhalt and provided information about the locations' profiles, markets and the innovation potential for sustainable logistics (Landesvertretung Sachsen-Anhalt bei der Europäischen Union 2013(1): 5-6).

In May 2012, the second external cabinet session of Saxony-Anhalt's government took place in Brussels. The members of the government discussed with officials of the Committee of permanent representatives, Commissioners and other COM officials on topics of: the Commission's working programme, the programming process for the funding period 2014-2020, solutions for the Euro-crisis, and the energy concept for Saxony-Anhalt. The interconnection between the regional policies and European policies was emphasised. Institutional cooperation between the European Council and the CoR was continued in May 2012, when president van Rompuy attended another CoR plenary session. The main topics of the plenary session were connected with the ERDF regulation that was already in the final stages of the decision-making process (Landesvertretung Sachsen-Anhalt bei der Europäischen Union 2013(1): 13-14, 30-31).

The 41st conference of the minister-presidents of the East-German *Länder* took place on the 13th September 2012 in Köthen under the presidency of Saxony-Anhalt. At the conference, significant actors from the federal government, such as the Chancellor Angela Merkel, the federal minister of the Interior Hans-Peter Friedrich, and the authorised representative of the federal government for the new *Länder*, Christoph Bergner, took part. The main topics of the conference were: implementation of energy turn, allocation of the EU-funds among the poor and the rich regions after 2013 and the demographic strategy of the federal government. Minister-president Haseloff emphasised the insistence of the Eastern *Länder* that the federal government took stronger regard of the Eastern necessities and that it would plead for reasonable financial allocation in the Council's negotiations on the Multi-annual financial framework (Staatskanzlei Sachsen-Anhalt 2012b; see Sălăgeanu 2014a).

In April 2013, the 100th Plenary session of the CoR took place at which the president of the EP, Martin Schulz, attended and emphasised the importance of the CoR's contribution to the EU decision-making processes, bringing the EU closer to citizens and informing them on the developments at European level. In June 2013, the topic of the MFF decisions dominated both the CoR plenary session and the 18th European People's Party (EPP) summit. The already mentioned institutionalised cooperation between the EP and the CoR could be positively assessed through the existence of the category of transition regions for the funding period 2014-2020, according to Danuta Hübner, former president of EP-REGI committee (Landesvertretung Sachsen-Anhalt bei der Europäischen Union 2014(1): 14-15). The EU funds financial contribution for the operational programmes of Saxony-Anhalt for 2014-2020 is: 1.427 billion € for the ERDF OP; 777 million € for rural development; 612 million € for the ESF OP (Schlüter 2017: 359).

In December 2013, the EPP political group within the CoR had a special meeting, at which actors from the scientific arena pointed out that the CoR should maintain its special role in representing the subnational levels and contributing to the further economic growth through solutions that are adapted to the local needs (Landesvertretung Sachsen-Anhalt bei der Europäischen Union 2014(1): 14-5).

5.3.4 The actors' functions and the policy content connection

During his first statement in May 2011, minister-president Haseloff presented the need for the coalition agreement to bring continuity and reliability to the settled goals and priorities of Saxony-Anhalt. His credo was that through a strong economy the government would be able to fulfil its goals. In his declaration, Haseloff stressed the importance of the EU membership experience, of having constant contact with European officials and of Saxony-Anhalt being acknowledged in Brussels. He stressed the objective to prepare the Europe- and internationalisation strategy and to strengthen the EU-competence of the administration (Staatskanzlei Sachsen-Anhalt 2011a: 31-32).

In July 2011, the minister-president visited Brussels. He met with regional partners from Poland, MEPs, Commission's president Barroso, European Council's president van Rompuy, and Commissioners Lewandowski, Oettinger and Hahn (Staatskanzlei Sachsen-Anhalt 2011a: 40-43). The newsletter of the Brussels representation of Saxony-Anhalt provided information about activities and discussions that took place in Brussels (see Landesvertretung Sachsen-Anhalt bei der Europäischen Union 2012(1): 23-24, 27-28, 42-44).

The cooperation between the EP and the CoR took place in the form of meetings between the EP-EPP political group and of the COTER committee of CoR in order to develop common positions with regard to the Cohesion Policy. On the same note, MEPs from Eastern Germany also met with colleagues from the Eastern German representations to the EU within their informal consultation procedures. The European Regional Policy regulations' package proposed in 2011 contained important stipulations for Saxony-Anhalt for the funding period 2014-2020. The stipulations were: the safety net of 2/3 funds allocation for transition regions, 30% reduction of funds for transition regions for SMEs and innovation projects, the 5% use of structural funds for the development of cities; reduction to 5% of the cross financing and others (Landesvertretung Sachsen-Anhalt bei der Europäischen Union 2012(1): 49, 53-54).

In January 2012, the internationalisation strategy of Saxony-Anhalt was adopted. The government joined the internationalisation strategy with the one for the European Union affairs. The strategy provided a basis for the activities of the regional government within EMLG. Its purpose was to increase the networking and participation of Saxony-Anhalt in international processes. The main purposes stated in the strategy were: intensifying the relations between partners and cooperation regions, Brussels journeys of members from different departments of the government, support for non-state actors in international cooperation in order to implement the Europe 2020 strategy by developing the R&D scene, and making use of the Cohesion Policy for the region's development, tackling the demographic and environment challenges (Landesregierung Sachsen-Anhalt 2012).

The international dimension was considered important for attracting investors, representing the interests and goals of the industry at European level, and elaborating an innovation strategy for Saxony-Anhalt with a European dimension. The goal regarding territorial cooperation was to make use of the INTERREG funds and to develop the economy based on innovation. Enhanced cooperation with other regions and implementation of the European goals such as TEN-T were among the elements of Saxony-Anhalt's internationalisation strategy (Landesregierung Sachsen-Anhalt 2012).

In April 2014, an external Saxony-Anhalt state secretaries' conference took place at the region's representation in Brussels. They met with members of the COM and discussed the innovation dimension for the funding period 2014-2020 and the programming process for the operational programmes. 2014 also brought personal changes in regard to the relations with the EP. After the election, MEP Horst Schnellhardt was replaced by two new MEPs from Saxony-Anhalt, Sven Schulze and Arne Lietz. In October 2014 – during the Open Days event, a seminar relevant for Saxony-Anhalt took place on the topic of demographic change (Landesvertretung Sachsen-Anhalt bei der Europäischen Union 2015(1): 16, 25, 29, 40-41).

The newsletter of the Brussels representation of Saxony-Anhalt informed about fewer and fewer events in the last two years. The reduced number of events might indicate the effect of the financial consolidation. Nevertheless, the presence and activity of Saxony-Anhalt at European level was still considered important and it was carried on according to the set priorities.

In 2015 the CoR started its 6th mandate. For Saxony-Anhalt, statesecretary Michael Schneider continued his activity, also as president of the CoR EPP political group. Next to Schneider, Tilman Tögel – member of the *Landtag* of Saxony-Anhalt, became again a member of the CoR (Landesvertretung Sachsen-Anhalt bei der Europäischen Union 2015(5): 4-5).

During the 6th legislative period, Saxony-Anhalt was the location for the establishment of several companies in the field of economy and science (IBM, T-Systems, Novelis), which created more than 500 new jobs. Research facilities were also developed, such as the institute for competence in auto mobility in Magdeburg, the Fraunhofer centre for chemical-biotechnological processes in Leuna, and the Fraunhofer centre for Silicon-Photovoltaic in Halle.

In order to increase the innovation potential of the SMEs, the government continued to promote the cooperation between science and economy. With regard to the development of companies, the government pursued the goal of achieving high qualifications for employees. For this purpose, it used 62 Million € from the ESF for qualification training (Staatskanzlei Sachsen-Anhalt 2013a).

Within EMLG, the government managed to position the Eastern German *Länder* in preparation works of the funding period 2014-2020, resulting in the existence of transition regions as a category of the European Regional

Policy 2014-2020 and in Saxony-Anhalt being one transition region. The idea of EU as part of the domestic policy has been pursued during the analysed period. It intensified each year, especially due to the connections created by participation in the HLG. There were not only political declarations but also evidence of the activities of Saxony-Anhalt within EMLG.

Authorities of Saxony-Anhalt needed to make sure that the *Land* managed to develop and tackle the challenges of migration and unemployment at the same time. Finding the balance among the multitude of EU regulations that needed implementation, such as the environment requirements, was a challenge for the government. The assessment of the government's achievements during the 6th legislative period emphasised the financial consolidation, the reduced unemployment, below 10% (Staatskanzlei Sachsen-Anhalt 2015a: 5), and the investments in the research infrastructure. The authorities achieved the goal of not making new debt and the finance ministry managed to even cut back the debt (Staatskanzlei Sachsen-Anhalt 2015b).

The government of Saxony-Anhalt could handle the Europeanisation only by involving the region's actors actively in the processes of the EMLG. The next chapters bring out the activity of Saxony-Anhalt and its strong mobilisation in the field of the European Regional Policy and of the European Chemicals Policy.

6 Regional participation of Saxony-Anhalt within European Multi-Level Governance: the complement of the European Regional Policy

The analysed hypothesis in this chapter is that the EU top-down incentives, for regions, contribute to subnational mobilisation of Saxony-Anhalt within EMLG. The analysis focuses on how the EU funding incentives triggered subnational participation within the EU policy-making processes of the European Regional Policy. This policy is based on European regulations that provide the context and purposes for use of the European Structural and Investments funds, leaving the process of programming and implementation in the hands of the Member States and their regions.

This section continues the analysis based on the interplay of the variables: goals, resources and their functions, and the participation processes. This chapter summarises the activities of Saxony-Anhalt focusing on elements of MLG type I. The advocated interest of Saxony-Anhalt was that the European Commission needed to take into consideration that the EU enlargements from 2004 and 2007 triggered a statistical change that affected the allocation of European funds for several regions. The main change was of the EU GDP average, based on which the eligibility categories for funds allocation were decided.

As mentioned in the second chapter, the MLG concept was developed because of the multi-level character of the European Regional Policy. Even though EMLG takes into account the importance of regions mainly in the implementation of the European Regional Policy, the participation of the regions in policy-making processes was possible as well.

Recently, a special attention has been given to the regional activity of interests' representation and the subnational contribution to the European policies content at European level (Tatham 2013, 2016; Beyers/Donas 2013; Rowe 2011). The mobilisation for the early interests' representation was the main contribution of Saxony-Anhalt to EMLG that was analysed and it is presented in this chapter. Therefore, the analysis of the subnational contribution to the European Regional policy-making fits in MLG type I as presented by Marks and Hooghe (2010). In addition, to the competition between the European, national and subnational level of MLG type, there was also a domestic competition between the sixteen *Länder* that boosted the subnational mobilisation.

6.1 The European Regional Policy

The European Regional Policy was set up in 1975 with the creation of the European Regional Development Fund. During the 1972 Paris Summit, the UK pressured other European members to channel funds into a European Regional Policy, similar to the one that had a strong tradition in the UK. The UK had several weak regions that needed financial help from the European level. Even though the proposal for the ERDF regulation was regarded as a regional policy instrument of the European Community, the Council of Ministers made sure that the ERDF was structured in such a matter that it allowed the individual MS to exert a strong influence on the allocation of funds. That left no room to the Commission to decide upon the distribution of funds where the need was greater (Armstrong 1995: 35-37).

Regional policy is a "system of joint finance linking budgetary policies of different levels of government" (Benz/Eberlein 1999: 335). This policy received much attention due to its redistributive character that discriminated between the Member States and the subnational units. The discrimination brought further conflicts over the advantages and disadvantages of the redistributive actions. The main players in this multi-level system of regional policy are the administrations that determine the agendas (Benz/Eberlein 1999; Benz 2003: 333, 340).

The 1988 reform of the European Regional Policy brought significant changes to the procedures and practices of the planning and to the policy implementation. The European Commission became an active participant in framing and monitoring the regional development programs. The partnership principle was also codified as a regulatory requirement, calling for the involvement of the regional and local authorities in the processes of programme formulation and implementation for the first time (European Parliament 2014: 10).

The territorial aspect was a highly debated subject in the 1990s. In 1999 the European Spatial Development Perspective was adopted which led to the establishment of a transnational cooperation programmes INTERREG and later to the European Spatial Planning Observatory Network, in order to support the policy development (Official Journal of the European Communities 2001: 10; Commission of the European Communities 2008: 10-11).

In 2007, the Member States committed themselves to add the territorial dimension to the social and economic cohesion dimension. The topic was of great interest for the ministers responsible for the spatial planning (Commission of the European Communities 2008: 10). The Territorial Agenda prepared the debate on territoriality, "an action-oriented political framework for [the] future cooperation" (Bundesministerium für Umwelt, Naturschutz, Bau und Reaktorsicherheit 2007:1). The Agenda promoted a polycentric territorial development through the better use of resources and cooperation, involving "various actors and stakeholders of territorial development at political, administrative and technical levels", by considering the history, culture and institutional frameworks of each Member State (Bundesministerium für Umwelt, Naturschutz, Bau und Reaktorsicherheit 2007: 1).

The issue of the EU enlargement's statistical effect was tackled by the European Commission for the period 2007-2013 as follows:

> (17) A Convergence objective is to cover the Member States and regions whose development is lagging behind. The regions targeted by the Convergence objective are those whose per capita gross domestic product (GDP) measured in purchasing power parities is less than 75 % of the Community average. The regions suffering from the statistical effect linked to the reduction in the Community average following the enlargement of the European Union are to benefit for that reason from substantial transitional aid in order to complete their convergence process. This aid is to end in 2013 and is not to be followed by a further transitional period. [...] The regions eligible are those under Objective 1 in the 2000 to 2006 programming period which no longer satisfy the regional eligibility criteria of the Convergence objective and which therefore benefit from a transitional aid, as well as all the other regions of the Community (Official Journal of the European Union 2006: L210/26).

The 2006 regulation contained the provision that the transitional aid would end in 2013. However, the new regulation for the 2014-2020 funding period contained a new set of eligible regions, among which the "transition regions" was one category. The next sections provide the proof of Saxony-Anhalt's participation, in partnership with other regions and actors, in the policy-making processes of the European Regional Policy. This participation was driven by the goal to ensure the continuance of the transitional aid within the European funding regulations.

The European Commission adopted in 2008 the Green Paper on territorial cohesion. The Green Paper emphasised the elements that contributed to the enhanced competitiveness of territory. That consisted of links with other territories, coordination of goods, services and capital, bridging economic effectiveness with social cohesion and with ecological balance, concentration on economic activity vs. concentration on the population; overcoming distance by connecting territories (intermodal transport connections, access to services such as health–care, education, energy, links between business and research centres); overcoming division by cooperating at different levels (environment, commuting – administrative cooperation); specific geographic features. Therefore, the implications of the territorial cohesion affected several policies, such as: the transport policy, the energy policy, the high-speed internet connection, the first pillar of Common Agriculture Policy, the European employment strategy, the maritime basins, the environmental policy, the high-quality research, and the competition policy, thus the territorial dimension gained importance.

The instruments that a territory has at its disposal (institutions, budget, and political legitimacy through elected officials) shape both activities within the state and within the EU (Commission of the European Communities 2008: 5-9). The legal framework is required especially for binding actors to their tasks and for the accountability of their actions. Hence, the overall political, institutional and juridical framework shapes the context of the political goals setting and their pursuit.

The European Regional Policy is an essential investment policy of the EU, delivered for the funding period 2014-2020 through the European Structural and Investment Funds (ESI): the ERDF, the CF, the ESF, the EAFRD and the EMFF. The objectives of the policy are to support the smart, sustainable and inclusive growth in the regions and cities of the MS, meeting the targets of the Europe 2020 strategy. The growth targets the job creation, the business competitiveness and the improvement of the citizens' quality of life (European Commission 2016d; see Appendix 5).

Since the European funds are investments, the regulations for the use of these funds have to take into consideration other European regulations of the internal market. The ESI regulations provide the rules, the funding priorities and the framework for the programming processes that occur in every MS. Provisions of the state aid and of the public procurement regulations must be respected in the implementation of the European funds. There is another regulation that provides the existence of resources necessary for the European funds, the multi-annual financial framework. This regulation sets the ground budget of the European Union for a seven-year period.

The reform and changes brought to the 2014-2020 European Regional Policy aim to maximise the impact of investments, and to deliver the Europe 2020 Strategy goals by investing in growth and people. Among the changes, a different categorisation of eligible regions[14] can be observed, as well as a refocused allocation of funds according to the 11 thematic objectives, a regular monitoring of the states' objective achievement, the use of the smart specialisation strategy, simplifying procedures (European Commission 2013).

The 2014-2020 funding period is constructed on long-term objectives of the Europe 2020 Strategy, on aligning the policy to the specific goals and targets in the fields of employment, education, innovation, research and development, climate. The European Regional Policy common regulation stipulates that the partnership agreements set out the commitments of the MS and

---

[14] Less Developed regions (GDP < 75% of EU-27 average); Transition regions (GDP 75% to 90% of EU-27 GDP average); More Developed regions (GDP > 90% of EU-27 average (Official Journal of the European Union 2013b).

the regions to the objectives of the Europe 2020 Strategy (see Appendix 5). These commitments are bound to financial allocations that depend on the types of eligible regions. (Official Journal of the European Union 2013: Article 20).

The 2014-2020 regulations' package for European funds introduced the category of transition regions, next to less developed and more developed regions. These new categories replaced the eligibility criteria used during the 2007-2013 funding period. The regions' category change reflects that those with an initial GDP/head < 75% EU GDP/head average managed to grow and improve their economic situation. However, exceeding the 75% margin did not mean that those regions exceeded the 90% EU GDP/head average threshold as well. Hence, the regions, whose GDP/head was between the 75% and 90% margins of the EU GDP/head average were the ones that required the transition aid (Sălăgeanu 2016: 62). The improved economic situation of the regions in need of transition aid did not mean that they did not still depend much on the contribution of the European funds for development projects.

Similar to the proposal of the CoR's WP on MLG, all Member States (not regions) must adopt together with the European Commission a Partnership Agreement for the financial period 2014-2020 in order to contribute to the implementation of the partnership principle. The agreement provides for:

> [...] arrangements to ensure alignment with the Union strategy for smart, sustainable and inclusive growth as well as with the Fund-specific missions pursuant to their Treaty-based objectives, arrangements to ensure effective and efficient implementation of the ESI Funds and arrangements for the partnership principle and an integrated approach to territorial development (Official Journal of the European Union 2013: Article 20).

The purpose of the new exercise for the Member States was to ensure that the MLG principles and the principles of subsidiarity and proportionality were respected and that experience and relevant know-how were used for planned interventions according to the specific challenges of the Member States (Official Journal of the European Union 2013: Article 11).

The common provisions regulation for the use of European funds explicitly introduced MLG elements. In addition, the European Commission adopted a European Code of Conduct on partnership in the form of a delegated regulation. The code specified the conditions to be taken into consideration regarding the partners' involvement in the preparation and implementation of the 2014-2020 partnership agreements and programmes. Accordingly, Member States needed to ensure: the transparency of the partners' selection, the provision of adequate information services, and the efficient involvement of partners in all phases and improvement of competencies of the partners (European Commission 2014a).

6.2 Political goals of Saxony-Anhalt regarding the European Regional Policy

The determination of the political goals has been guiding the activities of Saxony-Anhalt and its participation within EMLG. Resources available were used through the access channels available in order to intervene in the European policy-making processes at an early stage. The European Regional Policy provided a great opportunity for the regional participation within EMLG.

The political priorities set by the government of the 6th legislative period included investments in: innovation, energy, education, the demographic development and the quality of live. The EU funding criteria change for 2014-2020 according to the category of transition regions meant for Saxony-Anhalt a loss of about 1/3 of the former allocation. The European co-financing of projects was set to 80% (Kabinetsvorlage Sachsen-Anhalt 2013: 42-43). In that context, the government welcomed every investor in the region, such as the new site of the chemical company Paralube, an actor of the chemical industry sector (Staatskanzlei Sachsen-Anhalt 2013b).

The *Landtag* of Saxony-Anhalt prepared a resolution on the arrangements of the financing period 2014-2020. The *Landtag* requested the government to keep it informed and to specially regard the aspects emphasised in the resolution. The *CDU* and *SPD* requested the government to ensure the necessary co-financing from the *Land* budget and to consider the demographic changes (Landtag Sachsen-Anhalt 2011b: 1). The political group *DIE LINKE* requested the government to consider the matters it proposed during the negotiations at the federal and European level for the funding period 2014-2020. Among those matters, the support for the category of transition regions was clarified (Landtag Sachsen-Anhalt 2011c: 1). The political group *BÜNDNIS 90/DIE GRÜNEN* pointed out the need to consider the implementation of the resource-efficient Europe initiative, which was one of the flagships of the EU 2020 Strategy (Landtag Sachsen-Anhalt 2011d: 1).

The different requests from political groups of the *Landtag* were gathered in the resolution's recommendation of the committee for the federal and European affairs and for the media (Landtag Sachsen-Anhalt 2012a). All the requests to the government were later entailed in a resolution of the *Landtag* regarding the Cohesion Policy 2014-2020 in Saxony-Anhalt (Landtag Sachsen-Anhalt 2012b). Following the resolution of the *Landtag*, the government prepared a briefing for the parliament about the programming process and its stages according to a specific schedule (Landtag Sachsen-Anhalt 2012c: 3-4).

Saxony-Anhalt's political goals were not only determined at the beginning of the legislative period in the coalition agreement. They were further enforced by the *Landtag* and the *Landesregierung*. Therefore, the pursuit of the transition regions goal was followed by the actors, especially the one of achieving the Europe 2020 strategy.

6.3 Resources of Saxony-Anhalt and their functions regarding the European Regional Policy

The regions' categories are a crucial element of the European Regional Policy and of the multi-annual financial framework. There is a significant interest to ease a significant drop of the available funding by mobilising and bringing specific regional interests at the European level. Such is the case for transition regions, which were firstly considered to gain transitional aid only until 2014. Nevertheless, the progress of regions within these categories is a sign of success of the European Regional Policy.

Saxony-Anhalt dedicated resources to the topic of transition aid and transition regions since the beginning of the 2000s. A position paper of the *Landesregierung* underlined the success of Saxony-Anhalt's efforts for the transitional aid (Landesregierung Sachsen-Anhalt 2004: 10). The continued use of the region's resources for the pursuit of goals set by the parliament and the government shows the characteristics of the MLG Type I.

The institutional architecture maintained the structure of the elected legislature, the executive and the judicial system. Decision-making powers were dispersed across the jurisdictions. But participation within EMLG occurred through the available channels. For Saxony-Anhalt those channels were the direct communication with national and European actors (federal government, the *Bundesrat*, the horizontal cooperation with the other German *Länder*, the European Commission, the European Parliament, and the Committee of the Regions) and the interregional cooperation with the actors who share the same goals. Thus, participation within EMLG was multidimensional, both horizontally and vertically.

The activities of Saxony-Anhalt spanned across many territorial levels and across different policies because the European decision-making processes are interdependent. The European Regional Policy defines what type of regions receives what percentage of funds and what priorities need to be financed by those funds. But, the exact numbers were decided by members of the national governments together with the European Parliament. The funds are used to achieve the goals of the overall strategy of the EU. Therefore, the processes of preparing and making policies that ensure the achievement of the EU strategy and implementation of those policies is what EMLG is all about.

The document analysis focused on the following resources: the actors engaged in the participation of Saxony-Anhalt within EMLG, the information provided by subnational actors to the European level, the events organised to gather and coordinate the information, the partnerships and the cooperation among regions. The activities' results were the position papers the regions prepared and delivered to the European Commission. The Commission also delivered relevant information to the regions and national governments, based on which they could develop the position papers.

The analysis highlighted elements that show the continuity of Saxony-Anhalt's participation within EMLG. These were the repeated activities and contacts maintenance according to the multi-dimensional framework, and the consistent representation of Saxony-Anhalt by the same actors. For instance, the CoR member of Saxony-Anhalt, Michael Schneider has been active the entire period that was empirically analysed. He has been State Secretary for the Federal and European affairs and the Envoy of Saxony-Anhalt to the Federal Government within the Federal Republic of Germany, and a member of the Committee of the Regions at European level.

The functions and activities performed by Michel Schneider embody EMLG characteristics. His active engagement and commitment within the CoR in important matters for the regions have given him the possibility to play a major role in the activity of the CoR. Schneider served as the Chairman of the CoR's Commission for the Territorial Cohesion Policy (2008-2011) and as the European People's Party Group Vice-President (2004-2010). He was the rapporteur for several of the Commission's reports related to the Cohesion Policy. Since 2010, he has been the President of the EPP Group in the CoR (Committee of the Regions 2016b).

Another relevant actor is the Europe-minister, Rainer Robra, who has been in charge of the state chancellery since 2002. Former director of the representation to the EU, Thomas Wobben, was also a long-term partner in the communication and dialogue strategies with the European institutions. The current minister-president of Saxony-Anhalt, Reiner Haseloff, has been also a long-term political actor. He was state-secretary in the ministry of economy and labour of Saxony-Anhalt from 2002 to 2006, minister for economy and labour of Saxony-Anhalt and president of the ECRN from 2006 to 2011. Since 2011, he has been the minister-president of Saxony-Anhalt. Since 2016, after the *Landtag* election, he has been leading the government coalition between the *CDU*, the *SPD* and the *BÜNDNIS 90/DIE GRÜNEN* political groups (Haseloff 2016).

6.4 The participation processes of Saxony-Anhalt regarding the European Regional Policy

This section takes a closer look into the activities of Saxony-Anhalt related to the topic of transition regions from the perspective of MLG character of the EU. In 2003, Saxony-Anhalt engaged in many activities about the statistical effect of the EU enlargement, heard by the European decision-makers. A summary of the activities comprises:

- Discussions between minister-president Böhmer and commissioner Verheugen about the design of the Cohesion Policy and the effect of the EU enlargement (Landesvertretung Sachsen-Anhalt bei der Europäischen Union 2004(1): 8),
- The position paper of Saxony-Anhalt and other regions affected by the statistical effect requesting transitional aid (European Commission 2003; Staatskanzlei Sachsen-Anhalt 2003; Landesvertretung Sachsen-Anhalt bei der Europäischen Union 2004(1): 10),
- A round table about the needs and challenges of regions and the contribution of the European Regional Policy (Landesvertretung Sachsen-Anhalt bei der Europäischen Union 2002(3): 7),
- The CoR's reports of Michael Schneider (Landesvertretung Sachsen-Anhalt bei der Europäischen Union 2004(1): 9; Sălăgeanu 2014c),
- A panel discussion with members of the EP, the CoR and of Saxony-Anhalt,
- Commissioner Barnier confirmed to the Eastern German *Länder* that the 2007-2013 funding period would entail reasonable solutions for the statistically affected regions by the EU enlargement (Landesvertretung Sachsen-Anhalt bei der Europäischen Union 2004(1): 14); the same confirmation delivered Commissioner Danuta Hübner in direct discussions between her and minister-president Böhmer in 2004 (Landesvertretung Sachsen-Anhalt bei der Europäischen Union 2005(1): 38-39).

The institute for structural policy in Halle (*ISW*) prepared a mid-term review of the implementation of European funds and achievements for the period 2002-2006. The review accounted for a funding scheme that extended and modernised the corporate capital stock in Saxony-Anhalt. According to the review, the use of European funds contributed to the construction of new plants, to extension of businesses and modernisation of existing businesses. However, the review emphasised the need of prioritisation during the programming phase. It also made recommendations for the implementation and management of programmes (Institut für Strukturpolitik und Wirtschaftsförderung gGmbH 2003: 18-20). These recommendations targeted especially the financial planning and co-funding schemes, such as:

- Setting up a financial plan close to reality for the rest of the programme period (2006/08),
- Finding new possibilities of co-financing apart from the state budget,
- Achieving a better agreement between the programme actions of the OP and the grants given by the state,
- Preventing multiple assignments,
- Better interlocking of the financial budgeting of the OP with the state budget (Institut für Strukturpolitik und Wirtschaftsförderung gGmbH 2003: 20-22).

The review pointed out that the management of the financial allocation for Saxony-Anhalt could be improved in order to target the goals of development. Hence, Saxony-Anhalt needed to make sure that the European funds were properly used and the goals of the policy were achieved in order to make their case for the transition rules and to avoid a major decrease in funds allocation.

In 2004, CoR's member, Michael Schneider, prepared a paper as basis for the CoR's report to the COM's second interim report on cohesion (Landesvertretung Sachsen-Anhalt bei der Europäischen Union 2004(1): 10-11). The *Bund* and the *Länder* prepared a joint position paper to the 4th COM's report on economic and social cohesion presented by Schneider in the CoR (Bund und Länder 2008). In 2005, Saxony-Anhalt and the CoR organised a joint seminar about the programming process of the 2007-2013 European Regional Policy (Landesvertretung Sachsen-Anhalt bei der Europäischen Union 2006(1): 47; Sălăgeanu 2014c: 137).

DG Regio organised in January 2007 a conference on the topic of regional policy and demographic challenges. The rural development and transport minister of Saxony-Anhalt, Karl-Heinz Daehre, presented that the challenges posed by the demographic development were connected to the austerity policy, territorial reform and accomplishment of the infrastructure projects imposed on the regions (Landesvertretung Sachsen-Anhalt bei der Europäischen Union 2008(1): 3-4). From that perspective, the European Regional Policy played an important role for the regions that were struggling with negative demographic changes.

The demographic challenge was among the political priorities acknowledged by the *Landtag* of Saxony-Anhalt in its 2006 coalition agreement. The pursuit of strategies for tackling this challenge was connected with the 2014-2020 programming process (see chapter 5). Events like the conference on demographic challenges showed the interconnectedness of European policies with economic realities within the territories.

The European Commission needed to be able to correctly assess the problems in the territories. Regional authorities needed to be heard by European decision-makers. Providing both elements, the cooperation between the actors at the different levels, solutions and instruments could be developed so that the regions could tackle the challenges. But, the European institutions could not replace the work that needed to be done in the territory. For that reason, the implementation of the European Regional Policy required the involvement of regional authorities.

In 2007, the representations of the Eastern *Länder* to the EU initiated discussions with the new director of DG Regio, Dirk Ahner, about the future design of the European Regional Policy (Landesvertretung Sachsen-Anhalt bei der Europäischen Union 2008(1): 3). In 2007 and 2008, the *Länder* delivered resolutions about the future of the Cohesion Policy. In 2009, another resolution of the Europe-minister conference enforced the position of the *Länder* about the role of the Cohesion Policy (Rheinland-Pfalz 2010).

In 2008, Saxony-Anhalt together with other regions sent to the European Commission a position paper on the simplification of administrative procedures for the implementation of the Regional Policy. The Directorate-General Regional Policy highly appreciated the position paper and requested a further position paper on territorial cooperation. In 2009, Saxony-Anhalt prepared together with other 20 regions the requested position paper by DG Regional Policy (Landesvertretung Sachsen-Anhalt bei der Europäischen Union 2010(1): 12). The position paper was prepared within the framework of the Round Table of Practitioners in Structural Funds Implementation (ROTOPI-network). Further discussions of the network were held with the DG's General Director Ahner, followed by a seminar organised by the Czech presidency (Landesvertretung Sachsen-Anhalt bei der Europäischen Union 2010(1): 22).

The Consortium for the partnership of transition regions held a meeting during the 2009 Open Days (Landesvertretung Sachsen-Anhalt bei der Europäischen Union 2010(1): 58-9). Further discussions between minister-president Böhmer and MEPs also took place in Brussels (Landesvertretung Sachsen-Anhalt bei der Europäischen Union 2010(1): 61-62). These particular activities showed the very active engagement of Saxony-Anhalt with other involved actors, and their willingness to learn.

In June 2010, state-secretary Schneider participated at the High-Level Group for the Cohesion Policy future where he presented the position of the CoR to the topic (Landesvertretung Sachsen-Anhalt bei der Europäischen Union 2011(1): 37). He emphasised, in particular, the need for transitional rules on several occasions (Committee of the Regions 2010, 2012c, Schneider 2012).

With regard to the Cohesion Policy, Saxony-Anhalt engaged in wide cooperation, bringing together cohesion experts from the Commission, the Council, the federal government of Germany and the *Länder* to an event hosted by Saxony-Anhalt. At the event, the Commissioner for Regional Policy, Johannes Hahn, emphasised the importance of the cooperation between the federal and regional level in the policy-making process of the future Cohesion Policy (Landesvertretung Sachsen-Anhalt bei der Europäischen Union 2011(1): 56-58). In 2011, a *Bundesrat* position paper enforced the common position of the *Bund* and *Länder* to the 5th COM's report on the economic, social and territorial cohesion (Bund und Länder 2011). The *Bundesrat* did not support the category of transition regions but it did encourage the transitional aid (Bundesrat 2011).

At European level, the institutional cooperation between the European Council and the Committee of the Regions intensified, when the president of the European Council, Herman van Rompuy, attended the plenary session of the CoR; he enabled the direct opinion exchange on the implementation of the Europe 2020 strategy (Landesvertretung Sachsen-Anhalt bei der Europäischen Union 2012(1): 24-25; see Sălăgeanu 2014c).

6.5 Findings

MLG characteristics of the European Regional Policy's implementation triggered the research of the effects and benefits of this policy. The research highlighted its direct and indirect benefits. Direct performance was derived from the enterprises and companies that won EU-funded projects. Indirect effects were the increase in export outcomes, goods or services. On the other hand, the EMLG model of implementation was considered "one of the policy's main areas of added value and was credited with having a significant impact on regional policy practice in Member States and regions" (Polverari/Bachtler et al. 2014: 8). But the actual assessment of regional development as a direct result of the European policy was difficult to quantify.

Therefore, MLG contributed to the increase in efficiency, legitimacy and transparency of decision-making processes but it also brought administrative workload and extra bureaucracy, especially for the programme managers. Hence, the subnational involvement within EMLG might be costly before the benefits can be achieved. Nevertheless, the practice of governance at different levels increases the efficiency and transparency of the subnational activity (Polverari/Bachtler et al. 2014).

The information gathering processes involved the communication between the European and subnational level, between the national and subnational level, and communication between different types of actors, governmental, social, and private. The representation of interests was performed through the intrastate channel of the *Bundesrat* and through the European access channel of the Committee of the Regions. Saxony-Anhalt was involved in shaping the European Regional Policy at different levels, through the intrastate negotiations on the common position papers via the *Bundesrat* and through the Committee of the Regions. Information exchange and position papers were exchanged between the *Landesregierung* and the *Landtag*, based on the socio-economic analysis performed by the institute for structural policy in Halle (Landtag Sachsen-Anhalt 2012d). All these encompass the participation process within EMLG.

The newsletter of the Brussels representation of Saxony-Anhalt, *EU-Wochenspiegel*, briefed about the meetings and discussions between members of the *Landtag* of Saxony-Anhalt – the committee for federal and European affairs and for the media – and the officers of the European Commission. The actors presented their interests in the cooperation with the political, economic and social partners of the region in order to prepare the funding period 2007-2013. A diverse range of actors from Saxony-Anhalt mobilised for achieving their goals. In this context, the success of picking up the Halle area of Saxony-Anhalt into the framework of depreciating the transitional aid for the regions affected by the statistical effect was addressed as well (Landesvertretung Sachsen-Anhalt bei der Europäischen Union 2007(1): 28-30).

Even though the CoR has no legal decision-making power, interinstitutional cooperation increased in the last years. Through the ongoing exchange with the Commission, the EP and lately with the European Council, the CoR provided an active channel for the subnational participation within EMLG. The CoR's positions spoke for all the members, not only for Saxony-Anhalt. Therefore, the use of the CoR can be perceived as an important element in designing the strategy for a region's participation within EMLG.

The category of transition regions was initially not endorsed by actors at the European and national level. This category is, however, entailed in the cohesion package regulations for 2014-2020 and sees for a specific aid allocation method, a higher co-financing rate and more flexibility for the choice of investment priorities. Saxony-Anhalt approached the topics of the statistical effect on its own a few years before the EU enlargement generated the changes. But their continued engagement with many partners to this topic enhanced their regional voice.

The historical background and institutional framework were considered independent variables for Saxony-Anhalt. In the case of Central and Eastern Europe, the institutional and legal framework of the subnational level was conditioned by the European integration. There was no tradition of a strong subnational level. However, that did not impede the cooperation among regions of the new MS. The mobilisation of actors occurred. The regionalisation and decentralisation processes in the new MS are still relevant for the efficient implementation of the European Regional Policy. The activities of Saxony-Anhalt stimulated the cooperation of other regions being helpful for regions with weaker positions within their national state.

A region can pursue a strategic course of action for its participation within EMLG by making use of its resources, primarily gathering the necessary information for establishing its goals. A thorough understanding of the functioning of the EU and identification of the access channels can ease the access to information and improve the contacts between the European and subnational level. Due to specific time guidelines, such as the financing periods or the Commission's consultation processes, the subnational mobilisation should take into consideration the timeline of the European governance processes and proceed according to a timetable in order to facilitate early engagement within EMLG.

7 Regional participation of Saxony-Anhalt within European Multi-Level Governance: the complement of the European Chemicals Policy

This chapter offers a closer analysis of what EMLG can offer for the regional participation within it. The pursuit of mobilisation's goals for a particular policy can be very fruitful for a region that struggles with limited resources. Saxony-Anhalt has been struggling with a structural weakness of its economy after the unification. In the pursuit to reduce unemployment and to increase the attractiveness of Saxony-Anhalt as a science and business location, the chemical industry has played an important role. Making use of one of the region's historical industries, the authorities and private stakeholders have developed the potential of the Saxony-Anhalt chemical industry into a well-known player at European level.

The fourth hypothesis presented in the second chapter is that top-down incentives from the EU contribute to the mobilisation of Saxony-Anhalt, allowing it to become part of a European stakeholder such as the European Chemical Regions Network. This hypothesis is validated by the actions that Saxony-Anhalt undertook in the area of the chemicals policy, presented in this chapter. In addition, the incentives provided by the EU and the use of access channels to the European policy-making are discussed in the next sections.

7.1 European dimension of the chemicals industry

The Single European Act formally recognised the environmental protection as a legislative competence of the European Community. New stipulations of the treaty formalised legal activities that were already being implemented for years. Further treaty reforms established the goals of the European Environmental Policy such as the sustainable growth in the Treaty of Maastricht and the sustainable development in the Treaty of Amsterdam. The European Environment Policy is an example of positive integration (Scharpf 1997) that describes and determines a model by regulating the allocation of goods and activities. European regulatory measures are usually connected to the costs of their implementation. This way, developing European regulations creates incentives for private and public actors to bring forward alternatives and ways of increasing the efficiency of the policy implementation. Policy learning is favoured through the de-politicisation and the emphasis on expertise

(Haverland 2003: 25). Furthermore, the communication and consultation processes are considered highly important for the EMLG.

Setting environmental standards is a technocratic process, which usually involves experts such as scientists, civil engineers and economists. However, the number of affected actors exceeds the number of involved actors. There is also the difference between the interests of polluters and of those who develop new environmental technologies. Nevertheless, the regulatory procedure of the EU is interested in gaining as much information from all the involved parts, in order to create legislation that satisfies governments and companies that bring innovative environmental technology on the market, as well as polluter companies, which have to implement measures for the protection of the (working-) environment (Haverland 2003).

The chemical policy is not part of the exclusive legislative competence of the *Bund*. Due to the German intertwined policy-making competencies, the chemical policy is a multi-level policy. There are different authorities at both levels; policy-making and policy implementation are closely connected. The top-down incentive for the subnational mobilisation, created by the European regulatory measures, requires the use of resources within a region. These are needed for establishing the goals of the regional actors and their functions, and for planning their mobilisation strategy so that participation within EMLG can be pursued.

The environmental policy is decentralised and it involves the horizontal cooperation between ministries, and the vertical cooperation, between different levels of government. This is an area where especially problem-solving approaches of policy-content and policy instruments are pursued. These instruments need to be adaptable to the specific regional needs, to the industrial and market characteristics of the units, which need to implement the regulations. Thus, it is advisable to exert influence on the content of the European legislation in order to ease the process of implementation and to improve competition chances for companies within subnational units. Such activities suit Type II MLG because they are task-specific and comprise flexible jurisdictions. Type II MLG can be found in the private-public partnerships that pursue specific tasks and involve collective decision-making processes (Hooghe/Marks 2010: 18). These characteristics are suitable for the environmental and chemical policy because of their multi-level nature.

The industry's actors are potential relevant partners for the public authorities. Their cooperation can play a crucial role in the promotion of regional interests, enabling an impact on European decision-making. Cooperation between subnational authorities and industrial and corporate actors usually succeeds when it is built on the existing cooperation between the subnational authorities and the European institutions. These are instruments that allow further development of regions and facilitate the collective influence exertion on European institutions. Considering such lobby activities, subnational actors are rarely powerful on their own. The sectorial interests based on businesses located in the region or the specific links that a sector has with the specialised actors within the European Commission enhances the power of lobby activities (Keating 1998: 170). Lobby or interest representation does not immediately guarantee influence (Jeffery 2000), but a goal-oriented cooperation among several actors that share the goals and challenges can make a difference, as this chapter shows.

The environmental policy is one kind of policy that creates two types of misfit: a policy and an institutional one, because European environmental policies primarily regulate the content of policy and hardly give any specific details on the administrative structures which need to deal with the policy content (Börzel 2008: 231). A pattern of representation of interests between public authorities, societal and economic actors in the policy-making process can be noticed, it follows exactly the logic of influencing policy-content. Thus, the institutional framework of the implementing administrative structures may provide the opportunity for participation in the EMLG or it can hinder it, depending on the intrastate rules.

The chemical industry's regulation is part of the EU environment policy and of the industry policy. The environment policy has been developing during the last decades to a policy by itself and it is one of the best examples of Multi-Level Governance due to its cross-border effects and the need of local solutions. These solutions are decided upon through the cooperation at different levels and involving private, corporate, and public actors.

In the 1980s, the recognition of the central governments limits increased. This coincided with the increasing general trust in the responsibilities for the subnational levels of governments. Especially in the federal EU Member States, some environmental responsibilities were handed back to the subnational governments (Wälti 2010: 411). The EU environmental acquis (over 300 regulated issues) indicates a high degree of institutionalisation and regulatory density (Börzel 2008: 226). The high number of European rules for this policy area also indicates that there are many actors involved in the implementation of these binding decisions.

Towards the end of the 1990s the topic of the EU chemicals policy started a debate at European level due to the forthcoming EU regulatory measures. The Commission consulted around one hundred stakeholders. The result of the consultations was the White Paper Strategy for a future Chemicals Policy from 2001 that laid down the deficiencies of the existing system. It pointed out the general lack of knowledge about the properties and the uses of substances, the slow risk assessment process, the inappropriate allocation of responsibilities and the deficient legislation of the sector. The political objectives stated in the White Paper were:

- Protection of the human health and of the environment,
- Maintenance and enhancement of the competitiveness of the European Chemicals Industry,
- Prevention of the fragmentation of the internal market,
- Increasing transparency,
- Integration with international efforts and in conformity with the EU international obligations under the World Trade Organization,
- Promotion of non-animal testing (Commission of the European Communities 2001: 7).

The increasing number of new substances had created the need for a new system of the chemicals' control. In order to provide an appropriate assessment of the risks of chemical products, a reliable basis for deciding the adequate safety measures was necessary. A new system able to cope with a large amount of existing substances had to be developed that would "ensure adequate information, made publicly available, and appropriate risk management of existing and new substances" (Commission of the European Communities 2001: 11, 16).

The European Commission prepared four important legal instruments for the governing of chemicals. These instruments regulated the testing of substances, the determination of risk reduction measures, and safety duties such as the labelling and the safety data sheets. For the accelerated risk assessment system, the White Paper proposed the REACH framework composed of:

- Registration of basic information,
- Evaluation of the registered information for all substances,
- Authorisation of substances with certain hazardous properties.

The decision-making process for the REACH regulation comprised two processes: decision-making for the evaluation stage and decision-making for the authorisation stage. Both decision-making processes depended on the preliminary risk assessment data provided by actors from the industry. Therefore, the policy-making process in such a specific domain had to rely on a multitude of actors, national, sub-national authorities and private actors from the industry. The next sections present the activities within Saxony-Anhalt and the involved actors that contributed to an enhanced mobilisation for the participation of Saxony-Anhalt in EMLG with the focus on the EU's chemicals policy.

7.2 The chemicals industry in Saxony-Anhalt and its role for the participation within European Multi-Level Governance

Saxony-Anhalt entails an important location of the "Chemical Triangle" of Central Germany. The chemical industry has been subject to a deep restructuring process after the German unification. If in 1989, 117.000 people worked in the chemical industry, in 2007, there were about 10% of them employed in the chemical sector (Wobben 2007: 78). The contributing elements for the mobilisation of the private and public actors in this area have been the goals of developing the chemical sector as a vital element of the economy of Saxony-Anhalt and the development of the available private and public resources.

In order to plan further investments and their financial and economic future, the chemical companies addressed to Saxony-Anhalt authorities. In 1999, they proposed a strategic dialogue with the regional government. Both the government and the representatives of the chemical industry were interested in discussing and coordinating the chemical industry with the policies of the *Land*. Thus, they could jointly maintain and improve the growth chances of the regional chemical industry. The cooperation between the government and the companies followed on a regular basis. As a consequence the actors agreed upon different initiatives and their implementation, such as:

- Joint initiative for training professionals in the chemical industry,
- Close cooperation between the research institutions and the chemical companies,
- Initiatives for the *Bundesrat*, in order to promote federal regulations (Wobben 2007: 79).

The authorities of Saxony-Anhalt prepared a strategy for the chemical policy development in the region. In November 2000, discussions among Saxony-Anhalt's representative, state-secretary Ralf Nagel, and Peter Schweiger, cabinet member of Loyola de Palacio, Commissioner for Inter-Institutional Relations and Administration, Transport and Energy, took place concerning the EU's support for the cooperation among chemical sites from Central Europe. State-secretary Nagel presented the cooperation concept among sites from Poland, the Czech Republic and Central Germany, and he emphasised the regional, economic and European dimensions of such a project.

The initiative showed the trans-regional characteristic of improving the economy of a region. However, the use of the European pre-accession funds and the mobilisation for such cooperation depended also on the domestic mobilisation of the financial means and actors, especially the ones of the national authorities in the states that joined the EU only in 2004 (Landesvertretung Sachsen-Anhalt bei der Europäischen Union 2000: 23; 2002(1): 5).

The strategic dialogue between politics and economy was pursued in December 2000 after talks between the minister-president and representatives of the chemical industry in Saxony-Anhalt took place. The foundation for this cooperation was the result of the analysis showing that the chemical industry would be faced with new challenges due to globalisation and the regulatory impact of the EU membership. The cooperation was successful due to binding reached agreements regarding the goals, the means and the way between politics and economy that functioned as a benchmark (Institut für Strukturpolitik und Wirtschaftsförderung gGmbH 2001: 1).

Some of the key elements of the private-public cooperation covered the management of chemical parks, the raw materials situation safeguard, the development of transport infrastructure, adapted to the chemical relevant safety requirements and of the networks for innovation measures. Further measures concerned the analysis of the consequences that the COM's WP on chemicals policy would have. Those concerns facilitated the increased cooperation with other European chemical regions, such as Mazovia and North-Bohemia and the initiative of establishing a network of chemical regions that would act as regional interest network (Institut für Strukturpolitik und Wirtschaftsförderung gGmbH 2001: 1).

As part of the cooperation strategy with the chemical industry, the government of Saxony-Anhalt looked into its activities concerning the EU legislation on the chemical policy. It was noticed that a clear strategy for representing the interests of the *Land* as a chemical region was deficient. Moreover, the advisory opinions prepared by the *Land* were only discussed within the proceedings of the *Bundesrat*, in a late stage of the EU policy-making process. The practice was classified as inefficient and reactive. Thus, the dialogue strategy between the government of Saxony-Anhalt and the chemical companies aimed to jointly influence the European decision-making processes during the preparatory process (Wobben 2007).

The convenient location, which allowed access to the markets of the new EU Member States, relatively low costs of production, high education level and open-mindedness of the people towards the chemical industry were crucial elements for the success of the chemical industry in Saxony-Anhalt. These factors favoured the successful restructuring, which was completed by the end of the 1990s. However, restructuring did not eliminate further concerns about the future perspectives for this particular branch (Wobben 2007: 79).

The European level played a crucial role for the local chemical industry because it was the level where actually 80% of the guidelines on the chemical industry and environment policy were defined. Thus, the upcoming decision of the European institutions on the regulation of the chemical policy drove the cooperation between the regional government and the companies, thereby challenging the competitiveness of the whole European Chemicals Industry (Wobben 2007: 80). The chemical companies learned to take into consideration that the European level had a substantive influence on their business development. They were interested in what could influence their investments in the chemical parks and raised questions concerning:

- Legislative changes of the EU funding period 2007-2013,
- Government aid regulations and the grants for Eastern Germany,
- Legislative changes of the European environmental and industrial policy,
- Opportunities for enlargement of the existing chemical parks (Wobben 2007: 79).

The establishment of the office of Saxony-Anhalt in Brussels took place at the same time as the private-public cooperation started to develop around the chemical industry. This was a consequence of an internal development of a pro-active Europe policy of the *Land*. This strategy was combined with the external network strategy of the chemical industry. The strategy's insight aimed to influence the European legislation on the chemical policy, especially due to the complex effects of this legislation on the local and regional authorities (Wobben 2007: 80). In addition, the Brussels office of Saxony-Anhalt contributed to the strategy's implementation through:

- Keeping contact with the representatives of the European Commission,
- Maintaining discussions with them over the White Paper – Strategies for a future Chemicals Policy,
- Preparing a position paper representing the interests of Saxony-Anhalt,
- Establishing contacts with other chemical regions,
- Constituting a network for the chemical regions,
- Reporting to the *Bundesrat* and preparing a position paper of the *Bundesrat*,
- Participating in high-level discussions about the chemical policy in Brussels (Wobben 2004: 62).

The EU regulated the security measures, the environment protection and the competition regulations. These influenced the development opportunities of the local and regional industry structure. The implementation of the European regulations involved the regional authorities. Thus, the cooperation between regional authorities and participants in the implementation was of the utmost importance and needed to be notified to the European actors responsible for this policy (Wobben 2007: 81).

Saxony-Anhalt offered 10 advantages for the chemical industry that contributed to the development of the area and to the cooperation between the public authorities and companies:

1. Flexibility. With short approval and project implementation periods will fast-track your market entry.
2. Competence. Highly motivated and qualified workforce ensures long-time success.
3. Investment Safety. Political and financial stability make Saxony-Anhalt a reliable investment partner for the future.
4. Infrastructure. The most modern transport and logistics infrastructure enable you a rapid trans-shipment of goods.
5. Investment Incentives. Due to an excellent mix of subsidies you can expect noticeable reductions of capital expenditure and of operating costs.
6. Productivity. The lowest unit labour costs within Germany in combination with a stable and secure legal system give you a decisive competitive advantage.
7. Access to the Market. In the course of the eastern European expansion of the EU the central location within Europe ensures an optimal access to the East European economies.
8. Quality and Innovation - Made in Germany. Today numerous impulses for the high technology label come from Saxony-Anhalt.
9. Dynamic Economy. Out of the New *Länder* Saxony-Anhalt has the highest economic dynamic and generates the highest amount of direct investments abroad.
10. Service Free of Charge. The free professional business siting support of IMG allows you to fully concentrate on your core competencies (Institut für Strukturpolitik und Wirtschaftsförderung gGmbH 2009: 27).

All those advantages were considered valuable resources for Saxony-Anhalt and they contributed to the determination of the strategy pursued by its actors and implemented in the EMLG participation.

7.3 The European Chemical Regions Network

The working system of projects financed by the EU INTERREG instruments differs from other projects and programs financed by the European funds. The INTERREG infrastructure is part of the community initiatives, meaning that such cooperation has been endorsed and implemented by the European Commission. From this perspective, the required partnership expressed by the Commission in its WP on European Governance and further participation principles were endorsed, in order to pursue the effectiveness, legitimacy and transparency of the European Regional Policy throughout EMLG. Saxony-Anhalt used this instrument to promote the interregional cooperation among regions with chemical industries. The cooperation initiated by Saxony-Anhalt led to the emergence of the European Chemical Regions Network (ECRN), a network that has been implementing the EMLG principles.

During the 1990s, the body of literature dealing with the networks specifics within European governance processes emerged. The policy dimension of the governance processes triggered the research that combined the elements of polity and networks with those of the regional development strategies. As in many cases regarding European Union issues, Western Europe had been setting trends regarding the research and governance practices. The same applied to the concept of modern polity as network polity.

Ansell summarised the concept of networked polity as "a structure of governance in which both state and societal organisation [are] vertically and horizontally disaggregated (as in pluralism) but linked together by cooperative exchange (as in corporatism)" (2000: 311). Knowledge and initiative are often at the subnational levels. Thus, governance structure can bring together "unique configurations of actors around specific projects oriented toward integrative solutions rather than dedicated programs" (Ansel 2000: 311).

The centrality of a network points out to the lead organisation that plays "a critical brokerage role in bringing actors together" (Ansell 2000: 310). The required mobilisation of the involved brokerage comprises both the public administration and the private economy actors. An emerging semiautonomous organisation may become the network centrality element (Ansell 2000: 310). Saxony-Anhalt has been playing a crucial role for the mobilisation of other regional actors since the creation of the European Chemical Regions Network. Saxony-Anhalt has been the central element of the ECRN, providing the presidency of the network until 2016 and bringing it to the status of European stakeholder through participation processes of the network within EMLG.

The resources analysed for this chapter comprise: actors, representatives of the public institutions and the private sector, involved in the ECRN activities, the financial means needed for the preparation of activities and the information provided by the ECRN in the form of Congress declarations, position papers, publications, studies and communication materials. The exchanged information between the actors is valuable especially as part of the consultations at European level and of the learning activities for the involved actors.

The White Paper for the EU future Chemicals Policy was adopted in February 2001. During the same period, the *Landtag* of Saxony-Anhalt emphasised the fundamental role of the WP for the chemical sector in Saxony-

Anhalt and demanded a continuing interest representation in that area (Landesvertretung Sachsen-Anhalt bei der Europäischen Union 2001(8): 1).

The government of the third legislative period (1998-2002) started cooperation with the chemical regions, such as the region Mazovia in Poland. Minister-president Höppner started the discussions with the European Commission and with the European Parliament on the topic of the chemicals policy and the use of European funds for the cooperation of the chemical sector (Landesvertretung Sachsen-Anhalt bei der Europäischen Union 2002 (1): 16-18, 23).

The cooperation was continued by all the other governments of Saxony-Anhalt. The cooperation extended beyond the borders of the EU, at that time. However, the use of European funds for facilitating the interregional cooperation was a common denominator for all involved regions. In addition, the possibilities to use European funds showed the intertwinement of the European policies. Building partnerships and cooperation were among the European Governance goals, as envisioned by the European Commission.

In March 2001, representatives of Saxony-Anhalt and of the chemical enterprises from Saxony-Anhalt attended several events in Brussels. The delegation of Saxony-Anhalt met with European officials from DG Enterprise and DG Environment to discuss changes proposed by the WP and problems that would arise from the WP requirements for the small and medium enterprises of the chemical industry in Saxony-Anhalt. Through the joint approach of the government and the private industry, common concerns were expressed. This way, a future dialogue with the Commission was started (Landesvertretung Sachsen-Anhalt bei der Europäischen Union 2002(1): 5).

In March 2001, a meeting of representatives of the chemical regions also took place in Brussels. A consensus was met over the similar effects of the European legislation on all regions with the chemical industry. Representatives of the chemical sites located in regions with a deficient regional structure were opened to the cooperation strategy. The European Commission regarded the association of the chemical sites as a wise development, next to already existing networks of industry, civil society and European unions (Wobben 2007: 82).

The explicit interest of Saxony-Anhalt in establishing an interregional cooperation among the chemical locations was much appreciated by the director of the Brussels representation of the German Chemical Industry Association (*Verband der Chemischen Industrie*). The basis for further cooperation with the *VCI* was laid down in Brussels through discussions between the directors of the Brussels offices of Saxony-Anhalt and of the *VCI* (Landesvertretung Sachsen-Anhalt bei der Europäischen Union 2002(1): 2).

At the beginning of 2002, the president of DOW Europe, Luciano Respini, welcomed an initiative of Saxony-Anhalt to develop a network of the chemical locations in Europe. He expressed the special interest of DOW for the cooperation with Central and Eastern Europe. The Saxony-Anhalt's government and companies' efforts within the Chemistry dialogue strategy, a model in Europe and a cornerstone of the cooperation between politics and economy, were highly appreciated by the president of DOW Europe (Landesvertretung Sachsen-Anhalt bei der Europäischen Union 2002(3): 8). Hence, actors were deployed to mobilise and to cooperate with Saxony-Anhalt in pursuit of an interregional cooperation.

A network of subnational and European contacts and actors emerged. Rowe argued that such networking dynamics in Brussels could lead to "ad hoc or issue-specific alliance which emerges in relation to a specific piece of EU legislation" (2011: 107). The access to policy groups and the links created between individual chemicals companies across Europe were the benefits of the interregional cooperation (Rowe 2011: 108).

The year 2002 was a good one for the network's development initiative of the chemical sites' cooperation. The activities of Saxony-Anhalt and of the partner regions aimed to help the Commission with its decision of the WP's implementation (Landesvertretung Sachsen-Anhalt bei der Europäischen Union 2002(7): 9-10). In 2002, the government of North Rhine-Westphalia agreed to contribute to the establishment of ECRN. The English chemical locations were also preparing for the experience exchange and cooperation measures. Thomas Wobben, director of the Saxony-Anhalt office in Brussels, assessed those developments as a clear sign that the European Chemical Regions Network was on the right track (Landesvertretung Sachsen-Anhalt bei der Europäischen Union 2002(10): 1).

In October 2002, Wobben initiated and managed a meeting of the chemical regions. Representatives of the following regions attended this meeting: Mazovia, Catalonia, Piedmont, Asturia, Cheshire, North Rhine-Westphalia, Saxony, Brandenburg, Rhineland-Palatine and Saxony-Anhalt. The European Commission was represented by Jürgen Wettig, from DG Environment. Among the presentations from the regions and of the EU legislative progress on the SEVESO II directive[15], the set-up of a European network of chemical regions was the main discussed goal. Participants laid out the steps for the organisation of the first European Congress of Chemical Regions in 2003. The Congress gathered relevant actors from the chemical industry in Europe, members of the EP and European Commission's officials, and representatives

---

[15] The directive was about the control of major-accident hazards involving dangerous substances (European Commission 2016e).

of chemical regions and national governments (Landesvertretung Sachsen-Anhalt bei der Europäischen Union 2002(38): 5).

The Commission requested the chemical regions to deal with innovation, research promotion and technological trends. For this purpose, Saxony-Anhalt together with other 13 regions[16] applied in 2003 for the INTERREG funding for developing the network of chemical regions in Europe. The network was set to contribute to the experience exchange and to facilitate the cooperation among the administrations and economy of the involved regions. In 2003, the Polish chemical region Mazovia and the Italian region Veneto joined the interregional cooperation of the chemical regions (Landesvertretung Sachsen-Anhalt bei der Europäichen Union 2003(1): 2, 6, 20, 22).

The interregional cooperation started its network activities with the first Congress in 2003, in Brussels. It gave the opportunity for corporation boards, regional ministers and representatives of the European institutions to exchange opinions and to take a position on issues relevant for the chemical industry. The Congress was successful because it woke the interest in other actors to take part in the network and to expand the interregional cooperation (Wobben 2007: 81). Over 200 people attended the discussions about the future chemical policy proposed by the Commission.

Many actors from Saxony-Anhalt were involved in the Congress preparation, such as the institute for structural policy in Halle (*ISW*), the chemical enterprises and the *VCI Nordost*. The CeChemNet[17] project and its involved actors also proposed the emergence of an independent competence platform for chemical parks (Bratzke 2003: 11). The Congress released a declaration of the chemical regions to the European Commission and the European Parliament.

The ECRN Congresses have been organised yearly ever since. Ideas from the Congresses and their content are discussed in the following pages because they are related to the processes of determining goals for the ECRN member regions and their mobilisation. The goals were relevant for the allocation of resources and the settlement of common strategies, the problems or solutions the regions could tackle. Therefore, the yearly Congress of ECRN can be conceived as a public relations instrument, promoting not only the member regions but also creating connections for new members and opening the communication channels to actors and stakeholders from the chemical industry sector.

---

[16] The regions were: Lower-Saxony, North Rhine-Westphalia, Piedmont, Lombardia, North East and North West England, Limburg (NE), Mazovia, a county in Estonia, Catalonia, Asturia and Huelva.

[17] CeChemNet is the Central European Chemical Network and it gathers chemical parks from the Central German Triangle (CeChemNet 2016).

The ECRN followed the EU goals not only from the perspective of the chemicals policy but also from the perspective of the general strategies proposed by the European Commission. In 2004, the Joint Declaration of the ECRN Presidium emphasised that in order to meet the Lisbon Strategy's objectives, the innovation conditions in the regions had to be improved, especially since the chemical industry provided a good source for innovation and competitive advantages in Europe. The declaration called on the COM and the EP to provide more support for the regions with an economy based on small and medium enterprises (ECRN 2004b).

Meanwhile, the ECRN offered relevant data onto the development of new legislative measures and for the assessment of the implementation of REACH regulations. Pilot projects were implemented in the ECRN regions that provided information on the impact assessment of the new legislation and feedback that could be used by the European Chemicals Agency. For example, the ECRN demanded to the European Commission to find alternatives for the emissions reduction measures because those measures could jeopardise the regions' growth (ECRN 2004b).

The European Commission declared its intention to work closely with the ECRN in regard to the European chemicals policy. The Commission's invitation for the ECRN to participate in future EU proceedings of the chemicals policy as an official partner that represented the regional interests in the chemical sector was welcomed by the network's presidium (Landesvertretung Sachsen-Anhalt bei der Europäischen Union 2005(1): 15).

In February 2005, dynamics of the political debate over the chemical policy developed because the Council and the EP made changes in the legislative proposals made by the Commission. The new Commission chose REACH to be the core element of the strategy for improving Europe's competitiveness, insisting on the industrial dimension of the chemicals policy (Landesvertretung Sachsen-Anhalt bei der Europäischen Union 2006(1): 4-5). The ECRN continued to assess the REACH regulation and the future possibilities of cooperation between industry and research institutions (Landesvertretung Sachsen-Anhalt bei der Europäischen Union 2006(1): 6).

The ECRN charter was adopted at the third Congress, in 2005, which led to the development of the ECRN as an association based in Magdeburg, according to German law, providing Saxony-Anhalt a central role in the network. The network's emergence as an association provided the possibility to continue the interregional cooperation after the end of the financing period as an INTERREG project. As a consequence of this intense cooperation within the network, the bilateral cooperation between companies from Central Germany and those from Lombardy intensified (Wobben 2005: 8-10).

In April 2006, the ECRN permanent working group, where only the members of the network meet, decided to pursue the topics of education and further training for the area of chemicals. That area went beyond the REACH regulation. The study of training models from the UK, Spain and Italy, and the prospect of future involvement in the 2007 announced strategy dialogue with the chemical industry at the European level were the priorities for the network's activity (Landesvertretung Sachsen-Anhalt bei der Europäischen Union 2007(1): 15-16).

According to the 2006 Joint Position, the ECRN recognised that many of their amendments regarding the REACH system were taken into consideration in the Common Position of the EU Council from June 2006. However, the ECRN further demanded the implementation's simplification for the SMEs (ECRN 2006a). Therefore, the goal to contribute to the European policy-making process in the area of chemicals had shown results from the ECRN's perspective.

The INTERREG project ended after three years. The ECRN presented its results in December 2006. The network and its members identified many good-practices in relation to the structural funds and development strategies, for example, the idea of the chemical parks developed in Saxony-Anhalt. The work of the ECRN was considered valuable and the network emerged as a proper association in 2007 (ECRN 2006b). The challenging incentive provided by the COM in the form of regulating the chemicals sector contributed to a serious mobilisation at the subnational level, starting with Saxony-Anhalt and continuing with all involved regions.

A further top-down incentive was the acknowledgement of the subnational mobilisation within the ECRN and the invitation for ECRN to join the HLG, presented later in this chapter. The ECRN carried on its work and focused on further political ambitions. The goals for 2007 were: maintenance of the competitiveness of the European Chemicals Industry, stability of the energy supply, remediation of the climate change, "better regulation" of the European legislation, finalisation of the REACH debate, research and innovation in chemical regions, and interregional cooperation's strengthening (ECRN 2006b: 14). One of the issues related to the competitiveness of the European Chemicals Industry was the need to extend the existing strong network of the Western European chemicals industry towards Central and Eastern Europe (Landesvertretung Sachsen-Anhalt bei der Europäischen Union 2008(1): 40-42).

The interests of ECRN extended and in 2013, the ECRN Congress urged for the "timely agreement in EU's Cohesion Policy Package, Horizon 2020 and the multiannual financial framework for 2014-2020" and for the "consistent implementation across all levels" (ECRN 2013b). The implementation of the industrial policy goals, of the smart specialisation and innovation policy depended on those European decisions. Hence, the ECRN work and the determination of their work's goals were broadened to other European policies that were fundamental for the development of the member regions, such as European funding instruments for research or the European Regional Policy.

In 2014, the ECRN extended its working principles through the emergence of the ECRN project council initiative. The project council meant to be a "broker and mediator of European projects among the ECRN member regions and chemical institutions" (ECRN 2016a). Therefore, the goals and principles guiding the work of ECRN have been flexible and adapted to the European policy developments. The adaptation required resources and information on the instruments and policies that both the EU and the ECRN mobilisation within EMLG provided. Since the regional interests' representation to the European actors requires preparation, the next section provides an overview of the functions performed by the ECRN in order to enable the stakeholders' contribution to the EMLG.

7.4 The European Chemical Regions Network and its functions within EMLG

The actors in Saxony-Anhalt decided to contribute to the EU chemicals policy-making process. After the consultations on the White Paper on the European Chemicals Policy within the EU and after the discussions with the European officials and partners in other regions with a chemical industry, the European Chemical Regions Network emerged as an INTERREG project. The activities of this project were aiming the participation of the regional level in EMLG. For this purpose, the regions of ECRN conducted many events, where they met officials and representatives who listened to their concerns. All these events are considered activities that accomplish the functions of gathering information, representation of interests, partnership but also public relations in EMLG.

The focus of the ECRN analysis was on Saxony-Anhalt due to its initiative for the network's emergence and of the specific interregional cooperation within the ECRN. The actors from Saxony-Anhalt looked for partners from other regions who shared their concerns about upcoming effects of the European legislation on the chemical industry in their regions. The involvement of the authorities of Saxony-Anhalt was required by the need to take a position within the EU. The joint declarations of the regional governments were communicated to the European institutions.

The declarations of ECRN counted as resources used by the regions to participate within EMLG. They are the result of the functions performed by actors who collected the data within the member regions. The EU chemicals policy facilitated the regions' partnership engagement. At European level, the interregional cooperation contributed to the dynamic interplay of regional interests, creating the perception of regions as spaces for politics (Carter/Pasquier 2010).

The 2003 Congress made it clear that the regional dimension had a crucial importance. It highlighted the benefits of the cooperation and provided a forum for discussions, defining the future scope for the chemical regions network. The Congress took place during the 8-week period of the consultation process launched by the Commission for its new chemicals industry strategy (ECRN 2003: 7). Hence, the elements of the regional participation and of the identification of long-term objectives, called for by the Commission, started to take form.

Saxony-Anhalt prepared position documents for the yearly ECRN Congresses without relying on documents or information from the *Bundesrat*, which would be available for the *Länder* late in the EU policy-making processes. Through the position documents, the ECRN regions appointed their own common interests. The position documents were submitted and advocated for at European level. Some of those position documents were discussed in the *Bundesrat* as well, involving all German *Länder* in the debate. In addition, members of the European Commission were present at the network's events (Wobben 2007: 82).

In February 2002, an ECRN meeting took place at which representatives of the *VCI*, of the European Chemical Industry Council (CEFIC), officials from DG Enterprise, Reinhard Schulte-Braucks, and from DG Environment, Peter Zapfel, attended. The actors discussed the implementation of the WP on chemicals, further communications from the COM regarding substances such as PVC (polyvinyl chloride), and the COM's proposal for the emissions trading. As a result, the ECRN prepared a position paper and prepared a study about the consequences of the COM's legislative proposals. The study was presented at the 2nd Stakeholders' Conference on the business impact of the new Chemicals Policy (European Commission 2002a).

The ECRN was invited to take part in an EU research programme that measured the risks of chemical products exposure. The invitation came from the institute for protection and security of citizens in Italy (Landesvertretung Sachsen-Anhalt bei der Europäischen Union 2002(6): 12-13). Hence, the regions needed to gather further information on how European regulations were developing and also on the effects of chemical products.

The measures proposed in the WP on the future of the EU Chemicals Policy created disagreements between DG Environment and DG Industry, who were both responsible for the regulation of the Chemicals Policy. The regulations included sensitive points, such as the risks and high costs of the implementation. Many actors, the *VCI*, ECRN regions, unions and associations, were conducting costs assessments providing information to the European Commission (Landesvertretung Sachsen-Anhalt bei der Europäischen Union 2002(33): 5; 2002(35): 13-14).

In May 2004, the chair meeting of ECRN took place at the Saxony-Anhalt representation in Berlin. Representatives from Poland, UK, Netherlands, Italy, Spain, Belgium, and from *VCI-Nordost* were present. They debated the situation of the chemical industry in Eastern Germany. The participants prepared a declaration, stating their goal to enhance the dialogue among the chemical regions in Europe (Landesvertretung Sachsen-Anhalt bei der Europäischen Union 2005(1): 15).

The information and partnership functions of the ECRN led to the enhanced cooperation between the ECRN and other actors. In November 2004, the CEFIC offered the ECRN the opportunity to cooperate on research and innovation topics, through the European Technology Platform. In addition, the general secretary of CEFIC invited the ECRN, to be part of the strategy group for the future development of the chemical industry in Europe. That group gathered important actors, such as the president of the European Commission, relevant commissioners and CEOs of the chemical companies (Landesvertretung Sachsen-Anhalt bei der Europäischen Union 2005(1): 33, 37).

The 2nd Congress of the ECRN had as main discussion the future shape of the European Chemicals Policy. The debate involved the Commissioner for Environment, Margot Wallström. Even though the Congress highlighted the benefits of the cooperation among chemical regions, the topic of the EU legislation brought forward concerns, in particular, the burdens for the enterprises and administration. The declaration of the European Congress of chemical regions proposed that "the effects and feasibility of REACH should be sufficiently tested by means of concrete pilot projects involving enterprises of the value added chain and the authorities prior to the decision making in Parliament" (ECRN 2004a: 6, 15, 43).

The 4th European Congress took place in 2006 in Taragona and brought a new topic on the agenda, the research. The CEFIC contributed with ideas about the lack of engagement of the chemical industry in the 6th Research Framework Programme[18]. Further examples of the public communication with the chemical industry were presented by many regions. The vision for future strategies came from Klaus Behrend from DG Enterprise and Industry, who reported the state-of-play of HLG preparations (ECRN 2006c).

---

[18] The 6th Research Framework Programme gathered a collection of actions at the European level that funded and promoted research for the period 2002-2006 (European Commission 2002b: 1).

The ECRN declaration of the 8th Congress, in 2010, addressed three flagships[19] of the Europe 2020 strategy that were relevant for the chemical industry. The declaration emphasised the role of the Cohesion Policy and territorial cooperation for the implementation of the chemical regions' goals. The participants stressed the contribution of territorial cooperation to learning processes at regional level (ECRN 2010: 1-2). The topics of the ECRN Congresses showed the connection between the financial incentives provided by the European funding programmes and the implementation of EU's strategies.

In 2011, the ECRN transmitted a position paper to the European Commission within the public consultation on the Green Paper – From Challenges to Opportunities: Towards a Common Strategic Framework for EU Research and Innovation Funding to the Commission. The ECRN brought out the need for a "strategic multilayer approach" and a "more effective interaction between the different levels of projects operating on different scales" (ECRN 2011a: 1). Against the background of acknowledged advantages of the integration between research and development funds, ECRN considered that the European and the regional authorities ought to "work together to develop complementarities and close links between different funding programmes covering the entire research and innovation chain" (ECRN 2011a: 1). The position paper also underlined the "essential role of regional governments in contributing both to the development of the Common Strategic Framework for research and innovation and the future design of cohesion policies" (ECRN 2011a: 2-3).

The 9th Congress of the chemical regions emphasised the contribution of partnerships to the local and regional development through the coordinated strategies and use of structural funds. The chemical regions considered the European Regional Policy relevant, but they rejected the implementation of the "rigid requirements for thematic priorities from the European level or quotas for specific topics" because these could compromise the added value of the policy (ECRN 2011b: 2).

Regional actors endorsed the implementation of the partnership principle and the active involvement of local stakeholders in the planning and implementation phases. They emphasised the regional development challenge in the context of the demographic change and the challenge to achieve the environmental and climate policy objectives as stated in the Europe 2020 strategy (ECRN 2011b: 3).

The 10th ECRN Congress declaration focused on the Cohesion Policy and MFF negotiations. The declaration addressed both to the European Commis-

---

[19] The addressed flagships were: An industrial policy for the globalisation era, Innovation Union, and Resource Efficient Europe (see Appendix 5).

sion and regional authorities. The Commission was requested to "support and prioritise in their intended platforms value-added collaboration" comprising feedstock integration, new forms of cooperation and vital partnerships at the local level. Regional authorities were encouraged to take action to "reach out to SMEs and provide support for concrete initiatives encouraging entrepreneurialism and new start-ups". In addition, the regions were encouraged to "ensure a long-term vision in strategy and policy development and implementation, and to analyse and evaluate consequences and impacts of decisions to achieve sustainable solutions and results" (ECRN 2012: 2-3).

ECRN welcomed the Commission's clear strategic position for the industrial policy. In June 2013, it released its strategic position paper to the Europe 2020 flagship initiative in industrial policy. ECRN emphasised that a modern industrial policy combined the "different policy areas to an integrated economic, environmental and social policy strategy" (ECRN 2013a: 2). The ECRN strategic position clearly stated the role of the regions and the dialogue between the European level and regional authorities that "provide[d] superior knowledge of specific regional and local conditions" (ECRN 2013a: 5). Taking into consideration the implementation of the subsidiarity principle, ECRN demanded a "strong involvement of regional institutions, Local Economic Partnerships and representatives in a broad dialogue process" (ECRN 2013a: 5). Hence, the mobilisation of regional actors for an enhanced participation within EMLG had been set in motion through the ECRN.

7.5 The High Level Group for the Competitiveness of the European Chemicals Industry

Goals and principles guiding the chemical industry on Europe were developed at the European level, in the 2001 White Paper. Further policy recommendations were later prepared within the High Level Group for the Competitiveness of the European Chemicals Industry created by the European Commission. In May 2006, first talks about the HLG began when 22 representatives of the Commission, Member States, chemical companies, associations and the representative of ECRN exchanged thoughts (Landesvertretung Sachsen-Anhalt bei der Europäischen Union 2007(1): 16-17).

The work of the ECRN drew the public attention especially due to its presentation of the chemical industry parks. ECRN was acknowledged as a relevant and competent advisor for the European institutions. The Commission's invitation for ECRN to participate in EU proceedings regarding the chemicals policy was "unprecedented for a regional network at a European level" (Sachsen-Anhalt Ministerium für Landesentwicklung und Verkehr/Ministerium für Wirtschaft und Arbeit 2008: 31).

In September 2007 the Commission launched the work of the HLG. The HLG's tasks were to examine determinants of the "rapid structural change in the chemicals sector", to analyse "the competitive position of the European chemicals industry" and to formulate "a set of sector-specific recommendations" based on the requested analysis. The recommendations were to be put into action by private and public actors from the different levels "in order to enhance the competitiveness of the European chemicals industry in accordance with the principles of sustainable development" (European Commission 2014b). The HLG comprised members from different areas and institutions:

- European Commissioners, for: Enterprise and Industry, Environment, Science and research, External trade, Energy, and Transport,
- National ministers from: the Netherlands, Belgium, Poland, the Czech Republic, Germany, France and the UK, and two state-secretaries from Spain,
- High representatives of the chemical industry: the CEO of Maipei, the President of Bang & Bonsomer Group, the EVP of Shell Chemicals, the Chairman of the Board of Executive Directors of BASF, the CEO of Arkema, the Vice-Chairman of the Executive Committee and President of Chemicals, the Total and Group Managing Director of Contract Chemicals Ltd.,
- Representatives of regions, trade unions and other organisations: the secretary general of EMCEF, the President of Chalmers University of Technology, Sweden, the President of the European Environmental Bureau and Head of Policy, the Danish Consumer Council, and the president of ECRN (European Commission 2014b).

The ECRN was represented by its president, the Saxony-Anhalt minister for economy and labour, Reiner Haseloff, in the HLG meetings. The emissary of the ECRN president to the HLG working meetings was Thomas Wobben, director of the Brussels office of Saxony-Anhalt. The other ECRN member regions contributed with their input in the thematic ad-hoc groups of the HLG (ECRN 2016b).

The declaration of the 5th ECRN Congress, in Ludwigshafen in 2007, emphasised the importance of the regions' participation in the work of the HLG and their contribution to find adequate solutions for the energy intensive industries within the future European climate and energy policy. The extension of the discussions to the fields of energy and climate policies shows the spill-over effect of European policies, meaning that the EU policies influence themselves beyond the scope of individual policies.

The HLG had its work divided among the groups for innovation and human resources, trade, energy and raw materials, logistics and regional aspects, economy and social requirements. The implementation of the chemicals policy was endorsed by the use of European funds and it also had to take into consideration the implementation of other European policies that influenced it. ECRN invited the COM to use the "chemical regions as test beds for better regulation in the future" (ECRN 2007: 2) and presented its future cooperation plans:

- A lasting cooperation with CEFIC,
- A regional input into the European Technology Platform,
- The development of regional technology platform approaches in the participating regions,
- The development of a toolkit for setting up regional technology platforms,
- Identification of successful practices in research and innovation policies in the chemical regions,
- The development of 10 regional strategic research action plans in the participating regions and the development of a compilation out of the regional strategy plans (ECRN 2007: 4).

In 2007, the ECRN permanent working group prepared the network's positions in the HLG and in the sectoral social dialogue with the chemical industry organised by DG Employment, Social Affairs and Inclusion. The social dialogue covered the areas of manufacture of coke and refined petroleum-products, chemicals and chemical products, pharmaceutical products, rubber and plastic products, and non-metallic mineral products (ECRN 2007).

Identified challenges facing the chemical industry in Europe were the slow demand growth in Europe due to the increasing demand growth in Asia, the rising costs and heavy regulations of the environment and the implementation of the REACH system. Focusing on best-practice cases and health and safety management in the chemical and downstream user industries, the social dialogue delivered the following:

- A joint statement on the European Union emission trading scheme in 2008,
- A joint opinion on the global economic crisis in 2009,
- A European Framework Agreement on Competencies Profiles for Process Operators and First Line Supervisors in the Chemical Industry in 2011,
- A joint statement on the proposal for a directive on energy efficiency in 2012,
- A joint declaration on REACH and the inclusion of nanomaterial in its appendices in 2014,
- A European Chemical Social Partners' Roadmap 2015-2020 in 2015,
- A common position on energy and climate policy ahead of the 21st Conference of the Parties (COP21) of the United Nations Framework Convention on Climate Change in 2015, and others (European Commission 2016b).

The ECRN's participation in the HLG opened a direct communication channel between the ECRN and the European Commission. The early access to the problems and solutions definition on the policy agenda gave ECRN the chance to present the challenges its members were faced with, for example, the logistic development especially for the markets in Central and Eastern Europe. ECRN president Haseloff thanked the Commission for the invitation to participate within the HLG and underlined the need to find "adequate solutions for energy intensive industries in the future design of EU climate and energy policy" (ECRN 2016b). Haseloff presented the cooperation between ECRN and CEFIC to bring the European Technology Platform closer to the regions. On that note, he suggested that the HLG could be used for the integrated development of chemical sites in Central and Eastern Europe (ECRN 2016b).

The HLG met on several occasions and the ad-hoc groups contributed to the development of the debate and recommendations. The first discussion was about the ad-hoc group report on Innovation, Research and Human Resources. A consensus was found to widen the scope of the existing European Technology Platform by implementing recommendations related to the 7th Framework Programme. In 2008, the ECRN applied for a new INTERREG project, RegioSusChem, for the European Technology Platform (Landesvertretung Sachsen-Anhalt bei der Europäischen Union 2009(1): 2-3).

ECRN declarations and position papers prepared before the participation in the HLG were part of the resources that the network developed during its participation in the HLG. Not only through the information function performed during the yearly Congresses, but also the networking and partnership building practices enhanced the Europe-competence of the ECRN member regions.

At the second meeting of the HLG, in December 2007, the topic of innovation and research mastered the discussions. Those were the measures required for keeping the European chemicals industry at the level of a world leader. Haseloff pointed out the regions' role in organising a sector dialogue between the involved stake-holders and named the development of Suschem as part of such cooperation. He drew again the attention to the necessity of interconnecting the area of Central and Eastern Europe, needing to develop a common infrastructure and a material integration of the area (Landesvertretung Sachsen-Anhalt bei der Europäischen Union 2008(1): 60-62). The topics discussed within the HLG pointed to the intertwined content of the European policies and the interdependence between the policy goals of the industry competitiveness and the environment protection, and the different financial instruments the EU provided for achieving its goals (ECRN 2016b).

On 15.01.08, the first meeting of the subgroup on resources, energy and logistics of the HLG took place. ECRN was present through representatives from North Rhine-Westphalia and Northeast England. Another meeting took place in February. Within ECRN and later within the HLG, the initiative for improving the logistics within the area Eastern Germany – Poland – Czech

Republic was adopted (Landesvertretung Sachsen-Anhalt bei der Europäischen Union 2009(1): 3-4, 13-14).

The third meeting of the HLG took place in April 2008. The main subjects were energy, feedstock and logistics. The ECRN contributed especially to the topic of chemical logistics in Central and Eastern Europe. More about this topic is discussed in the next section. The fourth meeting took place in October 2008. The main subject was the trade and the competitiveness of other regions. A special feature of this topic was the export importance of the chemicals industry. Experts from DG Trade expressed the Commission's work on finding a possibility to abolish non-tariff measures. Many DGs were involved in the HLG proceedings because of the EU competence of the internal market and the goal to promote the economic competitiveness of the EU (ECRN 2016b).

The 6th ECRN Congress took place in 2008 in Brussels during the HLG proceedings. ECRN members discussed the preparation of a regional conference that would follow after the HLG finished its work. Commissioner Verheugen praised the work of the HLG and the conference organised by ECRN in Ústi (Landesvertretung Sachsen-Anhalt bei der Europäischen Union 2009(1): 63-64). ECRN extended its activity from the simple participation within the HLG to the dissemination of the results of the HLG with the help of the network's structure. Contributing to the dissemination of the results enhanced the output transparency of the HLG. In addition, the chemical regions facilitated an enhanced dialogue between the chemical companies and regional administrations to develop clustering strategies and the know-how transfer (ECRN 2008: 2).

In February 2009, the HLG for the competitiveness of European Chemicals Industry held its last meeting, at which the final report was presented. The final report of the HLG from July 2009 set out the facts and the situation of the European chemicals industry sector. The identified development needs that were touched: the areas of innovation and research as "key to securing the future of the European chemicals industry", the responsible use of natural resources and energy in order to ensure competitiveness and sustainability and the need of open markets (European Commission 2009: iv-vii).

The report identified three main problems for the chemical industry: 1. Increasing difficulty of energy and raw materials provision, 2. Climate change and global environment problems and 3. Strong competitiveness with the newly industrialised countries and the hampered access to markets in those countries (Landesvertretung Sachsen-Anhalt bei der Europäischen Union 2010(1): 14-15; European Commission 2009).

The report prepared recommendations for increasing the competitiveness of the European Chemicals Industry. The recommendations of the HLG included practices, such as the setup of innovation networks among industry and governments to foster best practice and knowledge exchange. The final report addressed the need of multi-stakeholder approach for cluster leadership and the need for multilateral free trade agreements that would enhance competitiveness (European Commission 2009: 40-46).

At the final meeting of the HLG, minister-president Haseloff underlined "the constructive role of the chemical regions in the work of the High Level Group and the many references to the regional level in the text of the conclusions and the final report of the HLG" (ECRN 2016b). From the ECRN's perspective, the regional level was highly involved in the work of the HLG. Subnational participation was enabled by cooperation between the regions that provided one voice for several regions under the umbrella of the ECRN.

In May 2009, the Competitiveness Council welcomed the HLG final report and invited the Commission, the Member States and industry to implement the HLG conclusions and to use those recommendations as a "roadmap for concrete and deliverable activities to be elaborated" (Council of the European Union 2009: 9). The Council called for a regular monitoring of the chemicals industry competitiveness and of the REACH regulation implementation (Council of the European Union 2009). The Council acknowledged the need to invest in logistics and infrastructure and invited the industry to expand the dialogue with stakeholders and to provide the necessary information about chemicals to the customers (Council of the European Union 2009: 8-9).

Participation within the HLG opened a direct channel of transmitting information directly to the Council and the Parliament, since they would further deal with the Commission's follow up on the goals' achievement. The ECRN regions organised further events to disseminate the results of the HLG, such as the conference in Düsseldorf in April 2009. Saxony-Anhalt organised another conference in Leuna, in July 2009 (ECRN 2016c). The report of the HLG was disseminated to all German *Länder* within the meeting of Ministers of Economy of the German *Länder* in June 2009 (ECRN 2016b). Those activities following the work of the HLG have been providing the change of the German intrastate cooperation.

Against the background of the HLG recommendations, the activity of ECRN reached the EP as well. ECRN shared information with MEPs during parliamentary events in Brussels. Such exchange events sought to get in touch with the MEPs relevant for the chemical regions and to "build a basis of mutual understanding and goodwill for future cooperation" (ECRN 2009: 11).

The Commission monitored the implementation of the HLG recommendations. In its 2011 report for the Council, each recommendation was analysed. An overview of the developed projects and initiatives, according to the

HLG recommendations mentioned two projects developed by the ECRN, ChemLog and ChemClust, which are discussed in the next section (European Commission 2011).

Participation of ECRN in EMLG did not cease after the HLG concluded its work. These projects and the continued cooperation in the ECRN showed the spill-over effect of European policies and the interdependency of those policies, of the EU 2020 strategy and the mobilisation of regional actors. Therefore, MLG type II unfolded through the subnational mobilisation initiated in Saxony-Anhalt. The determination of goals, the use of resources and the functions performed by actors enabled the regional participation within EMLG, targeting the development of the chemicals industry.

7.6 Spill-over of the European Chemical Regions Network within EMLG: ChemLog and ChemClust

The competitiveness of the European Chemicals Industry depended on the market possibilities for the companies and the infrastructure they could use in order to provide goods in different parts of the covered market. The need for a better infrastructure was acknowledged by the European institutions. The HLG recommendations contained the development of two projects initiated by ECRN. The first of them was the Chemical Industry Logistics Cooperation in Central and Eastern Europe (ChemLog). As presented in the next pages, the projects resulted from the subnational cooperation of chemical regions and their participation in EMLG.

Together with European policy-makers, regions identified areas that needed further policy development, such as logistics and transportation. Starting from the competitiveness of the chemicals industry in Europe, further policies needed development. Hence, the spill-over effect of subnational mobilisation and interregional cooperation is that from one policy that affected several regions other policies were developed within the EMLG cooperation process.

The ChemLog project was based on the cooperation between regional authorities, chemicals industry associations and research and science institutions from German *Länder*, Poland, Czech Republic, Slovakia, Hungary Austria, Slovenia and Italy. The objective of the project was "to strengthen [the] competitiveness of the chemical industry by improving framework conditions for supply chain management in Central and Eastern Europe" (ChemLog 2014). The logistics component was developed within the project and evolved towards the project ChemLog T&T – tracking and tracing (ChemLog 2014).

The lead partner of the project was Saxony-Anhalt, due to its "advantage of being [the] logistics hub of the entire European continent" (Sachsen-Anhalt Ministerium für Landesentwicklung und Verkehr/Ministerium für Wirtschaft und Arbeit 2008: 45). The project aimed to prepare a strategy for "the integration of materials distribution and the infrastructure in this region including chemical industry logistics up to and including the expanding Russian market" (Sachsen-Anhalt Ministerium für Landesentwicklung und Verkehr/Ministerium für Wirtschaft und Arbeit 2008: 45). Hence, the project extended beyond the EU borders, due to the EU's global player role.

The connection of the ECRN with the HLG, in conjunction with the ministries of economic affairs of the Czech Republic, Poland and Germany, and representatives of their chemical industry trade associations, provided the opportunity to launch an initiative to improve the logistics framework[20] for the chemical industry centres in Central and Eastern Europe (Sachsen-Anhalt Ministerium für Landesentwicklung und Verkehr/Ministerium für Wirtschaft und Arbeit 2008: 45). The ChemLog project aimed to overcome the barriers for the transnational transport of chemical goods (ChemLog 2011).

The SWOT analysis of the ChemLog project highlighted more weaknesses and threats than strengths and opportunities provided by the logistics situation. Acknowledged strengths were: strong integration of production processes, outsourcing and partnership, location development, contract logistics for storage of raw and packaging material and the pipeline networks. The identified opportunities were the central location in Europe, at the crossroads of transport axes, the good infrastructure in Central Germany, the positive economic development favoured the increase of the freight transport, and others (ChemLog 2011: 6).

The determined weaknesses covered: high supply chain costs, insufficient reliability of selling forecasts and insufficient ability to plan resources demand, high costs of new technologies transfer, and others. The identified threats included: lack of pipeline connections between chemical complexes, incompatibility between the rail systems in West- and East-Europe, lack of terminal structures for the Inter-Modal traffic, missing harmonisation of administrative and technical standards, bureaucracy in Customs Clearance, lack of common safety and security standards, absence of emergency response and crisis systems, and others (ChemLog 2011: 7). All these elements of the analysis performed within the project provided valuable information for the policy-making process at European level. The project used resources of the

---

[20] Waterways and railways needed to be bolstered. The facilitation of the intermodal transport was prioritised.

partner regions and produced relevant information for the development of strategies at European level.

The ChemLog project was funded by the EU through the Central Europe Programme. The project intended to find the obstacles for cross-border transport in Europe and to overcome them. Feasibility studies were implemented in the fields of pipeline, rail traffics, intermodal transport and inland waterway. Their purpose was to help build European intermodal transport networks. The scope of the ChemLog project extended beyond the EU borders as well. Russian stakeholders from the areas of politics, industry and science had the chance to represent their interests regarding the intermodal transport in a meeting organised in Moscow. The project identified areas that needed to be developed, such as the connections through the Czech Republic towards Russia, Belarus and Ukraine and towards the South-Eastern European countries (ChemLog 2011: 7).

The project also aimed to intensify the cooperation among public authorities from all levels and actors from the economy, such as the industry chambers, associations, producers and logistics service providers (Institut für Strukturpolitik und Wirtschaftsförderung gGmbH 2013: 31). The enhanced cooperation among the authorities and the incentive from the ECRN enforced the bottom-up mobilisation for contributing to European policy-making by linking the regional actors and developing coherent strategies.

Project partners discussed their recommendations with politics and administration representatives who were responsible for the transport planning at all levels within the EU. One of the mainstream activities was the Policy Advisory Group which forwarded the findings towards high-level stakeholders, especially the Commission, which was reviewing the EU transport policy at that time. Different meetings with the Commission's representatives helped shape the European TEN-T guidelines; hence the spill-over effect of ECRN in chemicals policy (ChemLog 2011: 18-20).

In 2012, a Marco-Polo workshop took place at the Saxony-Anhalt's representation in Brussels, co-organised by the ECRN and the Enterprise Europe Network. The Marco-Polo programme was looking for solutions how to divert the freight transport from the road to the rail and water transport infrastructure. On the same day, minister-president Haseloff visited the head of the cabinet of Commissioner Tajani[21] to discuss how the innovation potential could be increased with the use of European funds. On the occasion of the Brussels visit, minister-president Haseloff attended a CoR seminar about the role of the chemical industry within the European industry scenery. He emphasised the chemical parks pattern implemented in Saxony-Anhalt and the

---

[21] Antonio Tajani was the European Commissioner for Industry and Entrepreneurship from 2010 until 2014.

role of the interregional cooperation for the chemicals industry (Landesvertretung Sachsen-Anhalt bei der Europäischen Union 2013(1): 63-65).

The participation process through the project overlapped the functions that the project fulfilled, such as the information gathering, the representation of interests and the partnership. Through the top-down and bottom-up approach of using the project's findings, the implementation of ChemLog comprised the European access and participation process within EMLG.

During the Policy Advisory Group meeting in Brussels, in May 2011, Otto Linder from DG Enterprise emphasised the successful contribution of the ChemLog consortium to the implementation of the HLG recommendations, because the topic of logistics and transport infrastructure was an important one during the work of the HLG. This was an example of how decision-making within the EU was complemented by the contribution of the subnational level, empowering the EMLG patterns (ChemLog 2011: 22-24).

The contribution of ChemLog fits the profile of using the specificities of a territory in order to develop place-based approaches, through the use of bottom-up initiatives. It also fits the definition of MLG provided by the CoR, a coordinated action based on partnership and aimed at drawing up and implementing EU policies.

The ChemLog project was implemented by involving three types of institutions: regional administrations, industry associations and research facilities. The project ended in October 2011 through the establishment of the Central and Eastern European Chemical Logistics Network. The partners defined a Strategy and Action Plan according to which their follow-up activities were organised. Through ECRN, the partners continued to represent their interests at national and European level (ChemLog 2011: 3).

Political actors from Saxony-Anhalt and representatives of the project member regions presented the activities of the ChemLog project in a dissemination conference in Brussels. Further participants were officials from the European Commission, especially from DG Enterprise and Industry, who emphasised the role of regions in the implementation of partnerships, crucial instruments for the chemical industry. Another member of the Transport Commissioner's[22] cabinet discussed the challenges posed by the development of the transport infrastructure network, the so-called TEN. The regions were requested to make their voices heard and to contribute with their ideas (Landesvertretung Sachsen-Anhalt bei der Europäischen Union 2013(1): 54-55). Hence, the European policy-makers called for subnational mobilisation and participation in EMLG.

---

[22] Siim Kallas was vice-president of the European Commission and European Commissioner for Transport from 2010 until 2014.

The ChemLog project continued with a follow up, namely the ChemLog Tracking and Tracing project. The project's main objectives were to contribute to the development and implementation of Tracking and Tracing systems for transnational intermodal transport of dangerous goods. Thereby, it improved the safety, security, reliability and efficiency of intermodal transport of dangerous goods. ChemLog T&T brought together regional authorities, chemical industry associations and scientific institutions from Italy, Slovenia, Austria, Hungary, Slovakia, Czech Republic, Poland and Germany (Chemlog 2014). ChemLog provided a basis for further cooperation and partnership. Even though the ChemLog T&T project was aimed for the implementation of policies, its progress was also part of the participation within EMLG.

Through these projects, regional authorities, their partners from the private sector, and research institutions managed to participate both in the European policy-making processes and in the implementation of specific policies. The ChemLog project included the policy level, the stakeholder's level and the time-level. The time-horizon was essential for developing policies.

A further cooperation that emerged from the participation of ECRN in the HLG on the Competitiveness of European Chemicals Industry was the project ChemClust. This project pursued an improvement of "the effectiveness of regional development policies in the area of innovation and cluster policies for the chemical sector" (ChemClust 2014). The project was among the recommendations of the HLG regarding the cooperation of chemical clusters. By means of interregional exchange and on the basis of technology development, successful practices in innovation and cluster policies were the response to acknowledged problems in the chemical regions. The project was an extension of the partnership and cooperation among the ECRN member regions and other regions (ChemClust 2014).

The context for ChemClust was based on the chemical parks experience of Saxony-Anhalt and on CeChemNet, a network that provided a competence platform for the management of chemical parks in Central Germany. The need for this platform arose as the chemical industry started to develop in Central Germany. The platform's goals were to share the know-how, best-practices, to exchange experience and funding information, and to access international networks (CechemNet 2003). The need of resources triggered the subnational mobilisation and the intrastate cooperation, providing examples for regions from other EU MS.

Saxony-Anhalt coordinated the project with a budget of about 1.8 million €. This project tackled three topics: Chemical parks as Knowledge sites (coordinated by Saxony-Anhalt), Open Innovation and Skills Foresight. It delivered benchmarking data of clusters of the European Chemicals Industry and best-practice brochures (Institut für Strukturpolitik und Wirtschaftsförderung gGmbH 2013: 31). Among the project's outputs, there was the contribution to the improvement of regional policies in business innovation and clustering.

The identified best-practices for Saxony-Anhalt were: the development of the Innovation and Location Network of Central German Chemical Parks (CeChemNet), the development of the Frauenhofer Pilot Plant Centre for Polymer Processing and Synthesis, and the Integration of Lignite as an alternative raw material in the Chemical industry (IBI) (ChemClust 2012: 4). The cooperation of the ECRN projects, ChemLog (T&T) and ChemClust, provided further evidence of MLG Type II practices.[23]

7.7 Findings

The European Commission promoted its goal of harmonising the European legislation for the chemicals industry. Under those specific conditions, the authorities of Saxony-Anhalt analysed the situation of the chemical industry located in their jurisdiction. Chemical companies expressed their concerns and the specific problems of the industry with regard to the proposed European legislative measures. Processes that followed the private-public cooperation in Saxony-Anhalt were the strategic dialogue and the joint mobilisation for subnational participation within EMLG.

The chemicals industry is part of the jurisdiction of the Directorate-General for Environment and of the Directorate-General Industry for Internal Market, Industry, Entrepreneurship and SMEs (European Commission 2016c). Like every new government, the DG structure of the European Commission is reconfigured when the mandate of a new commission starts. That is why the Directorates-General may change their jurisdiction or name. However, the fact that the chemicals policy needs regulation and its implementation regards the rules from several domains shows the complexity of this particular sectorial policy and the multitude of actors that are involved in these policy-making processes.[24]

The actors involved in the chemicals policy are interdependent. Policies emerge from the interactions among them. Accordingly, ECRN has brought together actors from regions of the Member States to tackle together the chal-

---

[23] The ECRN provided a list of best-practice examples (see ECRN 2016d).
[24] Saxony-Anhalt faced environmental damages from the chemical industry before 1989. Those damages needed to be tackled (see Franke 2017). With the help of the federal government and of the EU, measures were taken and the chemical industry could further develop, developing even benchmarks such as the Chemical Parks.

lenges posed not only by the European regulation but also by the competitiveness challenges for all the European Chemicals Industry.

Through this cooperation and partnership with other regions, the European Chemical Regions Network emerged. The network originally started its work with 13 members. The main objective of the network was to simplify the cooperation between the chemical industry regions in order to find solutions to their common challenges. This way the chemical industry was strengthened by means of mutual learning processes. The network developed its interests to structural and development policy.

Cooperation among the regions with a similar economic profile or with a common industry sector, such as the chemical one, might not have been so attractive if it weren't for the INTERREG projects that provided the financial means for interregional cooperation. The interregional cooperation facilitated the access to actors from the European institutions.

The network has been promoting the interregional cooperation since the beginning. The ECRN projects brought the members of the project at the table with officials from the European Commission to improve governance practices of the European policies. The projects provided evidence for the functionality of the network and the spill-over effect that the mobilisation of subnational actors creates by their cooperation.

ECRN still plays a vital role by providing a voice for the chemical regions at European level. The fostering of its members' mobilisation resulted in a complex and substantive interregional cooperation that transcended the regional level. The ECRN got a seat at the policy-making table where the national level and the European agenda setter (the Commission) listened to the regional voice and made use of the gained information (see Council of the European Union 2009).

The establishment of the registered association European Chemical Regions Network, which is still very active, shows that the interregional cooperation was successful and worthwhile for the involved actors. ECRN currently comprises 18 regions: Baden-Württemberg, Bavaria, Brandenburg, Cheshire West and Chester, Flanders, Hesse, Ida Virumaa, Limburg, Lombardy, Mazovia, North Rhine-Westphalia, Novara, Rhineland Palatine, Saxony-Anhalt, Scottland, Ústí, Wallonia, and Yorkshire & the Humber (ECRN 2016e).

Network analysis reveals a continuous high level of interregional exchange relations (Kohler-Koch 2009). Networks are part of the regional participation process within EMLG. The ECRN document analysis looked at the goals, resources, functions and participation processes that were deployed by the regions. This chapter provided an overview of the many activities performed by the ECRN. The mobilisation of the actors can be acknowledged as best-practice for regional participation within EMLG.

The yearly Congresses, the training seminars, the dissemination conferences, and the ECRN working structure provided the empirical and practical elements needed in order to enable the theoretical aspects of the EMLG. ECRN has drawn the public attention through the presentation of its chemical industry clusters. The opened network meetings in Brussels have sparked the interest of European actors: "ECRN was perceived as a relevant, competent point of contact for European institutions and regional chemical industry policy" (Sachsen-Anhalt Ministerium für Landesentwicklung und Verkehr/Ministerium für Wirtschaft und Arbeit 2008: 31).

Accomplishments of the European Chemical Regions Network entail the following elements:

- The regional dimension of the chemical venture at the European level was strengthened,
- Saxony-Anhalt won a definitive role in the network through the presidency chair[25],
- The chemical regions provided relevant input for shaping the European chemicals policy,
- The REACH implementation simulations performed by the chemical regions revealed important details for the policy implementation,
- Saxony-Anhalt managed to create its profile as a chemical region,
- Contacts and new cooperation were initiated,
- Saxony-Anhalt provided relevant input during the preparatory European decision-making processes and actively participated within the EMLG (see Wobben 2007).

ECRN activities go beyond the High Level Group on the Competitiveness of the European Chemicals Industry within the European Commission. The ECRN was appointed observer of the implementation of the EU REACH regulation. The network provided consultation to the Commission in the fields of climate change, energy policy, research and even the use of the structural funds. Therefore, the initial mobilisation of Saxony-Anhalt resulted in a complex and substantial interregional cooperation. Beneficiaries of this close cooperation are the subnational authorities, the industry and the European policy-making process and its institutions.

The ECRN work occurs through group meetings, interregional events and the annual Congresses, which gather actors interested and involved in the chemicals policy and industry. ECRN organises regional partnership meet-

---

[25] Starting with June 2016, the president of the ECRN is no longer from Saxony-Anhalt. The curent president of the network is Fabrizio Sala from Lombardy (E-CRN 2016d).

ings that are attended by many stakeholders from private companies, public administration and research facilities. The main topics of such meetings are the development of companies, the qualitative implementation of the European legislation and the environment safety of the industrial activity (Sachsen-Anhalt Ministerium für Landesentwicklung und Verkehr/Ministerium für Wirtschaft und Arbeit 2008: 31). The results of ECRN cooperation are joint statements, policy papers adopted on different aspects of chemical and regional policy of the EU, and examples of best-practices (ECRN 2016e).

These primary conclusions of regional participation within European Multi-Level Governance take into consideration the study released by the European Commission in 2013 for the chemical industry as well. The study presents recommendations for the regional authorities that emphasise the need for active participation and identify key elements that need to be taken into consideration both by policy-makers and private economy actors when development policies need to be implemented. Some of the most important recommendations are mobilisation of resources at other levels, specific needs target, and effective identification of regional priorities (European Commission 2012: 12; see Appendix 7).

The study was presented a decade after the first ECRN Congress. In the meantime, Saxony-Anhalt has been involved in activities that are recommended by the study, being also one of the regions presented in the study. Elements, such as the recognition of weaknesses and strengths, new forms of interaction between the industry and the public authorities, have been part of the work of the ECRN, and of Saxony-Anhalt's participation in EMLG. These show the potential of subnational participation in EMLG.

8 The regional participation pattern of Saxony-Anhalt within European Multi-Level Governance

The German unification and the EU accession greatly changed the political, economic and social structure of the Eastern German *Länder*. These faced great transformation processes and a high need to adapt to the EU membership. In comparison to the other German *Länder*, the politics and implementation processes of the EU governance were not familiar for the new institutions of the Eastern *Länder*. But, that changed because the actors mobilised and learned how to be involved in European Multi-Level Governance.

Saxony-Anhalt was an interesting case for the analysis of regional participation within EMLG due to its artificial development as a territorial construction (Böhmer 2017: 15). The participation processes comprised a series of elements, starting from the goals' definition by political actors of Saxony-Anhalt, continuing with the horizontal and vertical intrastate cooperation and integrating common interests of the regions in a wide European multi-actor cooperation at European level, with the European actors and with the national actors.

The analysed period provided the elements of the regional participation framework within EMLG. The next pages summarise what this framework entails. The focus of the analysis is on the three legislative periods but the period before is also taken into consideration. The region's history was considered an asset and the chemical industry, as part of that history, was constantly encouraged to develop. The institutional framework of Saxony-Anhalt is the main element that provided opportunities and means for the regional participation. That is why the activities of Saxony-Anhalt's institutions and actors are relevant for the regional participation pattern.

As the previous chapters showed, the historical development of a region influences its present political and development priorities and guides the mobilisation of its actors. Mobilisation within EMLG gives an answer to the question of why is a region or an actor, be it a public authority or an enterprise, interested in taking action. There is actually a broad scope of policy fields where regional actors can engage. Looking at the EU 2020 strategy, the accomplishment of goals of different policies depends much on what local and regional actors can achieve by just creating jobs. However, the inception of a sustainable structure that could contribute substantially to the creation of jobs is much more difficult, when there are no means for investment and no ways to attract private investors. This is why the contribution of European funds within the territory played and continues to play a crucial role in the achievement of the EU 2020 strategy goals. The history of Saxony-Anhalt made a difference in that area. Saxony-Anhalt gave a lot of input and made efforts to really develop what could have been saved from the traditional economy drivers, such as the chemical industry.

Towards the end of the 1990s, the EU-policy of Saxony-Anhalt developed innovative ideas and made sure that the interests of Saxony-Anhalt were represented at European level. A successful implementation of its Europe policy was the success of Saxony-Anhalt in interregional projects. One initiative provided the connection between the chemical industry of the region and the regional administration's network-skills. Saxony-Anhalt gained access to bigger chemical regions and managed to be perceived at the same level as the other big chemical actors. Thus, participation in interregional projects became an instrument of the Europe policy of Saxony-Anhalt (Wobben/Heinke 2006: 222). The overview of the actions of Saxony-Anhalt reveals that the constellation of their participation within EMLG is endorsed by an early mobilisation.

The *Landtag* was concerned, since the beginning of the 1990s, about the democratic element of the European decision-making processes and the implementation of the subsidiarity principle. In this respect, the regional government organised information events, prepared many informational materials and began the financial support for the activities of unions and associations. The *Land* participated through the work of the representation office in Brussels in consultancy processes of the agenda setting and policy formulation phase at European level. Important areas for Saxony-Anhalt were: public services, greenhouse and gas emission allowance, the chemicals policy, services and the future European Regional Policy. The administration staff had the opportunity to observe the work of the European Commission for three months in order to familiarise with the European governance (Landesregierung Sachsen-Anhalt 2010a).

In 2002 the European Commission requested a study that showed the preoccupation of the Commission with the development of possibilities for regional parliaments to participate within EMLG processes. The study revealed both criticism and positive developments, e.g. members of regional parliaments preferred to take action at federal level through the practice of the *Bundesrat*. A need to increase Europe-awareness of the members of parliaments was acknowledged (see Müller/Mauren 2002).

The *Landtag* of Saxony-Anhalt was informed by the government about their European emphasised activities. Members of the committee for federal and European affairs and media increased their contact with the European level through their visits in Brussels. The yearly report of the government giving an account of the international and European activities was established in 2005 and provided the *Landtag* with an overview of the activities established to take place in the forthcoming year. Those activities were pivotal for their EU profile and comprised: regional cooperations, strategic partnerships, participation in INTERREG projects, horizontal and vertical institutionalised intrastate cooperation with the *Länder* and the *Bund*, and activities performed at European level.

The activity of the *Landtag* of Saxony-Anhalt regarding European affairs increased. Saxony-Anhalt's representation to the EU informed about the activities of the *Landtag*, such as the occasional evening meetings, where members of the EP or the *Landtag* and CoR-members, officials and experts of the European Commission, and representatives of the economy exchanged information, as the meetings of political groups of the *Landtag* in Brussels, or the committee's monthly meeting for federal and European affairs and media that was sometimes held in Brussels (or the media members and officers of Saxony-Anhalt who have been exchanging valuable information). The newsletter informed about the many activities that the government of Saxony-Anhalt pursued in the area of European affairs (Landesvertretung Sachsen-Anhalt bei der Europäischen Union 1999-2016).

Even though the *Landtag* was considered to be a rather passive player, when it comes to European affairs, the document analysis showed that its members and committees were active, working together with the government on policies under the European jurisdiction, such as the chemicals policy. During the 3rd legislative period, European affairs were tackled in the meetings of the *Landtag's* committee for the economy, technology and European affairs. Those meetings started the debate about the White Paper of the Commission regarding the future chemicals policy. The government provided the *Landtag* with information about visits of the European actors, such as commissioners, conferences with the industry chambers and companies.

Concerning the European Affairs, the German *Länder* had the possibility to exert their influence on national decision-making. There are several elements of the horizontal intergovernmental cooperation of the German *Länder*: the coordination between the *Länder* through the conferences of the minister-presidents of the *Länder*, or different ministers' conferences, or conferences of the presidents of the *Landtage*. The vertical cooperation entails regular conferences between the government leaders of the *Bund* and the *Länder*, and the relations between *Bund* and *Länder* at the federal level through the *Bundesrat*. Through the intrastate cooperation, the *Länder* prepared position papers stating the common interests. Saxony-Anhalt made use of these instruments to promote the goal of the transition regions and to gain support from the other *Länder* and the *Bund*. However, the intrastate channel did not allow any influence during the preparatory phase, such as the influence of the representation carried out at European level.

The *Bund – Länder* cooperation took place directly in Berlin and in Brussels, through the extended cooperation between the permanent representation of the Federal Republic of Germany and the representations of the *Länder* offices. The horizontal cooperation among the *Länder* developed in Brussels by establishing specialised working groups (Boest 2012: 81). The information and opinion exchange platform extended its focus on MEPs, on members of the permanent representation or on other representatives of different interests groups. Thus, participation of the *Länder*, including that of Saxony-Anhalt, extended beyond the national borders becoming a "cooperative paradiplomacy" (Tatham 2008) between the subnational, the national and European level.

The method of the Brussels's working groups was similar to that of the minister-conferences within Germany, namely through the presidency that mainly coordinated the work. Having the presidency, the *Land* organised the meetings and invited participants, being the main contact for the involved actors. That form of cooperation was a win-win situation for all the actors involved. The European Commission did not meet individually with representatives of all the *Länder*. At a single meeting, both concerns of the *Länder* as well as the ones of the *Bund* were tackled. Those working mechanisms have been increasingly appreciated (Holeschovsky 2012: 87-89). Therefore, by-passing the *Bund* in Brussels was merely a shift of the *Bund – Länder* cooperation on European affairs in a different city, but closely connected to the developments in Berlin. Close cooperation was important for the staff as well since the staff of the permanent representation of Germany to the EU had experience from working in one of the Brussels *Länder* representation, making use of the gathered experience (Boest 2012: 82).

One of the main parts of subnational participation of Saxony-Anhalt in EMLG was the so-called *Vorfeldarbeit*, the preliminary work – before the legislative proposals were presented to the legislators, the Council and the European Parliament. Its particular importance was emphasised in the newsletter of the *Landesregierung*, the *Europabrief*. The analysed participation of Saxony-Anhalt in EMLG concerning the transition regions and the European chemicals industry showed how subnational actors are encouraged to and how they can act early in EU decision-making processes. The governance part of EMLG is about the early strong interaction of the EU institutions with the regional and local actors.

The configuration of the Brussels representation of Saxony-Anhalt mirrored the structure of the government in Magdeburg. The staff maintained a close cooperation with their home-departments, increasing the EU-capacity of the administration at home. Saxony-Anhalt's representation to the EU brought together the different levels of EMLG and contributed to their involvement in governance processes, through knowledge transfer, staff exchange, joint trainings, networking activities and consultations related to policy-making processes. Löwe emphasised the promotion of the "Brussels way of thinking" among the *Land's* actors through activities such as the cabinet meetings in Brussels, seminars and workshops for employees of the *Land* administration (2012: 65).

Among the activities of the Brussels office of Saxony-Anhalt, a successful practice, from the perspective of Saxony-Anhalt's actors, was the organisation of occasional evening meetings, where members of the *Landtag* and the EP, and the CoR-member of Saxony-Anhalt, officials and experts of the European Commission, representatives of the economy, media members and the officers of the contact office of Saxony-Anhalt had the chance to exchange valuable information. In addition, the study trips to Brussels of different actors from the region brought the EU closer to them and them to EU actors.

It is important to make the difference between administration staff and political actors. The main steps of the interest representation within the EU were: the problem and its effect analysis; definition of its own interests, assessment of the political debate, the involvement of actors, search of partners, and actual participation in the decision-making process (Schmidt 2002; Wobben 2007). Subnational mobilisation required a long-term view of the strategy for the engagement in EMLG. The strategy needed to take into consideration the extent of the participatory process and the benefits that Saxony-Anhalt could enjoy, involving both political and administrative actors.

Saxony-Anhalt was involved in EMLG to help future EU members as well. It offered support and shared its experience of EU membership to other regions, such as information about the use of EU funds provided to Hungarian regions before Hungary's accession (Landesvertretung Sachsen-Anhalt bei der Europäischen Union 2002(1): 11).

Given the enormous debt level of Saxony-Anhalt due to the transition to democracy, the polity, policy and politics elements were challenged to balance and to stabilise the budget (Renzsch 2002: 177). The contribution of European funds through the European Regional Policy doubled the GDP of Saxony-Anhalt (Robra 2012: 29). Not only were the interests of Saxony-Anahlt to be brought to the knowledge of the European actors, but there was also the possibility to influence the decision-making processes in early drafting stages. There were a large number of different actors involved in representing their interests, which operated in different networks.

Participation processes of Saxony-Anhalt in EMLG were connected to the idea of competitiveness. Being part of networks, such as the Central German economic space, was promoted in order to increase the competitiveness. That can be seen put into action by projects such as ECRN and other interregional projects which go beyond the borders of a country.

The development at European level, as the Europe 2020 strategy showed, followed the pattern of enforced cooperation among political and administrative actors, science institutions and the industry (European Commission 2010: 3-4, 10, 14, 16). Similar patterns could be observed emerging at different levels within the EU. Those were further developed by the European institutions under the heading of EMLG. Being able to access European funds for interregional cooperation, subnational actors had the possibility to create networks and communication platforms. Those instruments allowed further developments and facilitated the collective representation of interests within the European institutions.

The College of Commissioners had the power to endorse or to censure the interests of regions. The CoR was a useful tool as ally and source of policy suggestions for the Commission (Tatham 2008: 506). The function of the CoR was to promote the partnership governance within the European multi-level system (Stahl/Degen 2012). The regions' Brussels offices were the "vital link" to the EU institutions and other stakeholders present in Brussels (Rowe 2011: 2). There was no direct legal settlement for the cooperation between the EP and the *Länder*. But the MEPs were a source of information regarding the state of EU legislative processes, which was enjoying a soft power. Due to their not yet institutionalised cooperation, the MEPs and the representations of the *Länder* could decide on how they wish to implement their information exchange (Schnellhardt/Böge 2012: 156).

The work of Saxony-Anhalt's Brussels office was conducted in the spirit of pragmatism and it depended on the particular skills of the representation's director as well (Rowe 2011: 190). The staff analysed the yearly work programmes of the COM and the agendas of council presidencies, providing the assessment of the "most relevant policy areas for the administrations" and making the "initial strategic selection process" (Rowe 2011: 190). The information is relevant in determining the policy goals and strategy that the region wishes to pursue. It is a process that "will map out the strategic priorities on Europe both for the regional administration and for the office in Brussels" (Rowe 2011: 190). The parliament is merely briefed by the government on the selection of these priorities.

The Brussels activities were part of the overall region's home strategy of the political contribution to the goals of the legislative majority and their purpose for the government's activity. The Brussels office enhanced the position of the region within the "Brussels policy networks" (Rowe 2011: 85). The document analysis confirmed Rowe's argument that the Brussels office operated according to the business plan determined within the region and that the activities complemented the strategy of the regional administration (2011: 170). In addition, the analysis showed the greater extent of the regional participation in Brussels that went beyond the office work.

Establishing transnational networks (e.g. ECRN) was a result of the participation and interaction of different actors involved in European affairs. It also constituted a starting point for further development and progress. Networking activities seemed to be one of the most promising elements of the EMLG strategy. Active participation of territorial actors, specialists and EU actors - throughout the policy cycle - was part of the strategy.

The added-value of networks that emerged through the Brussels office was that they mediated the access to offices of other regional governments and they facilitated the dissemination of best practices in areas such as policy coordination, strategy building, and interaction with the European institutions. The early access to information and mobilisation of resources led to joint policy positions which carry more weight. The existing relationships embodied the basis for the policy-oriented activities that were conducted. Therefore, the Brussels office's added-value represented the "soft" benefit of the contacts emerging that were "leveraged at some later stage to derive intelligence benefits or support in horizontal alliance-building on specific EU issues" (Rowe 2011: 103-104).

The representation of subnational interests improved the quality of information that supranational institutions received, enclosing the private actors' interests. Particularly within the early stages of the policy-shaping process, long-term relationships with officials of the European Commission were built on trust. The goal of the communication was the "strategic dialogue with Commission officials where they [could] channel their home administration's thinking on policy issues" (Rowe 2011: 91). The early stage of policy-making was the relevant one since it only involved few actors and the regions could be more effective.

Therefore, the framework of the European activities offered Saxony-Anhalt a large share of opportunities for action. The mobilisation of its actors depended on what the region needed within its territory. Saxony-Anhalt's actors took into consideration: who were the stakeholders at home, what were their needs and how could those be solved through the cooperation between the administration and political actors of Saxony-Anhalt and the stakeholders, and through the mobilisation of actors engaged in the pursuit of goals.

EMLG embraced the cooperation between the subnational authorities and the regional private actors from the industry. The industry was a relevant partner, who mobilised resources and cooperated with the public authorities. The cooperation between subnational authorities and industrial, respectively corporate actors, succeeded when it built itself on the existing cooperation between the subnational authorities and the European institutions.

In the case of multi-level policies, networks were the best hybrid form of governance for a large number of involved actors (Wald/Jensen 2007: 97). The network organisation could prevent the opportunistic behaviour and it helped the involved actors to cope with the information flow. The useful characteristics of these networks were the optional content, the voluntary membership, and the long-term relationships based on trust. Networks could bring their actors closer to the market and reduce bureaucracy, which favoured the subnational mobilisation and the planning of strategic regional cooperation and partnerships (Wald/Jensen 2007: 98). Hence, the incentives provided by the European Union contributed to the network development and networks facilitated the subnational mobilisation and the active engagement of regional actors within EMLG.

There is a difference between Saxony-Anhalt and many regions from the new MS. Saxony-Anhalt as a state of the Federal Republic of Germany has a strong institutional framework based on a constitution that legitimises the work of the parliament and of the government of Saxony-Anhalt. On the other hand, these institutions are accountable to the people living in Saxony-Anhalt, who can sanction them at the next election. The elections in Saxony-Anhalt showed that the population sanctioned the political parties for their policies. The specific intrastate framework of the subnational entity provides means for regional participation within EMLG. But the means are not sufficient. Actors have to mobilise and prepare their strategy for an active engagement. This is the recommendation for all subnational actors who wish to make a contribution or a difference in the EMLG.

The representations of regions at the EU level, that have no administrative or no constitutional status in their MS, are not controlled by a subnational elected authority. Because of this shortage, the information gathered from the European actors cannot be clearly used by a policy team that has no administration (Rowe 2011: 89). Hence, the variable of establishing goals and principles depends on the administrative structure of the subnational level.

Not many regions and actors from Central and Eastern Europe are involved in the ECRN. But those involved in the ECRN can experience how EMLG works and they can improve their participation. The asymmetry of resources allocated within a network might cause tensions but it might also encourage stronger mobilisation for a better allocation of resources. However, the mobilisation of social and economic actors in the regional networks and in close cooperation with the public authorities can be of use (Bafoil 2009: 85). Hence, it is crucial to realize that the subnational level can be empowered through both bottom-up and top-down cooperation, due to the interdependence of the levels for the implementation of European policies.

The regionalisation reform understood as the redistribution of power, position and significance of the involved actors, and the dimension of the dynamic of territorial regionalisation can introduce a high degree of tension between the central and local government levels – even though it should establish a balance of powers. Such tension between the government levels might lead to the emergence of confusion especially in regard to the financial rights and obligations that should be dispersed.

Rowe argues that the regions of the new Member States need to settle their internal problems in order to engage with a unified position at the European level (2011: 97-99). She makes the difference between contributing to MLG and simply stimulating or creating multi-level interactions. The relationships, exchange of knowledge and expertise are the activities of creating multi-level interactions (Rowe 2011: 123). Then, the contribution to MLG is connected to the development of a Europe-policy agenda within the home administration and decision-making actors and its pursuit, as the case of ECRN and the goal of the transition regions showed in the above-presented sections.

The new members lack a "fully-fledged civil service at the regional level such as is found in the larger Member States", creating for them a dependence on the "Brussels pool of talent" (Rowe 2011: 137). Hence, the cooperation with other regions and their staff can be a good start to developing the necessary skills for mastering the EMLG.

On the other hand, there is an indication of a "convergence of Western and Eastern European debates about subnational politics". They indicate the expectations of scholars of European regionalism, "to engage in comparing suitable constellations in Eastern and Western Europe". Such comparisons can enhance the analytical leverage for the scholars' specific research questions (Pitschel/Bauer 2009: 339).

The continuous engagement in the European affairs and the use of the framework that regions have at their disposal can enhance the contribution of regional politics to EMLG. A systematic pursuit and the dissemination of specific interests are advised when the resources of regional actors are limited. The timing of decision-making processes and the continuous use of resources and access channels can improve the chances of a region to achieve its goals within EMLG. However, the effectiveness of such actions cannot be guaranteed. The elements of Saxony-Anhalt's regional participation pattern in European Multi-Level Governance are summarised in the picture below.

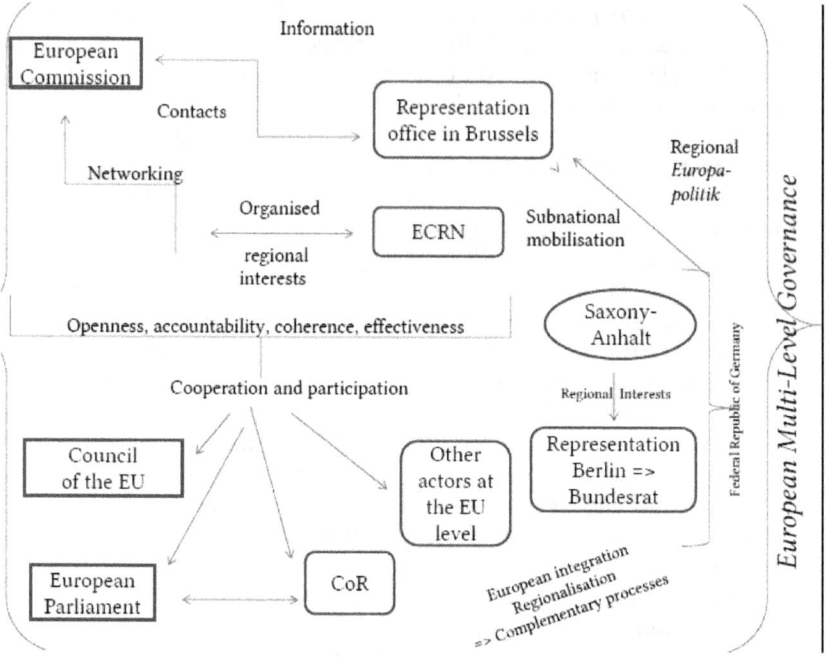

Figure 1: The regional participation of Saxony-Anhalt in the EMLG.

Author's figure based on the literature (Rowe 2011; Knodt/Corcaci 2012; Tatham 2008, 2010, 2013) and the document analysis.

9 Conclusions

The European Union provides the political and economic environment in which its Member States perform their everyday functions. These go beyond the government's activities and enter the reference of 'governance'. The EU governance system involves processes of regulation and interdependent interactions of private and public actors. The involvement of Member State administrations in EMLG requires their capacity to adapt to the EMLG principles and to expand their cooperation (see Appendix 1). Such cooperation extends to the subnational and local levels and across policy sectors towards the increased involvement of private actors and other non-state actors. In other words, the EU is enhancing its daily functions of Multi-Level Governance.

Due to the complex EMLG framework of institutions, actors and processes, this book only looked into the processes at the subnational level. Regions, being different, are understood as the intermediary structure between the national and the local government level within the MS of the EU. Their structure is embedded within an economic, political and cultural context, which provides them with their role within the state structure. This book analysed EMLG from an empirical and regional perspective.

The book emphasises the interconnectivity between European incentives and the ongoing mobilisation that takes place at the regional level. It stimulates a stronger mobilisation of the subnational actors, in particular, those from centralised countries, who do not benefit from specific constitutional frameworks. Moreover, the research presented in this book brings a window of opportunity for further research of subnational mobilisation from a bottom-up perspective.

The participation of regional actors occurs under the influence of a complex system, in which actors regard their specific interests. Even though actors act goal-oriented, the collaboration that is taking place is a result and a catalyst for the implementation of goals.

The Multi-Level Governance approach was used as a theoretical and empirical framework for the qualitative analyses because it directed the attention to the role and contribution of the regional level in the EU. MLG developed as a practice of the European institutions providing a working framework of the EU that enhanced the involvement of regions in the overall EU governance processes. Since regions are active within the EU, they mobilise and become part of the EMLG.

Multi-Level Governance gives an overview of the collective EU decision-making processes. There are two types of MLG. The first acknowledges MLG based on the federalist approach. The second type looks more into task-specific issues and their specific jurisdictions. The two types combine the perspectives of competence distribution and policy-related problem-solving frameworks. The regions' engagement in EMLG was intended to improve the implementation of the European Regional Policy. Increased participation of regional actors enlarged their contribution to the policy-making activities.

Saxony-Anhalt was chosen as a case study because it offers a model of regional participation in the European Multi-Level Governance. It shows the importance of understanding EMLG that allows subnational actors to use the channels and opportunities for their participation. The European institutions acknowledged the high determination of regions to mobilise and participate in EMLG. Participation was not understood as an institutionalised protest, but as a contribution to "more effective policy shaping based on early consultation and past experience" (Official Journal of the European Communities 2001: 12).

In the case of Central and Eastern Europe, such participation can contribute to the democracy development and to the European integration process. The CoR invited "councils of local and regional elected representatives to devote special sessions to European integration and European policies and to involve, in their debates, representatives of the various European institutions engaged in shared governance" (Committee of the Regions 2009: 12).

The research undertook the analysis of Saxony-Anhalt's regional participation in EMLG. The applied qualitative analysis of the mobilisation processes of Saxony-Anhalt developed a strategic activity framework from which regions can learn to enhance their own participation and contact with EMLG processes.

The empirical analysis of Saxony-Anhalt set off with its historical development and followed its particular mobilisation from 2002 to 2016. The analysis findings demonstrate the complexity of the EU functioning system and highlight how a region can establish itself as a stakeholder in the system.

The book answers several research questions presented in the second chapter. EMLG is the way the EU functions. All territorial levels are connected and interdependent. Their actors aim to increase the competitiveness of the EU as a unit by developing its smaller units, the regions. Regions are an adequate unit for the implementation of the EU policies and they provide valuable expertise for the European policy-makers. That is what regional participation within EMLG is all about. The access channels at the European level are provided by the European Commission, the European Parliament and the Committee of the Regions. The Member States also offer their own intrastate channels at the European level.

The mobilisation of Saxony-Anhalt was set by the effect of the European legislation on its economic development. Authorities assessed their needs and goals and decided to take a position and express their voice at the national and European level.

Regarding the first hypothesis, the historical development of Saxony-Anhalt was closely connected to the state's identity and the political actions of Saxony-Anhalt in the EU. The specificities of the region, such as the fertile soil and the chemically specialised south part, substantially contributed to the economy. Therefore, the historical development of the territory played a significant part in its development.

Regarding the second hypothesis, the institutional and legal framework of subnational actors was crucial for the way the actors engaged in the EMLG. The participation strategy of Saxony-Anhalt encompassed both the national and European level as access points for making their case in the process of interest representation. Even though it is argued that regional parliaments have mainly a passive role and the accountability of the government towards the parliament is restricted to the reporting process (Rowe 2011: 200), the analysis showed the active involvement of the parliament of Saxony-Anhalt. Members of the parliament met in Brussels maintaining contact with the European actors. The parliament endorsed the pursuit of goals set in the coalition agreements. The direct involvement in EMLG was enabled by the use of resources, the representations in Brussels and Berlin and by its representing actors, such as the members of the Committee of the Regions.

Regarding the third hypothesis, the interests articulated in political documents of Saxony-Anhalt functioned as binding elements of the participation in EMLG. Those interests regarded the principles of the European strategies, such as the Europe 2020 Strategy. The achievement of goals was pursued by an active engagement with the relevant stakeholders, with officials of the European Commission, the Commissioners, the European Parliament's committee for regional development, the Committee of the Regions and with other associations present in Brussels.

Regarding the fourth hypothesis, Saxony-Anhalt mobilised its actors and those of other regions within the EU that have a chemical industry and which were interested in the effect of the European policies for the European Chemicals Industry. Based on their mobilisation, several regions prepared an INTERREG project for their cooperation and representation of their specific interests related to the chemical industry and policy to the European level. The established project triggered a permanent interregional cooperation that takes place within the framework of the European Chemical Regions Network. The association was acknowledged as a stakeholder and has been active within the EMLG processes providing the added value of MLG by contributing with a regional perspective.

The Commission encouraged the use of INTERREG initiatives for the interregional cooperation. This is actually an area where Saxony-Anhalt has been successfully developing this cooperation. It was important for Saxony-Anhalt to become known among the European actors since it needed support for its later mobilisation for the transition rules of the Cohesion Policy. The importance of the Brussels office is connected to its efforts to connect the most important chemical sites in Central Europe. Representation of Saxony-Anhalt to the EU was a key actor that managed to bring actors from within the territory of the region to cooperate in the enlarged European framework.

Through development, regions can become the locations where the goals of European policies are achieved. The activities of the regions aim to solve problems addressed by those policies. The solutions need to be adequate and adapted to the specific problems of the regions. This is why it is important that subnational actors are aware of their needs and goals so that they can contribute to European policy-making processes. Both in the case of distributional and regulatory European policy-making processes, regions find themselves in competition with other regions. This is another reason why acknowledging their own problems, solutions and goals, the regions can improve their participation in EMLG. Regions can and are encouraged to make use of the opportunities of EMLG, being able to mobilise and organise their participation within European processes, so that they can gain more bargaining scope with the European institutions.

One should not take the participation of regions within the EU as a given standard. Even if there are elements that regions can use, actors can still learn from each other before deploying their own resources. Institutions solely cannot achieve these goals. Institutions need to be filled with motivated people, who pursue to make a difference in their territory.

Mobilisation can have different meanings and different implementation methods. However, the declared motivation and will of SNAs to be involved and to participate in the work of the EMLG is the first step. The second step of the active participation in EMLG is identifying the potential of the contribution within the EU policy-making processes and their implementation. According to such findings, regions can make use of the financial instruments the EU offers. On the other hand, such findings can ease the search for actors with similar goals and these could lay down the fundament for future cooperation that is also a European condition. The third step is to identify the communication and access channels and then to use them by deploying resources.

The findings of the analysis demonstrate the complexity of the EU functioning system and highlight how a region can establish itself as a stakeholder within the EMLG. The example of Saxony-Anhalt can be of use and inspiration for regions within Central and Eastern Europe, Saxony-Anhalt being an engaged actor in EMLG. It made use of the channels it has at its disposal in order to bring in political preferences and interests in the EMLG processes. Moreover, the active engagement of the regions from Central and Eastern Europe endorses their learning capacity and active engagement within EMLG. Nevertheless, the power of change relies on the intrastate channels.

Therefore, the research provides a constellation of variables that can be regarded as best-practice, provided by the case study of Saxony-Anhalt. Learning opportunities are provided for other regions in Central and Eastern Europe to have a more effective development of the subnational level. The EMLG outcome analysis provides the possibility for prospective research. A detailed analysis that would be welcomed includes a coordination analysis of subnational actors and their participation within EMLG using the methodology of social network analysis for Central and Eastern Europe.

10 Bibliography

*** (2002): Wahlen in Sachsen-Anhalt – Wahlen in Europa. In: Wolf, Jürgen/Rannenberg, Jens/Mattfeld, Harald/Giebel, Heiner (Hrsg.): Jahrbuch für Politik und Gesellschaft in Sachsen-Anhalt 2002. Halle: Mitteldeutscher Verlag, 40-51.

Ahner, Dirk (2012): Die Vertretung der ostdeutschen Bundesländer in Brüssel: Ein Erfahrungsbericht aus der Arbeit der Kommission. In: Renzsch, Wolfgang/Wobben, Thomas (Hrsg.): 20 Jahre ostdeutsche Landesvertretungen in Brüssel. Eine Bilanz der Interessenvertretung der Länder aus unterschiedlichen Blickwinkeln. Baden-Baden: Nomos, 145-149.

Ansell, Christopher K. (2000): The Networked Polity: Regional Development in Western Europe. In: Governance: An International Journal of Policy and Administration, Vol. 13, Issue 3, 303-330.

Arbeitgeber- und Wirtschaftsverbände Sachsen-Anhalt e.V. (2013): Hochschulpolitik als Kernbereich der Innovations- und Wachstumspolitik in Sachsen-Anhalt.

Armstrong, Harvey W. (1995): The Role and Evolution of European Community Regional Policy. In: Barry, Jones/Keating, Michael (eds.): The European Union and the Regions. Oxford: Clarendon Press, 23-64.

Bache, Ian (2004): Multi-level Governance and the European Union Regional Policy. In: Bache, Ian/Flinders, Matthew V. (eds.): Multi-level Governance. Oxford: Oxford University Press, 165-178.

Bache, Ian/George, Stephen (2006): Politics in the European Union. Oxford: Oxford University Press.

Bafoil, François (2009): Central and Eastern Europe: Europeanization and social change. Basinstoke: Palgrave.

Bango, Jenö (2003): Theorie der Sozialregion: Einführung durch systemische Beobachtungen in vier Welten. Berlin: Logos-Verlag.

Barmuß, Hans-Joachim/Kathe, Heinz (1992): Kleine Geschichte Sachsen-Anhalts. Halle: Mitteldeutscher Verlag.

Bauer, Michael/Börzel, Tanja A. (2010): Regions and the EU. In: Enderlein, Henrik/Wälti, Sonja/Zürn, Michael (eds.): Handbook on Multi-level governance. Cheltenham: Edward Elgar, 253-265.

Benz, Arthur (1998): German regions in the European Union – From joint policy-making to multi-level governance. In: Le Galès, Patrick/Lequesne, Christian (eds.): Regions in Europe. London: Routledge, 111-129.

Benz, Arthur (2003): Mehrebenenverpflechtung in der Europäischen Union. In: Jachtenfuchs, Markus/Kohler-Koch, Beate (eds.): Europäische Integration. Opladen: Leske+Budrich, 317-352.

Benz, Arthur (2004): Path-Dependent Institutions and Strategic Veto Players: National Parliaments in the European Union. In: Journal of European Public Policy, Vol. 27, Nr. 5, 875-900.

Benz, Arthur/Eberlein, Burkard (1999): The Europeanization of regional policies: patterns of multi-level governance. In: Journal of European Public Policy, Vol. 6, Nr. 2, 329-348.

Benz, Arthur/Zimmer, Christina (2010): The EU's competences: The 'vertical' perspective on the multi-level system. In: Living Reviews in European Governance, Vol. 5, Nr. 1, 5-31.

Beyers, Jan/Donas, Tom (2013): How Regions Assemble in Brussels: The Organizational Form of Territorial Representation in the European Union. In: Publius: The Journal of Federalism, Vol. 43, Nr. 4, 1-24.

Bickerton, James/Gagnon Alain-G. (2011): Regions. In: Caramani, Daniele (ed.): Comparative Politics. Oxford: Oxford University Press, second edition, 275-291.

Boest, Reinhard (2012): Die Zusammenarbeit von Bund und Länder in Brüssel. In: Renzsch, Wolfgang/Wobben, Thomas (Hrsg.): 20 Jahre ostdeutsche Landesvertretungen in Brüssel. Eine Bilanz der Interessenvertretung der Länder aus unterschiedlichen Blickwinkeln. Baden-Baden: Nomos, 80-85.

Böhmer, Wolfgang (2002): Den Menschen in Sachsen-Anhalt wieder eine Chance geben. In: Wolf, Jürgen/Rannenberg, Jens/Mattfeld, Harald/Giebel, Heiner (eds.): Jahrbuch für Politik und Gesellschaft in Sachsen-Anhalt 2002. Halle: Mitteldeutscher Verlag, 119-122.

Böhmer, Wolfgang Ministerpräsident a.D. (2017): Sachsen-Anhalt ist „kein politisches Schwergewicht". In: Träger, Hendrik/Priebus, Sonja (Hrsg.): Politik und Regieren in Sachsen-Anhalt. Wiesbaden: Springer Verlag, 15-29.

Böhmer, Wolfgang/Schneider, Michael (2001): Die besondere Lage der Opposition in Sachsen-Anhalt zwischen Vorwurf und Selbstbehauptung. In: Wolf, Jürgen et al. (Hrsg.): Jahrbuch für Politik und Gesellschaft in Sachsen-Anhalt 2001. Halle: Mitteldeutscher Verlag, 71-85.

Bomberg, Elisabeth/Peterson, John (1998): European decision-making: the role of sub-national authorities. In: Political Studies, Vol. 46, Issue 2, 219-235.

Börzel, Tanja (2002): Nations and Regions in the European Union: Institutional Adaptation in Germany and Spain. Cambridge: University Press.

Börzel, Tanja A. (2008): Environmental policy. In: Graziano, Paolo/Wink, Maarten P. (eds.): Europeanization New Research Agendas. Bakingstoke: Palgrave Macmillan, 226-238.

Börzel, Tanja A./Risse, Thomas (2003): Conceptualizing the domestic impact of Europe. In: Featherstone, K./Radaelli, Claudio M. (eds.): The politics of Europeanization. Oxford: Oxford University Press, 57-80.

Börzel, Tanja A./Risse, Thomas (2006): Europeanization: The Domestic Impact of European Union Politics. In: Jørgensen, Knud E. /Pollack, Mark A./Rosamond, Ben (eds.): Handbook of European Union politics. London: Thousand Oaks; California: Sage, 483-504.

Bratzke, Gunthard (2003): Erster Kongress der Europäischen Chemieregionen setzt Zeichen zum Aufbau des Netzwerkes der Chemieregionen Europas. In Europabrief, Nr. 14, 11.

Bratzke, Gunthard/Tobaben, Jörn-Heinrich (2012): Eine Region muss wissen, was sie will! Erfahrungen in der europapolitischen Interessenvertretung am Beispiel der Wirtschaftsinitiative Mitteldeutschland. In: Renzsch, Wolfgang/Wobben, Thomas (Hrsg.): 20 Jahre ostdeutsche Landesvertretungen in Brüssel. Eine Bilanz der Interessenvertretung der Länder aus unterschiedlichen Blickwinkeln. Baden-Baden: Nomos, 186-194.

Bullmann, Udo (2001): The politics of the Third Level. In: Jeffery, Charlie (ed.): The regional dimension of the European Union. Towards a third level in Europe? London: Frank Cass, 3-19.

Bulmer, Simon/Radaelli, Claudio M. (2004): The Europeanization of national policy? In: Queen's papers on Europeanization, No. 1, 1-22.

Bund und Länder (2008): Gemeinsame Stellungnahme von Bund und Ländern zum Vierten Bericht der Europäischen Kommission über den wirtschaftlichen und sozialen Zusammenhalt, (http://ec.europa.eu/regional_policy/archive/conferences/4thcohesionforu m/doc/contributions/gemeinsame_stellungnahme.pdf), [last access 08.12.2016].

Bund und Länder (2011): Gemeinsame Stellungnahme von Bund und Ländern zum Fünften Bericht der Europäischen Kommission über den wirtschaftlichen, sozialen und territorialen Zusammenarbeit.

Bundesministerium für Umwelt, Naturschutz, Bau und Reaktorsicherheit (2007): Territorial Agenda of the European Union. Towards a More Competitive and Sustainable Europe of Diverse Regions, Leipzig, (http://ec.europa.eu/regional_policy/en/information/publications/commun ications/2007/territorial-agenda-of-the-european-union-towards-a-more-competitive-and-sustainable-europe-of-diverse-regions), [last access 10.11.2016].

Bundesrat (2011): Beschluss des Bundesrates: Vorschlag für eine Verordnung des Europäischen Parlaments und des Rates mit gemeinsamen Bestimmungen über den Europäischen Fonds für regional Entwicklung, den Europäischen Sozialfonds, den Kohäsionfonds, den Europäischen

Landwirtschaftfonds für die Entwicklung des ländlichen Raums und den Europäischen Meeres- und Fischereifonds, für die der Gemeinsame Strategie Rahmen gilt, sowie mit allgemeinen Bestimmungen über den Europäischen Fonds für regionale Entwicklung, den Europäischen Sozialfonds und den Kohäsionsfonds und zur Aufhebung der Verordnung (EG) Nr. 1083/2006 KOM (2011) 615 endg.; Ratsdokument 15243/11 (629/11).

Bundesrat (2016): Europakammer, (http://www.bundesrat.de/DE/bundesrat/europakammer/europakammer.ht ml?nn=4353078), [last access 14.11.2016].

Bundestag (2009): Gesetz über die Zusammenarbeit von Bund und Länder in Angelegenheiten der Europäischen Union.

Bundestag (2014): Grundgesetz für die Bundesrepublik Deutschland.

Carter, Caitríona/Pasquier, Romain (2010): The Europeanization of Regions as 'Spaces for politics': A research agenda. In: Regional and Federal Studies, Vol. 20, Nr. 3, 295-314.

CechemNet (2003): CechemNet – Chemiestandorte in Sachsen-Anhalt kooperieren. In: Europabrief, Nr. 13, 22-23.

CeChemNet (2016): Partner, (http://www.cechemnet.de/Partner), [last access 16.12.2016].

ChemClust (2012): Best Practice Guide, September, (www.chemclust.eu/files/BEST_PRACTICE_GUIDE.pdf), [last access 16.12.2016].

ChemClust (2014): Welcome, (http://www.chemclust.eu/), [last access 03.12.2016].

ChemLog (2011): Final Brochure: Summary of Activities and Results.

ChemLog (2014): ChemLog Home, (http://www.chemlog.info/chemlog/index.html), [last access 03.12.2016].

Clement, Wolfgang (1996): The Committee of the Regions – More than an Alibi? In: Hesse, Joachim Jens (ed.): Regionen in Europa. Baden-Baden: Nomos,13-28.

Commission of the European Communities (2001): White Paper. Strategy for a future chemicals policy, COM (2011) 88.

Commission of the European Communities (2008): Communication from the Commission to the Council, The European Parliament, The Committee of the Regions and The European Economic and Social Committee. Green Paper on Territorial Cohesion. Turning territorial diversity into strength.

Committee of the Regions (2009): The Committee of the Regions' White Paper on Multilevel Governance, (http://cor.europa.eu/en/activities/governance/Pages/white-pape-on-multilevel-governance.aspx), [last access 10.11.2016].

Committee of the Regions (2010): Opinion of the Committee of the Regions on the contribution of Cohesion policy to the Europe 2020 strategy (CdR 223/2010 fin).

Committee of the Regions (2012a): Scoreboard for Monitoring Multilevel Governance (MLG) at the European Union Level – Is the principle of MLG being encouraged throughout the EU policy cycle? Report written by the European Institute of Public Administration, (http://cor.europa.eu/en/activities/governance/Documents/scoreboard-2012-executive-summary.pdf), [last access 10.11.2016].

Committee of the Regions (2012b): Building a European Culture of Multi-level Governance: Follow-Up to the Committee of the Regions' White Paper. Opinion, CdR 273/2011 fin.

Committee of the Regions (2012c): Opinion of the Committee of the Regions – Proposal for a regulation on the ERDF, CdR 5/2012 fin.

Committee of the Regions (2013): Scoreboard for Monitoring Multilevel Governance (MLG) at the European Union Level. Fact Sheets 2011-2012, (http://cor.europa.eu/en/activities/governance/Documents/mlg-scoreboard-fact-sheets.pdf), [last access 10.11.2016].

Committee of the Regions (2014): Resolution of the Committee of the Regions on the Charter for Multilevel Governance in Europe. RESOL-V-2012.

Committee of the Regions (2016a): The European Week of Regions and Cities – Open Days, (http://cor.europa.eu/en/events/opendays/Pages/opendays.aspx), [last access 28.11.2016].

Committee of the Regions (2016b): President Dr. Michael Schneider (http://web.cor.europa.eu/epp/Aboutus/Pages/President.aspx), [last access 07.12.2016].

Conzelmann, Thomas (2009): A new mode of governing? Multi-level Governance between Cooperation and Conflict. In: Conzelmann, Thomas/Smith, Randall (eds.): Multi-level Governance in the European Union: Taking Stock and Looking Ahead. Baden-Baden: Nomos, 11-30.

Council of the European Union (2009): An integrated approach to a competitive and sustainable industrial policy in the European Union, Conclusions of the 2945th Competitiveness (Internal Market, Industry and Research) Council meeting.

Crieckemans, David/Duran, Manuel (2010): Small State Diplomacy Compared to Sub-State Diplomacy: More of the Same or Different? In: Steinmetz, Robert/Wivel, Anders (eds.): Small States in Europe: Challenges and Opportunities. Farnham: Ashgate, 31-46.

De Propis, Lisa/Hamdouch, Abdelillah (2013): Editorial: Regions as Knowledge and Innovation Hubs. In: Regional Studies, Vol. 47, Nr. 7, 997-1000.

Der Beobachter der Länder bei der Europäischen Union (2016): Aufgaben, (http://www.laenderbeobachter.de/englishhome), [last access 16.11.2016].

Detterbeck, Klaus (2008): Die Landtagswahl in Sachsen-Anhalt 2006: Der landespolitische Parteienwettbewerb und der (ungewöhnlich kleine) Schatten der Bundespolitik. In: Tenscher, Jens/Batt, Helge (eds.): 100 Tage schonfrist. Bundespolitik und Landtagswahlen im Schatten der Größen Koalition. Wiesbaden: VS Verlag für Sozialwissenschaften, 177-195.

Detterbeck, Klaus (2010): Sachsen-Anhalt – von häufigen Regierungswechseln, einem gescheiterten Modell und einer christdemokraten Vormacht. In: Kost, Andreas/Rellecke, Werner/Weber, Reinhold (eds.): Parteien in den deutschen Ländern: Geschichte und Gegenwart. München: Beck Verlag, 360-374.

Detterbeck, Klaus (2012): When small becomes beautiful: Regionen und kleine Mitgliedstaaten in der EU. In: Renzsch, Wolfgang/Wobben, Thomas (Hrsg.): 20 Jahre ostdeutsche Landesvertretungen in Brüssel. Eine Bilanz der Interessenvertretung der Länder aus unterschiedlichen Blickwinkeln. Baden-Baden: Nomos, 169-172.

Enzensberger, Hans M. (2011): Brussels, the gentle monster: Or the disenfranchisement of Europe. London, New York: Seagull Books.

Eppler, Annegret (2008): Multi-level Governance in Europe – The implications of German Länder in the development of the Lisbon Treaty and the Strengthening of the regional level. In: International Law Forum of the Hebrew University of Jerusalem Law Faculty, Research Paper No. 09-08.

European Chemical Regions Network (2003): 1st European Congress of Regions – Congress Volume.

European Chemical Regions Network (2004a): 2nd European Congress of Chemical Regions – Congress Volume.

European Chemical Regions Network (2004b): Joint declaration of the ECRN Presidium, (www.ecrn.net/documents/ECRN_Joint_Pos_Joint_Declaration_ECRN_P residium_13_05_04.pdf), [last access 02.12.2016].

European Chemical Regions Network (2006a): Joint Position concerning the New European policy on Chemicals, (www.ecrn.net/documents/EcAJp14_Position_ECRN_REACH_END_22 0906.pdf), [last access 02.12.2016].

European Chemical Regions Network (2006b): Main Findings of the ECRN. Summary of Conclusions and outlook to the future.

European Chemical Regions Network (2006c): Joint Declaration of the fourth European Congress of Chemical Regions – Managing Change Together, (www.ecrn.net/documents/EcMC4_Declaration_final_071106_ENG.pdf), [last access 02.12.2016].

European Chemical Regions Network (2007): Joint Declaration of the fifth European Congress of Chemical Regions "Competitive Chemical Regions in Europe", (www.ecrn.net/documents/ludwigshafen_declaration.pdf), [last access 02.12.2016].

European Chemical Regions Network (2008): Enabling Solutions. Chemical Regions – A Driver for Competitiveness and Innovation in Europe, (www.ecrn.net/documents/ECRN_6_Congress_Declaration.pdf), [last access 03.12.2016].

European Chemical Regions Network (2009): Annual Report 2009, (http://www.ecrn.net/communicationanddownloads/annualreports.php), [last access 03.12.2016].

European Chemical Regions Network (2010): 8th Congress of European Chemical Regions – New Perspectives for concerted Actions (www.ecrn.net/documents/Congress_Resolution.pdf), [last access 02.12.2016].

European Chemical Regions Network (2011a): Response to the Commission Consultation on the Green Paper – From Challenges to Opportunities: Towards a Common Strategic Framework for EU Research and Innovation Funding.

European Chemical Regions Network (2011b): Congress Declaration: Sustainable growth and employment in the European Chemical Regions needs a strong cohesion policy, (www.ecrn.net/documents/ECRN_Congress_Declaration_9th_Congress_FINAL.pdf), [last access 02.12.2016].

European Chemical Regions Network (2012): Facing the changes – New challenges for the competitiveness of the European chemical industry, (www.ecrn.net/documents/10th_Congress_Declaration_2012.pdf), [last access 02.12.2016].

European Chemical Regions Network (2013a): Strategic Position to Europe 2020 flagship initiative on industrial policy – Taking the opportunity for a new integrated industrial policy to foster an economically, socially and environmentally sustainable development in Europe, (www.ecrn.net/documents/ECRN_Industrial_Policy_Paper_2013.pdf), [last access 02.12.2016].

European Chemical Regions Network (2013b): Demand Driven Innovations through Triple Helix Cooperation in Chemical Regions,

(www.ecrn.net/documents/ECRN_Congress_Declaration_2013.pdf), [last access 02.12.2016].
European Chemical Regions Network (2016a): ECRN Project Council (http://ecrn.net/abouttheecrn/projectcouncil.php), [last access 02.12.2016].
European Chemical Regions Network (2016b): High Level Group Archive, (http://www.ecrn.net/highlevelgroup/hlgarchive.php), [last access 03.12.2016].
European Chemical Regions Network (2016c): High Level Group follow-up process, (http://www.ecrn.net/highlevelgroup/hlgfollowupprocess.php), [last access 03.12.2016].
European Chemical Regions Network (2016d): President and Executive Board, (http://ecrn.net/abouttheecrn/president.php), [last access 05.12.2016].
European Chemical Regions Network (2016e): Member regions, (http://ecrn.net/abouttheecrn/memberregions.php), [last access 05.12.2016].
European Chemical Regions Network (2016f): Best practices, (http://ecrn.net/eventsandactivities/bestpractices.php), [last access 05.12.2016].
European Commission (2000): Regionalisation in Europe. DG Research Working Paper, Regional Policy Series REGI 108A XX/rev. 1.
European Commission (2002a): 2nd Stakeholders' Conference on the business impact of the new Chemicals Policy, DG Enterprise and Industry, (http://ec.europa.eu/enterprise/sectors/chemicals/documents/reach/archives/white-paper/2nd-stakeholder-conference_en.htm), [last access 04.01.2015].
European Commission (2002b): The Sixth Framework Programme in brief, (https://ec.europa.eu/research/fp6/pdf/fp6-in-brief_en.pdf), [last access 16.12.2016].
European Commission (2003): Positionspapier der vom "statistischen Effekt betroffenen Regionen zur Zukunft der EU-Strukturpolitik nach 2006", (http://ec.europa.eu/regional_policy/archive/debate/document/futur/member/stat_betroffene_regionen_apr_03_de.pdf), [last access 07.12.2016].
European Commission (2009): High Level Group on the Competitiveness of the European Chemicals Industry – Final Report, (www.ecrn.net/documents/hlg_final_report_july09.pdf), [last access 16.12.2016].
European Commission (2010): Europe 2020 A strategy for smart, sustainable and inclusive growth, COM (2010) 2020.

European Commission (2011): Report on the implementation of the recommendations of the High Level Group on the Competitiveness of the European Chemicals Industry.

European Commission (2012): Analysis of policies in chemical regions to support the competitiveness of the chemicals industry. Final report for DG Enterprise and industry, prepared by Kristina Dervojeda PwC, Bas Warmenhoven PwC, Mark Lengton PwC, reviewed by: Christian Ketels, Engagement partner: Jan-Hendrik Schretlen, PwC.

European Commission (2013): Refocusing EU Cohesion Policy for Maximum Impact on Growth and Jobs: The Reform in 10 points, (http://europa.eu/rapid/press-release_MEMO-13-1011_en.htm), [last access 14.11.2016].

European Commission (2014a): The European Code of Conduct on partnership,(http://ec.europa.eu/esf/BlobServlet?docId=443&langId=en&usg=AFQjCNF1GDKipHBi8yChHsLkg229DMT1Fw&cad=rja), [last access 14.11.2016].

European Commission (2014b): DG Enterprise and Industry – the High Level Group for the Competitiveness of the European Chemicals Industry, (http://ec.europa.eu/enterprise/sectors/chemicals/competitiveness/high-level-group/index_en.htm), [last access 15.06.2014].

European Commission (2016a): Regional Innovation Monitor Plus: Saxony-Anhalt (https://ec.europa.eu/growth/tools-databases/regional-innovation-monitor/base-profile/saxony-anhalt), [last access 30.11.2016].

European Commission (2016b): Sectoral social dialogue – Chemical industry, DG Employment, Social Affaisrs and Inclusion, (http://ec.europa.eu/social/main.jsp?catId=480&langId=en&intPageId=1828), [last access 03.12.2016].

European Commission (2016c): Departments (Directorates-General) and services, (http://ec.europa.eu/about/ds_en.htm), [last access 05.12.2016].

European Commission (2016d): Regional Policy (http://ec.europa.eu/regional_policy/en/policy/what/investment-policy/), [last access 06.12.2016].

European Commission (2016e): Industrial accidents, (http://ec.europa.eu/environment/seveso/legislation.htm), [last access 16.12.2016].

European Council (2000): The Lisbon Special European Council: Towards a Europe of Innovation and Knowledge, (http://eur-lex.europa.eu/legal-content/EN/TXT/HTML/?uri=URISERV:c10241&qid=1425827043877&from=EN), [last access 24.11.2016].

European Parliament (2008a): Governance and Partnership in Regional Policy. Ad-hoc note of DG For Internal Policies of the Union, Policy Department B: Structural and Cohesion Policy.

European Parliament (2008b): European Parliament Resolution of 21 October 2008 on governance and partnership at national and regional levels and a basis for projects in the sphere of regional policy, (http://www.europarl.europa.eu/sides/getDoc.do?pubRef=-//EP//TEXT+TA+P6-TA-2008-0492+0+DOC+XML+V0//EN), [last access 10.12.2016].

European Parliament (2012): The Partnership Contracts – how to implement multi-level governance and to guarantee the flexibility of Cohesion Policy. DG For Internal Policies of the Union, Policy Department: Structural and Cohesion Policy.

European Parliament (2014): An Assessment of Multilevel Governance in Cohesion Policy 2007-2013. Brussels: DG for Internal Policies, Policy Department B: Structural and Cohesion Policies.

European Parliament (2016): The "early warning mechanism", (http://www.europarl.europa.eu/webnp/cms/pid/1873), [last access 21.11.2016].

Fikentscher, Rüdiger (2002): Wahljahr 2002 – die SPD im Wettbewerb um Zustimmung. In: Wolf, Jürgen/Rannenberg, Jens/Mattfeld, Harald/Giebel, Heiner (eds.): Jahrbuch für Politik und Gesellschaft in Sachsen-Anhalt 2002. Halle: Mitteldeutscher Verlag, 123-132.

Fitjar, Rune Dahl (2010): The Rise of Regionalism – Causes of regional mobilization in Western Europe. Abington: Routledge.

Franke, Yvonne (2017): Umweltpolitik in Sachsen-Anhalt: ein vernachlässigtes Politikfeld mit großen Potentialen. In: Träger, Hendrik/Priebus, Sonja (Hrsg.): Politik und Regieren in Sachsen-Anhalt. Wiesbaden: Springer Verlag, 387-400.

Gabriel, Matthias (2003): Die Jahrhundertflut in Bitterfeld. Der ChemiePark – die Landzunge im Hochwasser. In: Wolf, Jürgen/Rannenberg, Jens/Mattfeld, Harald/Giebel, Heiner (eds.): Jahrbuch für Politik und Gesellschaft in Sachsen-Anhalt 2003. Halle: Mitteldeutscher Verlag, 225-229.

Gamble, Andrew (2004): Foreword. In: Bache, Ian/Flinders, Matthew V. (eds.): Multi-level Governance. Oxford: Oxford University Press, v-vii.

Goetz, Klaus (2006): Europäisierung der öffentlichen Verwaltung – oder europäische Verwaltung? In: Bogumil, Jörg/Werner, Jan/Nullmeier, Frank (eds.): Politik und Verwaltung. Wiesbaden: VS Verlag für Sozialwissenschaften, 472-490.

Grünert, Gerard MdL/Popp, Karsten (2009): Gemeindegebietsreform in Sachsen-Anhalt. Arbeitspapier für die Fraktionssitzung am 06. Oktober 2009.

Haseloff, Reiner (2016): Zu meiner Person, (http://reiner-haseloff.de/zu-meiner-person/), [last access 15.12.2016].

Haverland, Markus (2003): The Impact of Europeanization on Environmental Policies. In: Featherstone, Kevin/Radaelli, Claudio M. (eds.): The Politics of Europeanization. Oxford: Oxford University, 203-222.

Heimpold, Gerhard/Rosenfeld Martin T. W. (2003): Wirtschaftliche Indikatoren für Sachsen-Anhalt – welche Ausgangsbedingungen stellen sich für die Wirtschaftspolitik der neuen Landesregierung? In: Wolf, Jürgen/Rannenberg, Jens/Mattfeld, Harald/Giebel, Heiner (Hrsg.): Jahrbuch für Politik und Gesellschaft in Sachsen-Anhalt 2003. Halle: mdv Mitteldeutscher Verlag GmbH, 24-46.

Heller, Norbert (2005): Mechanismen der EFRE Programmierung/Schwerpunktsetzung der Kommission für das Thema Informationsgesellschaft. In: Ministerium für Wirtschaft und Arbeit des Landes Sachsen-Anhalt (Hrsg.): Europäische Strukturfonds Sachsen-Anhalt 2000-2006. Konferenzbericht 21. April 2005. Der Einsatz von Strukturfondsmitteln auf dem Gebiet der Informationsgesellschaft in Sachsen-Anhalt, 29.

Holeschovky, Christine (2012): Das Zusammenwirken der deutschen Ländervertretungen in Brüssel am Beispiel der Länderarbeiterkreise. In: Renzsch, Wolfgang/Wobben, Thomas (Hrsg.): 20 Jahre ostdeutsche Landesvertretungen in Brüssel. Eine Bilanz der Interessenvertretung der Länder aus unterschiedlichen Blickwinkeln. Baden-Baden: Nomos, 86-92.

Holtmann, Everhard/ Boll, Bernhard (1997): Sachsen-Anhalt: Eine politische Landeskunde. Opladen: Leske + Budrich.

Hooghe, Liesbet (1995): Subnational Mobilization in the European Union. In: West European Politics, Vol. 18, Issue 3, 175-198.

Hooghe, Liesbet (1996): Building a Europe with the Regions: The Changing Role of the European Commission. In: Hooghe, Liesbet (ed.): Cohesion policy and European integration: Building multi-level governance. New York: Oxford University Press, 89-128.

Hooghe, Liesbet/et al. (2016): Measuring Regional Authority. A Postfunctionalist Theory of Governance, Volume I. Oxford: Oxford University Press.

Hooghe, Liesbet/Marks, Gary (2010): Types of Multilevel Governance. In: Enderlein, Hendrik/Wälti, Sonja/Zürn, Michael (eds.): Handbook on Multilevel Governance. Cheltenham: Edward Edgar, 17-31.

Höppner, Reinhard (2002): Europapolitische Herausforderungen aus der Sicht Sachsen-Anhalts. In: Wolf, Jürgen/Rannenberg, Jens/Mattfeld, Harald/Giebel, Heiner (Hrsg.): Jahrbuch für Politik und Gesellschaft in Sachsen-Anhalt 2002. Halle: Mitteldeutscher Verlag, 160-168.

Hrbek, Rudolf (2010): Parliaments in EU Multi-Level Governance. In: Hrbek, Rudolf (ed.): Legislatures in Federal Systems and multi-level Governance. Baden-Baden: Nomos, 136-150.

Institut für Strukturpolitik und Wirtschaftsförderung gGmbH (2001): Strategiedialog Chemie ein Jahr ergebnisorientierter Zusammenarbeit zwischen Wirtschaft und Politik, Nr. 32, (http://isw-institut.de/doku-publikation/isw%20Report_32.pdf), [last access 01.12.2016].

Institut für Strukturpolitik und Wirtschaftsförderung gGmbH (2003): Halbzeitbewertung zum Einsatz der EU-Strukturfonds gemäß Operationellem Programm 2000-2006 des Landes Sachsen-Anhalt.

Institut für Strukturpolitik und Wirtschaftsförderung gGmbH (2009): Saxony-Anhalt – Land of Chemistry, Chemistry and plastics processing industry in Saxony-Anhalt.

Institut für Strukturpolitik und Wirtschaftsförderung gGmbH (2013): The Future Cluster Chemistry/Plastics Central Germany (Clusteratlas 2013), (http://www.cluster-chemie-kunststoffe.de/Download), [last access 20.04.2017].

Investment and Marketing Corporation Saxony-Anhalt (2016): Saxony-Anhalt – Highlights 2016/2017, (http://www.saxony-anhalt-tourism.eu/fileadmin/bilder/Broschueren/ENGLISCH/Sachsen-Anhalt_Highlights_2016_2017_englisch.pdf), [last access 14.12.2016].

IQ-NET (2016): IQ-NET Homepage, (http://www.eprc.strath.ac.uk/iqnet/), [last access 28.11.2016].

Jeffery, Charlie (2000): Sub-national Mobilization and European Integration: Does it make any difference? In: Journal of Common Market Studies, Vol. 38, Issue 1, 1-23.

Jeffery, Charlie (2001): Farewell the third level? The German Länder and the European Policy Process. In Jeffery, Charlie (ed.): The regional dimension of the European Union. Towards a third level in Europe? London: Frank Cass (reprint from 1997), 56-75.

Jessop, Bob (2004): Multi-level Governance and Multi-level Metagovernance. In: Bache, Ian/ Flinders, Matthew V. (eds.): Multi-level Governance. Oxford: Oxford University Press, 49-74.

Jones, Barry (1995): Conclusions. In: Jones, Barry/Keating, Michael (eds.): The European Union and the Regions. Oxford: Clarendon Press, 289-296.

Kabinetssvorlage Sachsen-Anhalt (2013): Aufstellung des Regierungsentwurfes für den Haushaltsplan 2014 und der Mittelfristigen Finanzplanung 2013 bis 2017.
Keating, Michael (1995): Europeanism and Regionalism. In: Jones, Barry/Keating, Michael (eds.): The European Union and the Regions. Oxford: Clarendon Press, 1-22.
Keating, Michael (1998): The new regionalism in Western Europe: territorial restructuring and political change. Cheltenham: Edward Edgar Publishing Ltd.
Kjær, Anne Mette (2010): Guvernanța (Governance), translated into Romanian by Natalia Cugleșan. Cluj-Napoca: CA Publishing (Cambridge: Polity Press 2004).
Knodt, Michèle (1998): Tiefenwirkung europäischer Politik. Eigensinn oder Anpassung regionalen Regierens? Baden-Baden: Nomos.
Knodt, Michèle (2000): Europäisierung à la Sinatra: Deutsche Länder im europäischen Mehrebenensystem. In: Knodt, Michèle/Kohler-Koch, Beate (Hrsg.): Deutschland zwischen Europäisierung und Selbstbehauptung. Mannheimer Jahrbuch zur Europäischen Sozialforschung 2000, Band 5. Frankfurt/M, N.Y.: Campus, 237-264.
Knodt, Michèle/Corcaci, Andreas (2012): Europäische Integration – Anleitung zur theoriegeleiteten Analyse. Stuttgart: UTB Stuttgart.
Knodt, Michèle/Große-Hüttmann, Martin (2006): Der Multi-level Governance Ansatz. In: Bieling, Hans-Jürgen/Lerch, Monika (eds.): Theorien der europäischen Integration. Wiesbaden: VS Verlag für Sozialwissenschaften, 2. Auflage, 223-248.
Kohler-Koch, Beate (1998): Interaktive Politik in Europa: Regionen im Netzwerk der Integration. Opladen: Leske+Budrich.
Kohler-Koch, Beate (2009): German Governance Research: Advanced but Monodisciplinary. In: Kohler-Koch, Beate/Larat, Fabrice (eds.): European Multi-level Governance. Contrasting Images in National Research. Cheltenham Northampton: Edward Elgar, 61-82.
Kohler-Koch, Beate/Rittberger, Berthold (2009): A Futile Quest for Coherence: The Many Frames of EU Governance. In: Kohler-Koch, Beate/Larat, Fabrice (eds.): European multi-level governance: Contrasting images in national research. Cheltenham Nordhampton: Edward Edgar, 3-18.
Krause-Heiber, Ulrich (2005): Europäische Strukturfonds und Lissabon – Die Rolle von Wissenschaft und Forschung. In: Ministerium für Wirtschaft und Arbeit des Landes Sachsen-Anhalt (ed.): Europäische Strukturfonds Sachsen-Anhalt 2000-2006. Konferenzbericht 21. April 2005. Der Einsatz

von Strukturfondsmitteln auf dem Gebiet der Informationsgesellschaft in Sachsen-Anhalt, 22.

Kregel, Bernd (2002): Strukturreform an Haupt und Gliedern. In: Wolf, Jürgen/Rannenberg, Jens/Mattfeld, Harald/Giebel, Heiner (Hrsg.): Jahrbuch für Politik und Gesellschaft in Sachsen-Anhalt 2002. Halle: Mitteldeutscher Verlag, 243-256.

Kregel, Bernd (2006): Kommunen zwischen Eigenverantwortung und Staatsauftrag. In: Holtmann, Everhard (Hrsg.): Landespolitik in Sachsen-Anhalt: Ein Handbuch. Halle: Mitteldeutscher Verlag, 126-145.

Landesregierung Sachsen-Anhalt (2004): Positionspapier des Landes Sachsen-Anhalt zum Dritten Bericht der Europäischen Kommission über wirtschaftlichen und sozialen Zusammenhalt.

Landesregierung Sachsen-Anhalt (2010a): Fondsübergreifende Halbbilanz der EU-Fonds in Sachsen-Anhalt. Strategiebericht 2010.

Landesregierung Sachsen-Anhalt (2010b): Zusammenarbeit von Landesregierung und Landtag in EU-Angelegenheiten: Bericht der Landesregierung gemäß Beschluss des Landtages vom 10. September 2010.

Landesregierung Sachsen-Anhalt (2011): Sachsen-Anhalt auf gutem Weg – Bilanz der Landesregierung 2006-2011.

Landesregierung Sachsen-Anhalt (2012): Internationalisierungs- und Europastrategie für Sachsen-Anhalt.

Landesvertretung Sachsen-Anhalt bei der Europäischen Union (1999-2016): EU-Wochenspiegel.

Landtag Sachsen-Anhalt (2002): Vereinbarung zwischen der Christlich Demokratischen Union Deutschlands Landesverband Sachsen-Anhalt und der Freien Demokratischen Partei Landesverband Sachsen-Anhalt über die Bildung einer Regierungskoalition für die 4. Legislaturperiode des Landtags Sachsen-Anhalt.

Landtag Sachsen-Anhalt (2003): EU-Strukturpolitik nach 2006. Beschluss des Landtages von Sachsen-Anhalt. Drucksache 4/19/721.

Landtag Sachsen-Anhalt (2004): Zukunft und Perspektive für die EU-Förderpolitik 2007 bis 2013. Beschluss des Landtages von Sachsen-Anhalt. Drucksache 4/43/1694 B.

Landtag Sachsen-Anhalt (2005a): Strategische Leitlinien, Konzepte und Schwerpunkte der Landesregierung zur EU-Förderpolitik 2007-2013. Beschluss des Landtages von Sachsen-Anhalt. Drucksache 4/60/2180B.

Landtag Sachsen-Anhalt (2005b): Stenografischer Bericht 60. Sitzung am Freitag, dem 27. Mai 2005, in Magdeburg. Plenarprotokoll 4/60.

Landtag Sachsen-Anhalt (2006): Vereinbarung zwischen der Christlich Demokratischen Union Deutschlands Landesverband Sachsen-Anhalt und der Sozialdemokratischen Partei Deutschlands Landesverband Sachsen-

Anhalt über die Bildung einer Koalition in der fünften Legislaturperiode des Landtags von Sachsen-Anhalt 2006 bis 2011: Sachsen-Anhalt Land mit Zukunft.
Landtag Sachsen-Anhalt (2009): Geschäftsordnung des Landestages Sachsen-Anhalt.
Landtag Sachsen-Anhalt (2010): Unterrichtung – Innovationsprogramm Sachsen-Anhalt 2010/2011. Drucksache 5/2965.
Landtag Sachsen-Anhalt (2011a): Vereinbarung zwischen der Christlich Demokratischen Union Deutschlands Landesverband Sachsen-Anhalt und der Sozialdemokratischen Partei Deutschlands Landesverband Sachsen-Anhalt über die Bildung einer Koalition in der sechsten Legislaturperiode des Landtags von Sachsen-Anhalt 2011 bis 2016: Sachsen-Anhalt geht seinen Weg – Wachstum Gerechtigkeit Nachhaltigkeit.
Landtag Sachsen-Anhalt (2011b): Antrag Fraktionen CDU und SPD – Neu Programmierung der Strukturfonds in der Förderperiode 2014 bis 2020. Drucksache 6/532.
Landtag Sachsen-Anhalt (2011c): Änderungsantrag Fraktion DIE LINKE – Neu Programmierung der Strukturfonds in der Förderperiode 2014 bis 2020. Drucksache 6/551.
Landtag Sachsen-Anhalt (2011d): Antrag BÜNDNIS 90/DIE GRÜNEN – Neu-Programmierung der Strukturfonds in der Förderperiode 2014 bis 2020. Drucksache 6/559.
Landtag Sachsen-Anhalt (2012a): Beschlussempfehlung – Ausschuss für Bundes- und Europaangelegenheiten sowie Medien – Neu-Programmierung der Strukturfonds in der Förderperiode 2014 bis 2020. Drucksache 6/814.
Landtag Sachsen-Anhalt (2012b): Beschluss des Landtages – Neu-Programmierung der Strukturfonds in der Förderperiode 2014 bis 2020. Drucksache 6/852.
Landtag Sachsen-Anhalt (2012c): Unterrichtung – Programmierung der EU-Förderperiode 2014 bis 2020; Zielstellungen sowie Verfahrensschritte und zeitliche Planung. Drucksache 6/1062.
Landtag Sachsen-Anhalt (2012d): Plenarprotokoll 6/31 – Stenographischer Bericht der 31. Sitzung vom 21.09.2012.
Loughlin, John (2011): Federal and local government institutions. In: Caramani, Daniele (ed.): Comparative Politics. Oxford: Oxford University Press, second edition, 198-215.
Löwe, Volker (2012): Die Funktion der Länderbüros als Bestandteil der Europapolitik der Länder. In: Renzsch, Wolfgang/Wobben, Thomas (Hrsg.): 20 Jahre ostdeutsche Landesvertretungen in Brüssel. Eine Bilanz der In-

teressenvertretung der Länder aus unterschiedlichen Blickwinkeln. Baden-Baden: Nomos, 65-71.
Magone, Jose M. (2011): Contemporany European politics: A comparative introduction. London: Routledge.
Managing Authority of European Structural Funds of Saxony-Anhalt (2005): European Structural Funds 2000-2006 Competititve Regions – Shaping Best Practice III. Magdeburg.
Marks, Gary (1993): Structural Policy and Multilevel Governance in the EC. In: Cafruny, Alan/Rosenthal, Glenda (eds.): The State and the European Community. New York: Lynne Rinner, 391-410.
Marks, Gary (1996): Competencies, Cracks and Conflicts: Regional Mobilization in the European Union. In: Marks, Gary/Schrarpf, Fritz/Schmitter, Phillipe/Streeck, Wolfgang (eds.): Governance in the European Union. London: Sage Publications, 40-63.
Marks, Gary/Hooghe, Liesbet (2001): Multilevel Governance and European Integration. Boulder: Rowman and Littlefield.
Marks, Gary/Hooghe, Liesbet/Blank, Kermit (1996): European integration from the 1980s: State-centric v. multi-level governance. In: Journal of Common Market Studies, Vol. 34, Issue 3, 341-378.
Marks, Gary/Hooghe, Liesbet/Schakel, Arjan H. (2008): Patterns of Regional Authority. In: Regional and Federal Studies, Vol. 18, Issues 2-3, 167-181.
Mayntz, Renate (2004): Governance im modernen Staat. In: Benz, Arthur (ed.): Regieren in komplexen Regelsystemen. Eine Einführung. Wiesbaden: Verlag für Sozialwissenschaften, 65-75.
Mayntz, Renate/Scharpf, F.W. (1995): Steuerung und Selbstorgnization in staatsnahen Sektoren. In: Mayntz, Renate/Scharpf, F.W. (eds.): Gesellschaftliche Selbstregulierung und politische Steuerung. Frankfurt/New York: Campus Verlag, 9-38.
Ministerium der Finanzen Sachsen-Anhalt (2005): Europäische Strukturfonds Sachsen-Anhalt 2000-2006.
Ministerium für Wirtschaft und Arbeit des Landes Sachsen-Anhalt (2005): Europäische Strukturfonds Sachsen-Anhalt 2000-2006. Konferenzbericht 21. April 2005. Der Einsatz von Structurfondsmitteln auf dem Gebiet der Informationsgesellschaft in Sachsen-Anhalt.
Ministerium für Wirtschaft und Arbeit Sachsen-Anhalt (2010): 300 Euro pro Monat 9 Studenten/Stiftungsprofessur an HS Merseburg. Erstmal Stipendien der Zukunftsstiftung überreicht/Haseloff: „Bildung schafft Zukunft". Pressemitteilung Nr. 235/2010.
Ministerium für Wissenschaft und Wirtschaft des Landes Sachsen-Anhalt (2014): Regionale Innovationsstrategie Sachsen-Anhalt 2014-2020.

Müller, Henrike/Mauren, Norbert (2002): Regional parliaments and good governance in Europe: New Communication Technologies for Enhancing Social Representation and European Public Spheres. CEuS Working Paper Nr. 9.

Nagel, Klaus-Jürgen (2007): Still Mid-term Elections? On the 2006 Eletions in Baden-Württemberg, Rhineland-Palatine and Saxony-Anhalt. In: Regional and Federal Studies, Vol. 17, Nr. 3, 375-383.

Niemann, Arne/Schmitter, Phillipe C. (2009): Neofunctionalism. In: Wiener, Antje/Diez, Thomas (eds.): European Integration Theory. Oxford: Oxford University Press, second edition, 45-66.

Official Journal of the European Communities (2001), White Paper on European Governance, COM (2001) 428 final, (http://eur-lex.europa.eu/legal-content/EN/TXT/?qid=1402389136979&uri=CELEX:52001DC0428), [last access 04.11.2016].

Official Journal of the European Union (2006): Council Regulation (EC) No 1083/2006 of 11 July 2006 laying down general provisions on the European Regional Development Fund, the European Social Fund and the Cohesion Fund and repealing Regulation (EC) No 1260/1999.

Official Journal of the European Union (2013): Regulation (EU) No 1303/2013 of the European Parliament and of the Council of 17 December 2013 laying down common provisions on the European Regional Development Fund, the European Social Fund and the Cohesion Fund, the European Agricultural Fund for Rural Development and the European Maritime and Fisheries Fund and laying down general provisions on the European Regional Development Fund, the European Social Fund and the Cohesion Fund and the European Maritime and Fisheries Fund and repealing Council Regulation (EC) No 1083/2006.

Olsen, Johan P. (2002): The many faces of Europeanization. In: Journal of Common Market Studies, Vol. 40, Issue 5, 921-952.

Panara, Carlos (2011): Germany: A Cooperative Solution to the Challenge of the European Integration. In: Panara, Carlos/De Becker, Alexander (eds.): The Role of the Regions in EU Governance. Berlin: Springer Verlag, 133-156.

Peters, B. Guy/Pierre, Jon (2009): Governance Approaches. In: Wiener, Antje/Diez, Thomas (eds.): European Integration Theory. Oxford: Oxford University Press, second edition, 91-104.

Piattoni, Simona (2009): The Committee of the Regions' White Paper on Multilevel Governance: some reflections. In: Committee of the Regions: The Cahiers of the CoR – Vers une gouvernance à plusieurs niveaux en Europe? Towards Multi-level Governance in Europe?, Vol. I, 67-73.

Piattoni, Simona (2010): The Theory of Multi-Level Governance. Conceptual, Empirical and Normative Challenges. Oxford: Oxford University Press.

Pieper, Cornelia (2002): FDP-Kompetenz für Sachsen-Anhalt – damit hier endlich was passiert. In: Wolf, Jürgen/Rannenberg, Jens/Mattfeld, Harald/Giebel, Heiner (eds.): Jahrbuch für Politik und Gesellschaft in Sachsen-Anhalt 2002. Halle: Mitteldeutscher Verlag, 139-144.

Pitschel, Diana/Bauer, Michael W. (2009): Subnational governance Approaches on the Rise – Reviewing a Decade of Eastern European Regionalization Research. In: Regional and Federal Studies, Vol. 19, Nr. 3, 327-347.

Polverari, L./Bachlter, J. with Davies, S./Kah, S./Mendez, C./Michie, R./Vironen, H. (2014): Balance of Competences Cohesion Review: Literature Review on EU Cohesion Policy. Final Report to the UK Department for Business, Innovation and Skills, (https://www.gov.uk/government/uploads/system/uploads/attachment_dat a/file/336227/bis_14_988_BALANCE_OF_COMPETENCES_COHESI ON_REVIEW_2.pdf), [last access 08.12.2016].

Püchel, Manfred (2002): Die Gemeindereform in Sachsen-Anhalt. In: Wolf, Jürgen/Rannenberg, Jens/Mattfeld, Harald/Giebel, Heiner (eds.): Jahrbuch für Politik und Gesellschaft in Sachsen-Anhalt 2002. Halle: Mitteldeutscher Verlag, 237-242.

Putz, Sebastian (2006): Die Landesregierung als Zentrum politischer Steuerung. In: Holtmann, Everhard (Hg.): Landespolitik in Sachsen-Anhalt: Ein Handbuch. Halle: Mitteldeutscher Verlag, 80-103.

Rannenberg, Jens/ Wolf, Jürgen (2002): Sachsen-Anhalt und die Erweiterung der EU. In: Wolf, Jürgen/Rannenberg, Jens/Mattfeld, Harald/Giebel, Heiner (eds.): Jahrbuch für Politik und Gesellschaft in Sachsen-Anhalt 2002. Halle: Mitteldeutscher Verlag, 145-152.

Reich, Andreas (2004): Verfassung des Landes Sachsen-Anhalt: Kommentar. Bad Honnef: Verlag Boch, 2. völlig neu bearbeitete Fassung.

Renzsch, Wolfgang (2002): Solidarpakt II: Perspektiven für Sachsen-Anhalt in einem vereinigenden Europa. In: Wolf, Jürgen/ Ranennberg, Jens/Mattfeld, Harald/Heiner, Giebel (Hrsg.): Jahrbuch für Politik und Gesellschaft in Sachsen-Anhalt 2002. Halle: Mitteldeutscher Verlag, 177-187.

Renzsch, Wolfgang (2003): Wahlen in Sachsen-Anhalt in 2002. In: Wolf, Jürgen/Rannenberg, Jens/Mattfeld, Harald/Giebel, Heiner (Hrsg.): Jahrbuch für Politik und Gesellschaft in Sachsen-Anhalt 2003. Halle: Mitteldeutscher Verlag, 61-67.

Renzsch, Wolfgang (2012): Vertretung von Landesinteressen im europäichen Merhebenensystem. In: Renzsch, Wolfgang/Wobben, Thomas (Hrsg.): 20 Jahre ostdeutsche Landesvertretungen in Brüssel. Eine Bilanz der Interessenvertretung der Länder aus unterschiedlichen Blickwinkeln. Baden-Baden: Nomos, 117-128.

Renzsch, Wolfgang (2017): Der Haushalt des Landes Sachsen-Anhalt: „Freiheit statt Schuldenspirale". In: Träger, Hendrik/Priebus, Sonja (Hrsg.): Politik und Regieren in Sachsen-Anhalt. Wiesbaden: Springer Verlag, 259-269.

Rheinland-Pfalz (2010): Ergebnisse der 52. Europaministerkonferenz der Länder am 8. Dezember 2010 in Berlin.

Robra, Rainer (2012): EU-Kohäsionspolitik – ein Schwerpunkt ostdeutscher Europapolitik. In: Renzsch, Wolfgang/Wobben, Thomas (Hrsg.): 20 Jahre ostdeutsche Landesvertretungen in Brüssel. Eine Bilanz der Interessenvertretung der Länder aus unterschiedlichen Blickwinkeln. Baden-Baden: Nomos, 26-30.

Rowe, Carolyn (2011): Regional representation in the European Union – Between Diplomacy and Interest Representation. Hampshire: Palgrave Macmillan.

Sachsen-Anhalt (2005): Fortschrittsbericht „Aufbau Ost" 2005 des Landes Sachsen-Anhalt.

Sachsen-Anhalt (2010): Landtag Sachsen-Anhalt: Modernes Parlament mit Geschichte. Halle: Mitteldeutscher Verlag.

Sachsen-Anhalt (2016a): Vertretung des Landes Sachsen-Anhalt beim Bund, (http://www.lv.sachsen-anhalt.de/nc/landesvertretung/), [last access 15.11.2016].

Sachsen-Anhalt (2016b): Staatssekretär Dr. Michael Schneider, (http://www.lv.sachsen-anhalt.de/nc/landesvertretung/staatssekretaer/), [last access 15.11.2016].

Sachsen-Anhalt (2016c): Aufgabenbereiche der Europapolitik, (http://www.europa.sachsen-anhalt.de/europapolitik/aufgabenbereiche-der-europapolitik/), [last access 15.11.2016].

Sachsen-Anhalt (2016d): Landesvertretung in Brüssel, (http://www.europa.sachsen-anhalt.de/europapolitik/landesvertretung-in-bruessel/), [last access 16.11.2016].

Sachsen-Anhalt (2016e): Chemical and Plastics Industry, (http://www.invest-in-saxony-anhalt.com/chemical-and-plastics-industry), [last access 16.11.2016].

Sachsen-Anhalt Ministerium für Landesentwicklung und Verkehr/ Ministerium für Wirtschaft und Arbeit (2008): INTERREG B- and C-Projects in Saxony-Anhalt. Transnational and interregional cooperation.

Sachsen-Anhalt Online-Portal (2014): Regierungspolitik, (http://www.sachsen-anhalt.de/startseite/landesregierung/schwerpunkte-regierungsarbeit/), [last access 27.11.2014].

Sagan, Iwona/Halkier, Henrik (2005): Regional Contestations: Conclusions. In: Sagan, Iwona/Halkier, Henrik (eds.): Regionalism contested: institutions, society and governance. Farnham England: Ashgate, 265-272.

Sălăgeanu, Romana (2014a): The European Negotiations for the 2014-2020 Multi-annual Financial Framework – a State-Centric vs. Multi-level Governance Reflection. In: Studia Europaea, Studia Universitatis Babeș-Bolyai, Vol. 1, 177-193.

Sălăgeanu, Romana (2014b): The European Dimension of Sub-national Regionalism in the European Union. In: Studia Europaea, Studia Universitatis Babeș-Bolyai, Vol. 2, 117-129.

Sălăgeanu, Romana (2014c): Compiling European policy from a regional perspective – the innovation of transition regions within the Regional Policy of the EU – evidence from Saxony-Anhalt. In: Czech Journal of Political Science, Nr. 2, 131-150.

Sălăgeanu, Romana (2016): Regional implementation of Multi-level Governance Type I – the European Cohesion Policy. In: Federal Governance, Vol. 13, Nr. 1, 56-67.

Schaal, Dirk (2005): Die Modernisierung der mitteldeutschen Landwirtschaft im 19. Jahrhundert. In Tulner, Matthias (Hrsg.): Sachsen-Anhalt: Geschichte und Geschichten. Anderbeck: Anderbeck-Verlag, Nr. 2, 20-31.

Scharpf, Fritz W. (1997): Balancing positive and negative Integration: The Regulatory Options for Europe, Max Plank Institute for the Study of Societies, (http://www.mpi-fg-koeln.mpg.de/pu/workpap/wp97-8/wp97-8.html), [last access 1.12.2016].

Schieren, Stefan (2000): Fünf Jahre Magdeburger Modell – Eine zwiespältige Bilanz. In: Rannenberg, Jens/Mattfeld, Harald/Giebel, Heiner (eds.): Jahrbuch für Politik und Gesellschaft in Sachsen-Anhalt 2000 – „Geht uns die Luft aus? – Perspektiven für das Land". Halle: Mitteldeutscher Verlag GmbH, 29-40.

Schlangen, Kareen (2010): Regionalmanagement. Ein Governance-Konzept zur Steuerung regionaler Akteure. Hamburg: Kovač.

Schlüter, Karen (2017): Wirtschafts- und Innovationspolitik in Sachsen-Anhalt: S[4] – Smart Specialisation Strategy in Sachsen-Anhalt? In: Träger, Hendrik/Priebus, Sonja (Hrsg.): Politik und Regieren in Sachsen-Anhalt. Wiesbaden: Springer Verlag, 355-375.

Schmidt, Andrea (2002): New Governance – Politikverpflechtung am Beispiel europäischer Vorfeldarbeit. In: Sachsen-Anhalt: Europabrief, Nr. 10.

Schmidt, Vivian (2003): European Integration as Regional Variant of Globalization: The Challenges to National Democracy. In: Kathenhusen, Ines/Lamping, Wolfram (eds.): Demokratien in Europa. Der Einfluss der europäischen Integration auf Institutionenwandel und neue Konturen des demokratischen Verfassungsstaates. Opladen: Leske+Budrich, 205-228.

Schmitt-Egner, Peter (2005): Handbuch zur Europäischen Regionalismusforschung. Wiesbaden: VS Verlag für Sozialwissenschaften.

Schmuck, Otto (2009): Die Europaministerkonferenz der deutschen Länder – Strukturen, Aufgaben, Themenschwerpunkte. In: Europäisches Zentrum für Föderalismusforschung (Hrsg.): Jahrbuch des Föderalismus 2009. Föderalismus, Subsidiarität und Regionen in Europa. Baden-Baden: Nomos Verlagsgesellschaft, 489-502.

Schnapp, Kai-Uwe/Burchardt, Susann (2006): Politische Parteien in Sachsen-Anhalt. In Holtmann, Everhard (Hg.): Landespolitik in Sachsen-Anhalt: Ein Handbuch. Halle: Mitteldeutscher Verlag, 179-201.

Schneider, Michael (2009): The Increasing Importance of Territorial Governance to European Integration. In: Committee of the Regions: The Cahiers of the CoR – Vers une governance à plusieurs niveaux en Europe? Towards Multi-level Governance in Europe?, Vol. I, 37-39.

Schneider, Michael (2010): 5th Report on Economic, Social and Territorial Cohesion sets the course for a European Cohesion Policy after 2013, (http://web.cor.europa.eu/epp/News/Pages/10November2010.aspx#.Uhik Untqm51), [last access 15.12.2016].

Schnellhardt, Horst/Böge, Reimer (2012): Die Zusammenarbeit mit dem Europäischen Parlament. In: Renzsch, Wolfgang/Wobben, Thomas (Hrsg.): 20 Jahre ostdeutsche Landesvertretungen in Brüssel. Eine Bilanz der Interessenvertretung der Länder aus unterschiedlichen Blickwinkeln. Baden-Baden: Nomos, 150-157.

Sodupe, Kepa (1999): The European Union and Inter-regional cooperation. In: Aldecoa, Francisco/Keating, Michael (eds.): Paradiplomacy in Acttion. The foreign relations of subnational governments. London: Routledge, 58-81.

Staatskanzlei Sachsen-Anhalt (2003): Leipziger Konferenz "Die Zukunft der europäischen Kohäsionspolitik: Ministerpräsident Böhmer übergibt Erklärung von 13 europäischen Regionen an EU-Kommissar Barnier", Pressemitteilung Nr. 204/2003, (http://www.asp.sachsen-anhalt.de/presseapp/data/stk/2003/204_2003.htm), [last access 07.12.2016].

Staatskanzlei Sachsen-Anhalt (2005): Bilanz – Bericht der Landesregierung – Legislaturperiode 2002-2006.

Staatskanzlei Sachsen-Anhalt (2009): Europas Regionen stärken – Landesinteressen vertreten – Europawahl aktiv vorbereiten. Regierungserklärung des Europaministers des Landes Sachsen-Anhalt Rainer Robra am 20.02.2009.

Staatskanzlei Sachsen-Anhalt (2010): Der Beitrag Sachsen-Anhalts zur neuen EU-Strategie EUROPA 2020 – Sachsen-Anhalt – Hier ist Zukunft.

Staatskanzlei Sachsen-Anhalt (2011a): Arbeit schaffen, Wissen vermitteln, Verantwortung stärken. Regierungserklärung vom Ministerpräsident Dr. Reiner Haseloff, Pressemitteilung Nr. 260/2011, (www.asp.sachsen-anhalt.de/presseapp/data/stk/2011/260_2011_f271d073dbeff87c641fca88 b16256b6.htm), [last access 29.11.2016].

Staatskanzlei Sachsen-Anhalt (2011b): Regierungserklärung des Ministerpräsidenten des Landes Sachsen-Anhalt, Herrn Dr. Reiner Haseloff am 10. November 2011.

Staatskanzlei Sachsen-Anhalt (2012a): Landesregierung zieht Jahresbilanz/ Ministerpräsident Haseloff: Regierung auf festem Kurs: Koalitionsvertrag wird konsequent umgesetzt. Pressemitteilung Nr. 151/2012.

Staatskanzlei Sachsen-Anhalt (2012b): Ost-MPK in Köthen: Ostdeutsche Länder für stärkere Beachtung regionaler Aspekte in der Förderpolitik, Pressemitteilung Nr. 450/2012, (http://www.presse.sachsen-anhalt.de/index.php?&cmd=get&id=855926&identifier=b95bedd4f20036 b51aa0a43bc2226c52), [last access 15.12.2016].

Staatskanzlei Sachsen-Anhalt (2013a): Landesregierung zieht Halbzeit/Haseloff: Sachsen-Anhalt ist auf gutem Weg. Pressemitteilung Nr. 522/2013, (http://www.presse.sachsen-anhalt.de/index.php?&cmd=get&id=862649&identifier=760e8236db3ab1 01c744e6d815334b36), [last access 29.11.2016].

Staatskanzlei Sachsen-Anhalt (2013b): Erweiterungsinvestition von Puralube in Elsteraue/Ministerpräsident Haseloff betont Bedeutung der Investorenpflege, Pressemitteilung Nr. 241/2013, (www.presse.sachsen-anhalt.de/index.php?&cmd=get&id=860085&identifier=518cdf71c7a6b2 7d4e921b8769487f0e), [last access 29.11.2016].

Staatskanzlei Sachsen-Anhalt (2015a): Bilanz der Landesregierung Sachsen-Anhalt. Legislaturperiode 2011-2016.

Staatskanzlei Sachsen-Anhalt (2015b): Landesregierung präsentiert Bilanz ihrer Arbeit, Pressemitteilung Nr. 688/2015, (www.presse.sachsen-anhalt.de/index.php?cmd=get&id=874697&identifier=3c85988cb750518 efc813b589753c22e), [last access 30.11.2016].

Stahl, Gerhard/Degen, Manfred (2012): Die Rolle der deutschen Landesvertretungen für den Ausschuss der Regionen. In: Renzsch, Wolfgang/Wobben, Thomas (Hrsg.): 20 Jahre ostdeutsche Landesvertretungen in Brüssel. Eine Bilanz der Interessenvertretung der Länder aus unterschiedlichen Blickwinkeln. Baden-Baden: Nomos, 158-168.

Statistisches Amt Sachsen-Anhalt (2016): Gebietsinformationen und Wahlen, (http://www.statistik.sachsen-anhalt.de/wahlen/aktuell.html), [last access 28.11.2016].

Tatham, Michaël (2008): Going Solo: Direct Regional Representation in the European Union. In: Regional and Federal Studies, Vol. 18, Nr. 5, 493-515.

Tatham, Michaël (2010): 'With or Without You'? Revisiting territorial state-bypassing in EU interest representation. In: Journal of European Public Policy, Vol. 17, Nr. 1, 76-99.

Tatham, Michaël (2013): Paradiplomats against the State: Explaining Conflict in State and Substate Interest Representation in Brussels. In: Comparative Political Studies, Vol. 46, Nr. 1, 63-94.

Tatham, Michaël (2016): With, Without or Against the State? How European Regions Play the Brussels Game. Oxford: Oxford University Press.

Thierse, Wolfgang (2001): Von der Wiedervereinigung zur Neuvereinigung? In: Wolf, Jürgen/Rannenberg, Jens/Mattfeld, Harald/Giebel, Heiner (eds.): Jahrbuch für Politik und Gesellschaft in Sachsen-Anhalt 2001. Halle: Mitteldeutscher Verlag, 118-130.

Tömmel, Ingeborg/Verdun, Amy (2009): Innovative Governance in the European Union. In: Tömmel, Ingeborg/Verdun, Amy (eds.): Innovative Governance in the European Union – The Politics of Multilevel Policymaking. Boulder London: Lynne Rienner Publishers, 1-9.

Tricoire, André im Inteview (2000): Elf-Aquintaine in Sachsen-Anhalt. In: Wolf, Jürgen/Rannenberg, Jens/Mattfeld, Harald, Giebel, Heiner (Hrsg.): Jahrbuch für Politik und Gesellschaft in Sachsen-Anhalt 2000 – „Geht uns die Luft aus? – Perspektiven für das Land". Halle: mdv Mitteldeutscher Verlag, 125-130.

Tricoire, André/Wolf, Jürgen/Rannenberg, Jens (2000): Elf – a global player – ein Europäer – ein Sachsen-Anhalter. Wie zukunftsfähig ist das Paradepferd? In: Wolf, Jürgen/Rannenberg, Jens/Mattfeld, Harald, Giebel, Heiner (Hrsg.): Jahrbuch für Politik und Gesellschaft in Sachsen-Anhalt 2000 – „Geht uns die Luft aus? – Perspektiven für das Land". Halle: mdv Mitteldeutscher Verlag, 118-124.

Tullner, Mathias (2005): Die Landwirtschaft und die Herausbildung eines industriellen Wirtschaftsraums an Mittelelbe und unterer Saale im 19. Jahrhundert. In: Tullner, Mathias (ed.): Sachsen-Anhalt: Geschichte und Geschichten. Anderbeck: Anderbeck-Verlag, Nr. 2., 6-19.

Tullner, Mathias (2008): Geschichte Sachsen-Anhalts. München: Beck Verlag.

Tullner, Mathias (2012): Kleine Geschichte Sachsen-Anhalts. Von der Weimarer Republik bis zum Bundesland. Halle: Mitteldeutscher Verlag.

Van den Brande, Luc (2014): Multilevel Governance and Partnership – The Van den Brande Report. Prepared at the request of the Commissioner for Regional and Urban Policy Johannes Hahn, (https://portal.cor.europa.eu/mlgcharter/highlights/Documents/VandenBrandeReport_08102014.pdf); [last access 15.12.2016].

Wald, Andreas/Jensen, Dorothea (2007): Netzwerke. In: Benz, Arthur/Lütz. Sussane/Schimank, Uwe/Simonis, Georg (eds.): Handbook Governance – Theoretische Grundlagen und empirische Anwendungsfelder. Wiesbaden: VS Verlag für Sozialwissenschaften, 93-106.

Wälti, Sonja (2010): Multi-level Environmental Governance. In: Wälti, Sonja/Zürn, Michael (eds.): Handbook on Multi-level Governance. Cheltenham: Edward Elgar, 411-422.

Welz, Winfried (2004): Sachsen-Anhalt. In: Wehling, Hans-Georg (Hrsg.): Die deutschen Länder. Geschichte, Politik, Wirtschaft. Wiesbaden: VS Verlag für Sozialwissenschaften, 3. Auflage.

Wobben, Thomas (2004): Die Vertretung von Landesinteressen in Brüssel – die Arbeit des Verbindungsbüros des Landes Sachsen-Anhalt bei der EU. In: Renzsch, Wolfgang/Böhm, Wolfgang (eds.): Sachsen-Anhalt in Europa – Europa in Sachsen-Anhalt. Opladen: Leske+Budrich, 51-64.

Wobben, Thomas (2005): 3. Kongress der Chemieregionen stellt wichtige Weichen für das Netzwerk der Chemieregionen. In: Europabrief, Nr. 18, 8-10.

Wobben, Thomas (2007): Strategien der Vorfeldarbeit in Brüssel und der Interessenvertretung für Ostdeutschland am Beispiel der Chemieindustrie. In: Renzsch, Wolfgang (ed.): Perspektiven ostdeutscher Länder in der Europäischen Union (Schriftenreihe des Europäischen Zentrums für Föderalismusforschung). Baden-Baden: Nomos, 78-84.

Wobben, Thomas/Busse, Franziska (2012): Fakten und Zahlen über die Entwicklung der deutschen Länderbüros in den letzten 20 Jahren. In: Renszch, Wolfgang/Wobben, Thomas (Hrsg.): 20 Jahre ostdeutsche Landesvertretungen in Brüssel. Eine Bilanz der Interessenvertretung der Länder aus unterschiedlichen Blickwinkeln. Baden-Baden: Nomos, 58-64.

Wobben, Thomas/Heinke, Michael (2006): Europäisierung der Landespolitik: Sachsen-Anhalts Weg zu einer aktiven Interessenvertretung in Europa. In: Holtmann, Everhard (Hrsg.): Landespolitik in Sachsen-Anhalt: ein Handbuch. Halle: Mitteldeutscher Verlag, 221-246.

Wohland, Elisabeth (2008): Bundestag, Bundesrat und Landesparlamente im europäischen Integrationsprozess: Zur Auslegung von Art. 23 Grundgesetz unter Berücksichtigung des Verfassungsvertrags von Europa des Vertrags von Lissabon. Frankfurt a.M.: Peter Lang Verlag.

Wolf, Jürgen/Rannenberg, Jens (2000): Reeducation – Wie ein Standort wieder fit werden soll. DOW in Deutschland. In: Wolf, Jürgen/Rannenberg, Jens/Mattfeld, Harald, Giebel, Heiner (Hrsg.): Jahrbuch für Politik und Gesellschaft in Sachsen-Anhalt 2000 – „Geht uns die Luft aus? – Perspektiven für das Land". Halle: mdv Mitteldeutscher Verlag, 110-117.

Appendix 1: Extracts from the European Commission's White Paper on European Governance (2001)

The White Paper proposes opening up the policy-making process to get more people and organisations involved in shaping and delivering EU policy. It promotes greater openness, accountability and responsibility for all those involved. This should help people to see how Member States, by acting together within the Union, are able to tackle their concerns more effectively. [...]

Better involvement and more openness

No matter how EU policy is prepared and adopted, the way this is done must be more open and easier to follow and understand. The Commission will provide:

— up-to-date, on-line information on preparation of policy through all stages of decision-making.

There needs to be a stronger interaction with regional and local governments and civil society. Member States bear the principal responsibility for achieving this. But the Commission for its part will:

— establish a more systematic dialogue with representatives of regional and local governments through national and European associations at an early stage in shaping policy,

— bring greater flexibility into how Community legislation can be implemented in a way which take account of regional and local conditions,

— establish and publish minimum standards for consultation on EU policy,

— establish partnership arrangements going beyond the minimum standards in selected area committing the Commission to additional consultation in return for more guarantees of the openness and representatives of the organisations consulted" (Official Journal of the European Communities 2001: 2-3).

The Commission will:

— establish criteria to focus its work in investigating possible breaches of Community law,

— define the criteria for the creation of new regulatory agencies and the framework within which they should operate (Official Journal of the European Communities 2001: 4).

Democracy depends on people being able to take part in public debate. To do this, they must have access to reliable information on European issues and be able to scrutinise the policy process in its various stages. Major progress has been made in 2001 with the adoption of new rules giving citizens greater access to Community documents. But the institutions and Member States also need to communicate more actively with the general public on European issues. The communication policy of the Commission and the other institutions will promote efforts to deliver information at national and local level, where possible making use of networks, grassroots organisations and national, regional and local authorities. Information should be presented in a way adapted to local needs and concerns, and be available in all official languages if the Union is not to exclude a vast proportion of its population — a challenge which will become more acute in the context of enlargement (Official Journal of the European Communities 2001: 7-8).

The stronger involvement of regional and local authorities in the Union's policies also reflects both their growing responsibilities in some Member States and a stronger engagement of people and grass root organisations in local democracy. Yet the way in which the Union currently works does not allow for adequate interaction in a multi-level partnership; a partnership in which national governments involve their regions and cities fully in European policy-making. Regions and cities often feel that, in spite of their increased responsibility for implementing EU policies, their role as an elected and representative channel interacting with the public on EU policy is not exploited (Official Journal of the European Communities 2001: 9).

A complementary response at EU level is needed in three areas to build a better partnership across the various levels:

— involvement in policy shaping. At EU level, the Commission should ensure that regional and local knowledge and conditions are taken into account when developing policy proposals. For this purpose, it should organise a systematic dialogue with European and national associations of regional and local government, while respecting national constitutional and administrative arrangements. The Commission welcomes ongoing efforts to increase cooperation between those associations and the Committee of the Regions. Furthermore, exchange of staff and joint training between administrations at various levels would contribute to a better knowledge of each other's policy objectives, working methods and instruments,

— greater flexibility. Local conditions can make it difficult to establish one set of rules that covers the whole of the Union, without tying up the legislation in excessive complexity. There should be more flexibility in the means provided for implementing legislation and programmes with a strong territorial impact, provided the level playing field at the heart of the internal market can be maintained.

The Commission is also in favour of testing whether, while respecting the existing Treaty provisions, the implementation of certain EU policies could be better achieved by target-based, tripartite contracts. Such contracts should be between Member States, regions and localities designated by them for that purpose, and the Commission. Central government would play a key role in setting up such contracts and would remain responsible for their implementation. The contract would provide that the designated subnational authority in the Member States undertakes to implement identified actions in order to realise particular objectives defined in 'primary' legislation. The contract should include arrangements for monitoring. The approach concerns regulations or directives in fields where subnational public authorities are responsible for implementation within the national institutional or administrative system. The area of environmental policy might be a candidate for this pilot approach. Furthermore, the Commission has already committed itself to a more decentralised approach in future regional policy,

— overall policy coherence. The territorial impact of EU policies in areas such as transport, energy or environment should be addressed. These policies should form part of a coherent whole as stated in the EU's second cohesion report; there is a need to avoid a logic which is too sector-specific. In the same way, decisions taken at regional and local levels should be coherent with a broader set of principles that would underpin more sustainable and balanced territorial development within the Union.

The Commission intends to use the enhanced dialogue with Member States and their regions and cities to develop indicators to identify where coherence is needed. It will build on existing work, such as the European spatial development perspective adopted in 1999 by Ministers responsible for spatial planning and territorial development. This work of promoting better coherence between territorial development actions at different levels should also feed the review of policies in view of the sustainable development strategy (Official Journal of the European Communities 2001: 10).

The Commission will:

— establish from 2002 onwards a more systematic dialogue with European and national associations of regional and local government at an early stage of policy shaping,

— launch, from 2002 onwards, pilot 'target-based contracts' within one or more areas, as a more flexible means of ensuring implementation of EU policies.

The Committee of the Regions should:

— play a more proactive role in examining policy, for example through the preparation of exploratory reports in advance of Commission proposals,

— organise the exchange of best practice on how local and regional authorities are involved in the preparatory phase of European decision-making at national level,

— review the local and regional impact of certain directives, and report to the Commission by the end of 2002 on the possibilities for more flexible means of application. The Commission will then consider a more systematic approach to allow such flexibility for some parts of Community law.

The Member States should:

— examine how to improve the involvement of local and regional actors in EU policy-making,

— promote the use of contractual arrangements with their regions and localities (Official Journal of the European Communities 2001: 11).

European integration, new technologies, cultural changes and global interdependence have led to the creation of a tremendous variety of European and international networks, focused on specific objectives. Some have been supported by Community funding. These networks link businesses, communities, research centres, and regional and local authorities. They provide new foundations for integration within the Union and for building bridges to the applicant countries and to the world. They also act as multipliers spreading awareness of the EU and showing policies in action (Official Journal of the European Communities 2001: 14).

By making them more open and structuring better their relation with the institutions, networks could make a more effective contribution to EU policies. More specifically, regional and city networks that support transnational and cross-border cooperation, for example under the Structural Funds, are held back by the diverging administrative and legal conditions which apply to each individual participating authority (Official Journal of the European Communities 2001: 15).

Refocusing policies means that the Union should identify more clearly its longterm objectives. These may, with the overall objective of sustainable development, include improving human capital, knowledge and skills; strengthening both social cohesion and competitiveness; meeting the environmental challenge; supporting territorial diversity, and contributing to regional peace and stability. Improved focus will help to guide the reform of policies in preparation for a successful enlargement and ensure that expanding the Union does not lead to weakening or dilution of existing policies (Official Journal of the European Communities 2001: 24).

Appendix 2: Extracts from the European Parliament's Resolution on governance and partnership at a national, regional and project basis in the field of regional policy (2008)

The European Parliament [...]

5. Notes that transparent and clear procedures are factors of good governance and therefore calls on the Commission and the Member States, working together with regional and local authorities and taking due account of the suggestions of potential beneficiaries, to examine without delay – subject to a fixed timescale to be set by the Commission – how to simplify and rationalise procedures and how to divide more clearly responsibilities for implementing cohesion policy with a view to reducing the bureaucratic burden on the individuals and bodies involved; (European Parliament 2008b: 3-4).

7. Calls on the Commission to draw up and submit to it an assessment of the implementation of the partnership principle by the Member States in the context of the drafting of the National Strategic Reference Frameworks and the operational programmes, identifying the factors behind successful and unsuccessful governance, and also to examine in particular what account has been taken of opinions and proposals put forward by the partners in drawing up the operational programmes; [...]

9. Notes that the partnership process can work only with partners which have the necessary capabilities and resources, and calls on the managing authorities to contribute to the strengthening of those capabilities by providing the partners, at an early stage and in accordance with Article 11 of the General Regulation on Structural Funds with the same information as is available to the authorities and by allocating appropriate financial resources to technical assistance for implementing the partnership principle, for example training, building up social capital, and making their partnership activities more 'professional'; [...]

14. Recalls that partnership can contribute to effectiveness, efficiency, legitimacy and transparency in all the phases of Structural Fund programming and implementation and can increase commitment to and ownership of programme outputs; calls, therefore, on the Member States and managing authorities to involve the partners more closely at an early stage in all the phases of Structural Fund programming and implementation, with a view to making better use of their experience and knowledge; (European Parliament 2008b: 4-5).

18. Calls on the Member States to develop as quickly as possible the practical measures set out in the First Action Programme for the implementation of the Territorial Agenda of the European Union, in particular under heading 3.1, with a view to strengthening multi-level governance;

19. Proposes that governance should be included as a criterion under heading 4.1 of the First Action Programme for the implementation of the Territorial Agenda of the European Union, which calls on the European Spatial Planning Observation Network (ESPON) to develop new territorial cohesion indicators;

20. Takes the view that successful multi-level governance needs to be based on a 'bottom-up' approach; calls in this context upon local and regional authorities to investigate means to intensify their cooperation and contact with national governments as well as with the Commission, and recommends that regular meetings take place between officials from national, regional and local authorities;

21. Urges the Member States to decentralise the implementation of cohesion policy, so that the system of multi-level governance can work effectively and in keeping with the principles of partnership and subsidiarity, and calls on them to take the decentralisation measures required, at both legislative and budgetary levels;

22. Emphasises that regional and local administrative capacity as well as its stability and continuity constitute a precondition for the efficient absorption of funds and their impact maximisation; calls on Member States to ensure adequate administrative structures and human capital in terms of recruitment, remuneration, training, resources, procedures, transparency and accessibility; [...]

24. Urges the Member States to delegate responsibility for managing the Structural Funds to regional and local authorities on the basis of agreed terms and criteria which must be met by the authorities in question, with a view to involving them more closely and by means of formal coordination structures in the work of drafting and implementing the operational programmes, or, at the very least, to award them global grants; recommends that full use be made of the possibilities offered by these grants to enable regional and local authorities to play a full role in the multi-level governance arrangements; [...]

26. Calls on the Commission, while examining which NUTS level is most pertinent, to identify the area in which, on the basis of experience gained, an integrated policy for the development of territories might best be implemented, forming the basis of the following projects in particular:

– population and labour catchment areas, i.e. towns, suburban areas and the adjacent rural areas;

– territories which justify specific thematic approaches, such as mountain ranges, large wooded areas, national parks, river basins, coastal areas, island regions and environmentally degraded areas, to develop place-based approaches (European Parliament 2008b: 5-6).

Appendix 3: Extracts from the Committee of the Regions' White Paper on Multilevel Governance (2009)

Governance is one of the main keys to the success of the process of European integration. Europe will be strong, its institutions legitimate, its policies effective, and its citizens feeling involved and engaged if its mode of governance guarantees cooperation between the different tiers of government, in order to implement the Community agenda and meet the global challenges. This was acknowledged by the Heads of State or of Government in the Berlin Declaration on 25 March 2007. By recognising the scope of multilevel governance, they accepted the vision and conception of Europe that the Committee of the Regions had formulated a few days earlier in its Declaration of Rome.

Within the European Union nearly 95 000 local and regional authorities currently have significant powers in key sectors such as education, the environment, economic development, town and country planning, transport, public services and social policies. They also help ensure the exercise of European democracy and citizenship. Both the closeness to the citizens and the diversity of governance at local and regional level is a real asset to the Union. However, despite significant advances having been made in recent years in terms of recognising their role in the European process, substantial progress has yet to be achieved, both at Community level and within the Member States. Change will be gradual, but real efforts are now needed to do away with such administrative cultures that stand in the way of the ongoing processes of decentralisation (Committee of the Regions 2009: 3).

The EU's ability to adapt to the new global context actually depends largely on the potential of its regions to react, act and interact. [...] Multilevel governance actually serves the fundamental political objectives of the European Union: a Europe of citizens, economic growth and social progress, sustainable development, and the role of the European Union as a global player. It reinforces the democratic dimension of the European Union and increases the efficiency of its processes. It does not, however, apply to all EU policies, and when it does, it rarely applies symmetrically or homogenously.

The activities carried out by the Committee of the Regions and the recommendations made are based on the Treaties, but nevertheless reflect the prospect of the entry into force of the Lisbon Treaty, which enshrines the territorial dimension, notably territorial cohesion, as part of the process of European integration and strengthens the mechanisms of multilevel governance.

Establishing genuine multilevel governance in Europe has always been the strategic priority of the Committee of the Regions. It has now become a condition of good European governance. This White Paper acknowledges this priority, proposes clear policy options for improving European governance and recommends specific mechanisms and instruments for stimulating all stages of the European decision-making process. It identifies lines of action and discussion, which may facilitate, in the interests of the citizens, the design and implementation of Community policies, it makes commitments to develop these and it offers illustrations of shared governance. In addition, it represents an initial contribution by the Committee of the Regions to the Reflection Group that has been given the task by the European Council of helping the European Union to anticipate and meet challenges more effectively in the longer term (i.e. 2020-2030), taking the Berlin Declaration of 25 March 2007 as its starting point. [...]

The legitimacy, efficiency and visibility of the way the Community operates depend on contributions from all the various players. They are guaranteed if local and regional authorities are genuine "partners" rather than mere "intermediaries". Partnership goes beyond participation and consultation, promoting a more dynamic approach and greater responsibility for the various players. Accordingly, the challenge of multilevel governance is to ensure that there is a complementary balance between institutional governance and partnership-based governance. The development of political and administrative culture in the European Union must therefore be encouraged and stimulated. The European public seems to want it (Committee of the Regions 2009: 4-5).

The Committee of the Regions considers multilevel governance to mean coordinated action by the European Union, the Member States and local and regional authorities, based on partnership and aimed at drawing up and implementing EU policies. It leads to responsibility being shared between the different tiers of government concerned and is underpinned by all sources of democratic legitimacy and the representative nature of the different players involved. By means of an integrated approach, it entails the joint participation of the different tiers of government in the formulation of Community policies and legislation, with the aid of various mechanisms (consultation, territorial impact analyses, etc.).

Multilevel governance is a dynamic process with a horizontal and vertical dimension, which does not in any way dilute political responsibility. On the contrary, if the mechanisms and instruments are appropriate and applied correctly, it helps to increase joint ownership and implementation. Consequently, multilevel governance represents a political "action blueprint" rather than a legal instrument and cannot be understood solely through the lens of the division of powers (Committee of the Regions 2009: 6).

The implementation of multilevel governance depends on respect for the principle of subsidiarity, which prevents decisions from being restricted to a single tier of government and which guarantees that policies are conceived and applied at the most appropriate level. Respect for the principle of subsidiarity and multilevel governance are in dissociable: one indicates the responsibilities of the different tiers of government, whilst the other emphasises their interaction. [...]

Multilevel governance is not simply a question of translating European or national objectives into local or regional action, but must also be understood as a process for integrating the objectives of local and regional authorities within the strategies of the European Union. Moreover, multilevel governance should reinforce and shape the responsibilities of local and regional authorities at national level and encourage their participation in the coordination of European policy, in this way helping to design and implement Community policies. The conditions for good multilevel governance actually depend on the Member States themselves. Although there is a clear trend in Europe towards a process of decentralisation, which is certainly not uniform but nonetheless widespread, the conditions for this shared governance have not yet been met in full. The principles and mechanisms of consultation, coordination, cooperation and evaluation recommended at Community level must firstly be applied within the Member States (Committee of the Regions 2009: 7).

Guaranteed since the Treaty of Maastricht, institutional representation for local and regional authorities has been strengthened in the course of the successive institutional reforms. The entry into force of the Lisbon Treaty would represent an important step towards institutional recognition of multilevel governance in the way the European Union operates. In this respect, strengthening the representation and influence of local and regional authorities in the Community decision-making process must be encouraged both within the Committee of the Regions and in the activities of the Council of the European Union. Since 1994 the Treaties have allowed the regions, in accordance with the respective national constitutional structures, to participate in the activities of the Council of the European Union. This direct participation allows the representatives of the regions concerned to be included in Member State delegations, to be authorised to lead the national delegation and, where necessary, to assume the presidency of the Council (Committee of the Regions 2009: 9).

Multilevel governance presupposes the existence of mutual loyalty between all the various levels of government and the institutions to reach common goals. The institutional framework is fundamental but is not enough to guarantee good governance. On the contrary, good cooperation between the various levels of political power and the institutions is absolutely vital; it has to be based on trust, rather than on confrontation between the different legitimate political and democratic roles.

European democracy would be reinforced by more inclusive and flexible interinstitutional cooperation and by more sustained political cooperation between the various levels of power; European political parties, which are a particularly important element for strengthening the European political sphere and thus helping to develop a political culture of multilevel governance. Because of the political nature of the Committee of the Regions and the European Parliament, it is logical that they should work closely together to strengthen the democratic legitimacy of the process of European integration, both in the context of the European political groups and families, and also in the context of their various decision-making bodies.

Interparliamentary cooperation is gradually becoming a vital component of democratic legitimacy and of the process of drafting European legislation. Multilevel governance is a way of also involving all local and regional authorities more explicitly in the process. In particular, under the "early warning" mechanism proposed in the Lisbon Treaty, regional parliaments and regional legislative assemblies will be able to play a part in appraising the application of the subsidiarity principle (Committee of the Regions 2009: 10-11).

Territorial cohesion, which with the Treaty of Lisbon becomes a responsibility shared between the European Union and Member States, must be present in all sectoral policies and must become an incarnation of multilevel governance. Urban governance is also vital for the successful implementation of sustainable development strategies in urban areas, not only to coordinate all the tiers of government but also to involve local players. Urban governance in an integrated approach must tackle the three pillars of sustainable development – the environment, the economy and social issues – in order to guarantee real social and territorial cohesion. Other common policies are also appropriate to foster an integrated and coherent approach. Integrated strategies should be drawn up for rural areas which are based on multi-level governance and are designed to boost sustainable development and competitiveness. These strategies should contain measures designed to tackle the regions' natural handicaps, together with the imbalances between these areas and urban areas (Committee of the Regions 2009: 24).

Appendix 4: Extracts from the Committee of the Regions' Scoreboard Table with MLG best-practices and recommendations (2013)

Table 1 Overview of the CoR's MLG best-practice and recommendations

Process and Content	Best-practice	Recommendations
Information and consultation	Open, transparent and timely consultations that allow the LRAs to prepare a contribution. Developed longstanding information channels between the COM and LRAs. LRAs' awareness of the EU policy-making processes.	Raise awareness about the importance of the participation in the public consultations organised by the COM. Coordinate better the public contribution to consultation between the LRAs and the CoR. Prioritise policies relevant for the RLAs for efficient use of administrative resources. Establish a two-way communication with the Com by contributing to the surveys and questionnaires.
Stakeholders' involvement	Allocated administrative resources for the contribution to the consultations. Coordination of opinions between the CoR and the LRAs through CoR's network mechanisms.	Effective management of administrative resources for priority policies during the open consultations. Use of the existing networks mechanisms to foster interests and concerns of the regions.
Responsiveness	An informal dialogue between the CoR and the EP for better policy-making. Opened discussions between the COM and the EP on the integration of LRAs' proposals.	Monitor closely and assess the proposals of the public consultations. Analyse if such proposals were included in the policy drafts. Explain the rejected LRAs' proposals. Informal communication for a beneficial partnership with the EP and the COM.
Territorial	Extensive discus-	Respect territorial needs by streamlin-

209

and integrated approach	sion of the territorial dimension in the EU regulations.	ing a territorial and place-based approach that takes into account the territorial specificities and does not jeopardise the flexibility at the local and regional levels.
Innovative instruments for implementation in partnerships	Concrete instruments, e.g., territorial pacts were promoted. The CoR and the LRAs promoted the debate on innovative instruments, influencing the positions of the EU institutions.	Raise awareness and understanding of the partnership principle, the mutuality and the inter-institutional balance. Inform the EU institutions of the lacking resources for the implementation of innovative instruments that impede their effective use.

Author's table based on Committee of the Regions 2013: 23-26.

Appendix 5: Extracts from the Europe 2020 Strategy (2010)

Europe 2020 puts forward three mutually reinforcing priorities:
– Smart growth: developing an economy based on knowledge and innovation.
– Sustainable growth: promoting a more resource efficient, greener and more competitive economy.
– Inclusive growth: fostering a high-employment economy delivering social and territorial cohesion.

The EU needs to define where it wants to be by 2020. To this end, the Commission proposes the following EU headline targets:
– 75 % of the population aged 20-64 should be employed.
– 3% of the EU's GDP should be invested in R&D.
– The "20/20/20" climate/energy targets should be met (including an increase to 30% of emissions reduction if the conditions are right).
– The share of early school leavers should be under 10% and at least 40% of the younger generation should have a tertiary degree.
– 20 million less people should be at risk of poverty.

These targets are interrelated and critical to our overall success. To ensure that each Member State tailors the Europe 2020 strategy to its particular situation, the Commission proposes that EU goals are translated into national targets and trajectories. The targets are representative of the three priorities of smart, sustainable and inclusive growth but they are not exhaustive: a wide range of actions at national, EU and international levels will be necessary to underpin them. The Commission is putting forward seven flagship initiatives to catalyse progress under each priority theme:

– "Innovation Union" to improve framework conditions and access to finance for research and innovation so as to ensure that innovative ideas can be turned into products and services that create growth and jobs.
– "Youth on the move" to enhance the performance of education systems and to facilitate the entry of young people to the labour market.
– "A digital agenda for Europe" to speed up the roll-out of high-speed internet and reap the benefits of a digital single market for households and firms.
– "Resource efficient Europe" to help decouple economic growth from the use of resources, support the shift towards a low carbon economy, increase the use of renewable energy sources, modernise our transport sector and promote energy efficiency.
– "An industrial policy for the globalisation era" to improve the business environment, notably for SMEs, and to support the development of a strong and sustainable industrial base able to compete globally.
– "An agenda for new skills and jobs" to modernise labour markets and empower people by developing their of skills throughout the lifecycle with a view to increase labour participation and better match labour supply and demand, including through labour mobility.
– "European platform against poverty" to ensure social and territorial cohesion such that the benefits of growth and jobs are widely shared and people experiencing

poverty and social exclusion are enabled to live in dignity and take an active part in society (European Commission 2010: 3-4).

Smart growth means strengthening knowledge and innovation as drivers of our future growth. This requires improving the quality of our education, strengthening our research performance, promoting innovation and knowledge transfer throughout the Union, making full use of information and communication technologies and ensuring that innovative ideas can be turned into new products and services that create growth, quality jobs and help address European and global societal challenges. But, to succeed, this must be combined with entrepreneurship, finance, and a focus on user needs and market opportunities (European Commission 2010: 9-10).

Flagship Initiative: "Innovation Union"

The aim of this is to re-focus R&D and innovation policy on the challenges facing our society, such as climate change, energy and resource efficiency, health and demographic change. Every link should be strengthened in the innovation chain, from 'blue sky' research to commercialisation (European Commission 2010: 10).

Flagship initiative: "Youth on the move"

The aim is to enhance the performance and international attractiveness of Europe's higher education institutions and raise the overall quality of all levels of education and training in the EU, combining both excellence and equity, by promoting student mobility and trainees' mobility, and improve the employment situation of young people (European Commission 2010: 11).

Flagship Initiative: "A Digital Agenda for Europe"

The aim is to deliver sustainable economic and social benefits from a Digital Single Market based on fast and ultra-fast internet and interoperable applications, with broadband access for all by 2013, access for all to much higher internet speeds (30 Mbps or above) by 2020, and 50% or more of European households subscribing to internet connections above 100 Mbps. [...]

Sustainable growth – promoting a more resource efficient, greener and more competitive economy

Sustainable growth means building a resource efficient, sustainable and competitive economy, exploiting Europe's leadership in the race to develop new processes and technologies, including green technologies, accelerating the roll out of smart grids using ICTs, exploiting EU-scale networks, and reinforcing the competitive advantages of our businesses, particularly in manufacturing and within our SMEs, as well through assisting consumers to value resource efficiency. Such an approach will help the EU to prosper in a low-carbon, resource constrained world while preventing environmental degradation, biodiversity loss and unsustainable use of resources. It will also underpin economic, social and territorial cohesion (European Commission 2010: 12).

Flagship Initiative: "Resource efficient Europe"

The aim is to support the shift towards a resource efficient and low-carbon economy that is efficient in the way it uses all resources. The aim is to decouple our economic growth from resource and energy use, reduce CO_2 emissions, enhance competitiveness and promote greater energy security (European Commission 2010: 13).

Flagship Initiative: "An industrial policy for the globalisation era"

Industry and especially SMEs have been hit hard by the economic crisis and all sectors are facing the challenges of globalisation and adjusting their production processes and products to a low-carbon economy. The impact of these challenges will differ from sector to sector, some sectors might have to "reinvent" themselves but for others these challenges will present new business opportunities. The Commission will work closely with stakeholders in different sectors (business, trade unions, academics, NGOs, consumer organisations) and will draw up a framework for a modern industrial policy, to support entrepreneurship, to guide and help industry to become fit to meet these challenges, to promote the competitiveness of Europe's primary, manufacturing and service industries and help them seize the opportunities of globalisation and of the green economy. The framework will address all elements of the increasingly international value chain from access to raw materials to after-sales service (European Commission 2010: 14).

Inclusive growth – a high-employment economy delivering economic, social and territorial cohesion

Inclusive growth means empowering people through high levels of employment, investing in skills, fighting poverty and modernising labour markets, training and social protection systems so as to help people anticipate and manage change, and build a cohesive society. It is also essential that the benefits of economic growth spread to all parts of the Union, including its outermost regions, thus strengthening territorial cohesion. It is about ensuring access and opportunities for all throughout the lifecycle. Europe needs to make full use of its labour potential to face the challenges of an ageing population and rising global competition. Policies to promote gender equality will be needed to increase labour force participation thus adding to growth and social cohesion (European Commission 2010: 15).

Flagship Initiative: "An Agenda for new skills and jobs"

The aim is to create conditions for modernising labour markets with a view to raising employment levels and ensuring the sustainability of our social models. This means empowering people through the acquisition of new skills to enable our current and future workforce to adapt to new conditions and potential career shifts, reduce unemployment and raise labour productivity" (European Commission 2010: 16).

Flagship Initiative: "European Platform against Poverty"

The aim is to ensure economic, social and territorial cohesion, building on the current European year for combating poverty and social exclusion so as to raise awareness and recognise the fundamental rights of people experiencing poverty and social exclusion, enabling them to live in dignity and take an active part in society (European Commission 2010: 17).

Appendix 6: Article 5 Common Provisions Regulation (2013)

Article 5 Partnership and multi-level governance

1. For the Partnership Agreement and each programme, each Member State shall in accordance with its institutional and legal framework organise a partnership with the competent regional and local authorities. The partnership shall also include the following partners:

(a) competent urban and other public authorities;

(b) economic and social partners; and

(c) relevant bodies representing civil society, including environmental partners, non-governmental organisations, and bodies responsible for promoting social inclusion, gender equality and non-discrimination.

2. In accordance with the multi-level governance approach, the partners referred to in paragraph 1 shall be involved by Member States in the preparation of Partnership Agreements and progress reports and throughout the preparation and implementation of programmes, including through participation in the monitoring committees for programmes in accordance with Article 48.

3. The Commission shall be empowered to adopt a delegated act in accordance with Article 149 to provide for a European code of conduct on partnership (the 'code of conduct') in order to support and facilitate Member States in the organisation of partnership in accordance with paragraphs 1 and 2 of this Article. The code of conduct shall set out the framework within which the Member States, in accordance with their institutional and legal framework as well as their national and regional competences, shall pursue the implementation of partnership. The code of conduct, while fully respecting the principles of subsidiarity and proportionality, shall lay down the following elements:

(a) the main principles concerning transparent procedures to be followed for the identification of the relevant partners including, where appropriate, their umbrella organisations in order to facilitate Member States in designating the most representative relevant partners, in accordance with their institutional and legal framework;

(b) the main principles and good practices concerning the involvement of the different categories of relevant partners set out in paragraph 1 in the preparation of the Partnership Agreement and programmes, the information to be provided concerning their involvement, and at the various stages of implementation;

(c) the good practices concerning the formulation of the rules of membership and internal procedures of monitoring committees to be decided, as appropriate, by the Member States or the monitoring committees of programmes in accordance with the relevant provisions of this Regulation and the Fund-specific rules;

(d) the main objectives and good practices in cases where the managing authority involves the relevant partners in the preparation of calls for proposals and in particular good practices for avoiding potential conflicts of interest in cases where there is a possibility of relevant partners also being potential beneficiaries, and for the involvement of the relevant partners in the preparation of progress reports and in relation to monitoring and evaluation of programmes in accordance with the relevant provisions of this Regulation and the Fund-specific rules;

(e) the indicative areas, themes and good practices concerning how the competent authorities of the Member States may use the ESI Funds including technical assistance to strengthen the institutional capacity of relevant partners in accordance with the relevant provisions of this Regulation and the Fund-specific rules;

(f) the role of the Commission in the dissemination of good practices;

(g) the main principles and good practices that are apt to facilitate the Member States' assessment of the implementation of partnership and its added value. The provisions of the code of conduct shall not in any way contradict the relevant provisions of this Regulation or the Fund-specific rules.

4. The Commission shall notify the delegated act, referred to in paragraph 3 of this Article, on the European code of conduct on partnership, simultaneously to the European Parliament and to the Council by 18 April 2014. That delegated act shall not specify a date of application that is earlier than the date of its adoption.

5. An infringement of any obligation imposed on Member States either by this Article or by the delegated act adopted pursuant to paragraph 3 of this Article, shall not constitute an irregularity leading to a financial correction pursuant to Article 85.

6. At least once a year, for each ESI Fund, the Commission shall consult the organisations which represent the partners at Union level on the implementation of support from that ESI Fund and shall report to the European Parliament and the Council on the outcome (Official Journal of the European Union 2013: L347/341).

Appendix 7: Key recommendations for regional authorities in chemical regions (2012)

- Regional policy makers should aim at mobilising resources at other levels (national, EU, global) in a targeted way to best serve the specific needs of their chemical region. The connection to EU policies can be made through such existing platforms as ChemClust, ChemLog and ECRN.
- Regional authorities should aim at ensuring that regional policies and programs first support an effective process of identifying the action priorities, and evaluating their success perspectives, and then provide the right tools to address whatever those priorities are. Regional authorities should communicate with businesses in a service-oriented way to achieve the goals that underlie these priorities.
- Cluster policies should be discussed with local companies, and designed in a way that captures the interest of the companies. They should involve companies of all sizes, both large and small. Policies should be managed in a way to ensure trust among authorities and companies but also between the partners.
- The regional authorities should ensure their awareness of the relative strengths and weaknesses of related RDI policies and funding sources and use this information to design and continuously improve their own policies, and to advise companies in a service-oriented way.
- The regional authorities should ensure that a thorough and dynamic analysis of the gap between supply and demand of skills is conducted at the regional level. The regional authorities should actively involve the regional chemicals industry when conducting the gap analysis, so that the data and dynamics on the demand for skills are appropriately taken into account.
- Administrative and legal procedures need to be designed or amended in such a way that new forms of interaction between industry, regional and national government, and other stakeholders are encouraged, and that interaction is not hampered in its effectiveness.
- Regional authorities should aim to create a platform for public-private cooperation to achieve environmental and sustainability goals. These goals should be clearly defined and policies should be embedded in clear structures. Policies should aim at being concrete and fitting into company reality. Regional authorities should provide services to make policies, legal obligations and opportunities easily understood. Administrative burden should be eliminated as far as possible.
- Regional authorities and local industry need to engage in active dialogue to realise sustainable industry. The dialogue ensures that local needs are identified, and contributes to a common goal among the various stakeholders.
- Regional authorities need to ensure that there is strong external communication to clearly communicate the benefits of the policies. A clear presentation of the (expected) benefits that underlines the advantages for all stakeholder

groups ensures that expectations are aligned and helps to involve stakeholders.
- Regional authorities need to identify and address local (future) demand for logistics and infrastructure in order to both contribute effectively to national policies as well as design their own.
- Regional authorities should strive for transparent decision making to ensure the acceptance of new policies or regulation.
- Relevant stakeholder groups should be informed in an appropriate way, consulted and be invited to take part in the discussions.
- Regional authorities need to engage in active dialogue with both local industry and other relevant regional authorities, as well as with relevant local, national and international authorities, in order to address transregional infrastructural challenges in an effective manner (European Commission 2012: 12-14).

Index

Activity, 26, 27, 28, 31, 43, 55, 69, 72, 87, 92, 101, 106, 107, 109, 111, 116, 120, 136, 145, 146, 155, 159, 162, 168
Barnier, Michel, 97, 117
Barroso, Manuel, 94, 105
best-practice, 13, 37, 38, 43, 86, 143, 151, 152, 154, 155, 171
Böhmer, Wolfgang, 70, 72, 80, 81, 87, 88, 96, 98, 117, 119, 157
Bullerjahn, Jens, 89, 96
Bundesrat, 19, 45, 62, 64, 65, 66, 68, 69, 71, 72, 87, 94, 115, 120, 121, 127, 128, 129, 138, 158, 159
Bundesregierung, 19, 71
Bundestag, 19, 64, 65, 66, 71, 72, 79, 88
Cohesion Policy, 16, 35, 38, 40, 41, 84, 88, 93, 95, 96, 97, 105, 106, 114, 116, 117, 119, 120, 136, 140, 170
Commission, 17, 18, 21, 22, 25, 26, 31, 32, 34, 35, 39, 40, 41, 46, 63, 65, 69, 70, 72, 74, 77, 80, 81, 82, 84, 85, 87, 93, 94, 95, 96, 97, 103, 105, 109, 110, 111, 113, 115, 116, 118, 119, 121, 122, 125, 126, 129, 130, 132, 133, 134, 135, 138, 139, 140, 141, 142, 143, 144, 145, 146, 149, 150, 152, 153, 154, 155, 158, 160, 161, 162, 163, 168, 169, 170
Competencies, 15, 21, 22, 25, 27, 29, 31, 45, 49, 62, 63, 64, 65, 66, 67, 77, 83, 113, 124, 130, 143
Cooperation, 27, 29, 32, 34, 35, 36, 37, 39, 45, 56, 58, 59, 62, 64, 65, 68, 69, 71, 72, 74, 75, 78, 80, 83, 87, 88, 91, 92, 93, 96, 100, 101, 103, 104, 105, 106, 110, 111, 115, 116, 118, 119, 120, 121,122, 124, 125, 127, 128, 129, 130, 131, 132, 133, 134, 135, 136, 137, 138, 139, 140, 141, 143, 144, 146, 147, 149, 150, 151, 152, 153, 154, 155, 157, 159, 160, 162, 163, 164, 165, 167, 170
Coordination, 15, 17, 32, 71, 92, 94, 103, 111, 159, 163, 171
Council, 21, 27, 39, 43, 57, 58, 61, 63, 64, 65, 66, 69, 71, 72, 81, 93, 97, 104, 105, 110, 119, 120, 121, 135, 136, 137, 138, 142, 146, 153, 160, 162, 168
Development, 16, 17, 21, 22, 23, 24, 25, 26, 27, 28, 29, 32, 35, 36, 40, 42, 44, 49, 50, 51, 52, 53, 55, 56, 57, 58, 59, 61, 71, 72, 73, 74, 78, 79, 80, 81, 82, 83, 84, 85, 87, 89, 90, 91, 92, 93, 94, 95, 96, 98, 99, 100, 101, 102, 103, 104, 105, 106, 110, 111, 112, 113, 114, 118, 120, 123, 125, 127, 128, 129, 130, 131, 132, 133, 135, 136, 137, 139, 140, 141, 142, 143, 144, 145, 147, 148, 149, 150, 151, 152, 153, 155, 157, 158, 160, 162, 163, 164, 165, 168, 169, 170, 171
European Chemical Regions Network (ECRN), 45, 74, 85, 88, 97, 98, 100, 116, 123, 130,

131, 133, 134, 135, 136, 137, 138, 139, 140, 141, 142, 143, 144, 145, 146, 147, 148, 149, 150, 151, 152, 153, 154, 155, 162, 163, 164, 165, 169

European Chemicals Policy, 18, 107, 123, 135, 137, 139, 154

European integration, 13, 15, 16, 21, 23, 24, 26, 28, 29, 30, 31, 34, 47, 49, 61, 63, 66, 72, 121, 168

European Multi-Level Governance (EMLG), 13, 15, 16, 17, 18, 21, 22, 24, 26, 28, 29, 30, 32, 33, 34, 35, 36, 38, 39, 41, 42, 43, 44, 45, 46, 47, 49, 55, 69, 73, 75, 77, 79, 80, 83, 84, 85, 86, 88, 90, 91, 92, 93, 94, 95, 96, 97, 103, 105, 107, 109, 114, 115, 116, 120, 121, 122, 123, 124, 126, 127, 130, 131, 137, 141, 147, 150, 151, 152, 153, 154, 155, 157, 158, 160, 161, 162, 163, 164, 165, 166, 167, 168, 169, 170, 171

European Parliament, 18, 21, 35, 37, 39, 40, 41, 46, 63, 69, 85, 110, 115, 132, 134, 160, 168, 169

European Regional Policy, 13, 16, 17, 18, 21, 22, 23, 28, 31, 32, 33, 34, 39, 79, 82, 83, 84, 93, 99, 105, 107, 109, 110, 111, 112, 114, 115, 117, 118, 119, 120, 121, 122, 131, 137, 140, 141, 158, 161, 168

Europeanisation, 21, 24, 49, 62, 70, 102, 107

Federal government, 16, 25, 56, 62, 63, 64, 67, 72, 93, 104, 115, 116, 119, 152

Framework, 13, 18, 21, 23, 24, 25, 27, 28, 31, 33, 39, 41, 42, 44, 45, 47, 49, 58, 59, 61, 62, 66, 68, 69, 74, 82, 88, 89, 91, 92, 95, 98, 99, 104, 110, 112, 115, 116, 119, 121, 125, 126, 136, 139, 140, 143, 144, 147, 148, 157, 163, 164, 165, 167, 168, 169, 170

Genscher, Hans-Dietrich, 56, 58

Gies, Gerd, 58, 67

Goals, 17, 18, 23, 24, 28, 29, 30 32, 35, 44, 45, 47, 49, 61, 80, 81, 84, 85, 86, 88, 89, 92, 97, 98, 99, 102, 103, 105, 106, 109, 112, 114, 115, 118, 121, 122, 123, 124, 125, 127, 128, 132, 134, 136, 137, 140, 141, 144, 146, 147, 151, 153, 157, 162, 163, 164, 165, 167, 169, 170

Governance, 13, 15, 16, 17, 18, 21, 27, 30, 31, 32, 33, 34, 35, 36, 37, 38, 39, 40, 41, 42, 43, 45, 49, 64, 75, 77, 80, 94, 97, 109, 120, 122, 123, 125, 127, 130, 131, 132, 153, 155, 157, 158, 160, 161, 162, 164, 165, 167, 168

Grünwald, Siegfried, 57, 58

Hahn, Johannes, 40, 104, 120

Haseloff, Reiner, 97, 100, 101, 103, 104, 116, 142, 144, 146, 149

High Level Group (HLG), 81, 98, 100, 107, 136, 139, 141 142, 143, 144, 145, 146, 147, 148, 150, 151, 154

Höppner, Reinhard, 70, 78, 79, 132
Hübner, Danuta, 95, 104, 117
Incentive(s), 28, 42, 43, 45, 49, 59, 109, 123, 124, 130, 136, 140, 149, 164, 167
Information, 16, 27, 29, 31, 35, 38, 41, 45, 46, 64, 65, 67, 68, 70, 71, 72, 82, 84, 85, 86, 88, 92, 93, 94, 97, 98, 100, 102, 103, 105, 113, 116, 120, 121, 122, 124, 126, 131, 135, 137, 138, 139, 144, 146, 148, 149, 150, 151, 153, 158, 159, 160, 161, 162, 163, 164
Interdependence(ies), 15, 17, 22, 28, 31, 42, 43, 49, 83, 85, 90, 97, 115, 144, 147, 152, 165, 167, 168
Interests, 15, 16, 17, 21, 24, 25, 26, 27, 28, 29, 31, 32, 38, 42, 43, 45, 46, 49, 50, 53, 54, 57, 59, 61, 63, 64, 67, 70, 71, 72, 73, 74, 77, 80, 83, 84, 86, 87, 89, 92, 93, 94, 96, 97, 98, 100, 101, 106, 109, 110, 115, 121, 124, 125, 127, 128, 129, 132, 133, 134, 135, 136, 137, 138, 149, 150, 153, 154, 157, 158, 159, 160, 161, 162, 163, 165, 167, 169, 171
Jurisdiction, 15, 31, 32, 33, 63, 72, 115, 124, 152, 159, 168
Kolodniak, Alfred, 57, 58
Land, 19, 24, 25, 26, 40, 45, 50, 52, 53, 54, 55, 56, 57, 58, 59, 61, 63, 64, 65, 66, 67, 68, 69, 70, 71, 72, 74, 78, 79, 80, 81, 83, 84, 85, 86, 87, 88, 89, 90, 91, 92, 93, 94, 95, 96, 97, 98, 99, 100, 101, 102, 103, 104, 105, 106, 107, 111, 115, 116, 117, 118, 119, 120, 121, 124, 127, 128, 129, 131, 132, 133, 134, 135, 136, 138, 139, 141, 142, 144, 145, 147, 148, 149, 150, 151, 153, 154, 155, 158, 159, 160, 161
Länder, 15, 19, 25, 26, 31, 36, 49, 55, 57, 58, 59, 61, 62, 63, 64, 65, 66, 67, 68, 71, 72, 73, 74, 78, 84, 86, 87, 88, 89, 90, 94, 98, 99, 101, 104, 107, 109, 115, 117, 118, 119, 120, 130, 138, 146, 147, 157, 159, 160, 162
Landesregierung, 19, 45, 57, 68, 69, 70, 71, 72, 83, 84, 114, 115, 121, 160
Landtag, 19, 45, 55, 56, 65, 66, 67, 68, 69, 71, 72, 79, 80, 81, 83, 84, 85, 89, 92, 93, 94, 96, 97, 98, 99, 106, 114, 116, 118, 121, 131, 158, 159, 161
Meaning, 13, 18, 22, 27, 32, 38, 44, 77, 83, 91, 130, 142, 170
Merkel, Angela, 93, 94, 104
Mobilisation, 15, 16, 17, 18, 22, 23, 24, 25, 26, 27, 29, 31, 35, 36, 42, 43, 45, 49, 53, 55, 59, 61, 77, 83, 85, 107, 109, 122, 123, 124, 126, 127, 131, 134, 136, 137, 141, 147, 149, 150, 151, 152, 153, 154, 155, 157, 158, 161, 162, 163, 164, 167, 168, 169, 170
Network(s), 17, 27, 29, 30, 31, 32, 36, 37, 45, 51, 52, 54, 68, 74, 78, 81, 85, 88, 92, 97, 102, 105, 119, 123, 128, 129, 131, 132, 133, 134, 135, 136, 137, 138, 141, 143, 144, 145,

148, 149, 150, 151, 152, 153, 154, 158, 161, 162, 163, 164, 169, 171

Partnership(s), 34, 35, 36, 37, 39, 40, 41, 46, 58, 74, 78, 81, 84, 86, 87, 90, 95, 110, 111, 112, 113, 116, 119, 124, 130, 132, 137, 139, 140, 141, 144, 148, 150, 151, 153, 154, 159, 162, 164

Pattern(s), 13, 17, 18, 19, 29, 32, 42, 43, 44, 46, 47, 97, 125, 149, 150, 157, 162

Policy-making, 15, 16, 22, 25, 27, 28, 30, 32, 34, 37, 40, 45, 47, 49, 62, 63, 65, 82, 89, 95, 109, 114, 120, 123, 124, 125, 126, 128, 136, 137, 138, 148, 149, 151, 152, 153, 154, 161, 168, 170

Prioritisation, 18, 45, 77, 96, 103, 117

Private actors, 15, 59, 85, 126, 163, 167

Public actors, 15, 123, 125, 127, 142, 167

Qualitative analysis, 13, 18, 28, 43, 44, 168

Regional parliament(s), 46, 62, 66, 67, 68, 73, 158, 169

Regional participation, 13, 15, 16, 17, 18, 21, 22, 26, 28, 29, 30, 33, 35, 36, 41, 43, 44, 47, 49, 69, 80, 85, 97, 103, 109, 114, 123, 138, 147, 153, 154, 155, 157, 163, 164, 165, 166, 168

Resources, 17, 27, 29, 35, 37, 38, 39, 40, 44, 45, 46, 47, 55, 56, 80, 82, 88, 89, 96, 99, 102, 109, 111, 112, 114, 115, 116, 122, 123, 124, 127, 130, 131, 134, 137, 140, 142, 144, 145, 147, 148, 151, 153, 155, 163, 164, 165, 169, 170

Robra, Rainer, 71, 94, 116, 161

Schneider, Michael, 38, 39, 70, 71, 72, 86, 94, 106, 116, 117, 118, 119

Schnellhardt, Horst, 85, 105

Stakeholders, 18, 38, 39, 73, 96, 111, 123, 125, 134, 137, 138, 140, 146, 149, 155, 162, 163, 169

Strategy, 17, 18, 29, 38, 42, 43, 45, 46, 47, 52, 59, 61, 62, 65, 71, 77, 80, 81, 82, 83, 85, 86, 91, 92, 97, 98, 102, 103, 104, 105, 106, 111, 112, 113, 114, 115, 120, 121, 124, 125, 127, 128, 129, 130, 132, 133 135, 138, 139, 140, 141, 143, 147, 148, 150, 157, 161, 162, 163, 164, 169

Subnational actors, 25, 26, 27, 28, 29, 32, 33, 34, 49, 62, 77, 96, 116, 125, 153, 160, 162, 164, 167, 168, 169, 170, 171

Territorial, 16, 22, 23, 24, 25, 26, 28, 31, 32, 33, 34, 36, 38, 39, 40, 41, 42, 44, 53, 59, 62, 65, 80, 90, 91, 94, 95, 96, 106, 110, 111, 112, 113, 115, 116, 118, 119, 120, 140, 157, 163, 165, 168

van Rompuy, Herman, 104, 105, 120

Verheugen, Günter, 94, 117, 145

Wallström, Margot, 87, 139

Wobben, Thomas, 116, 133, 142

budrich journals

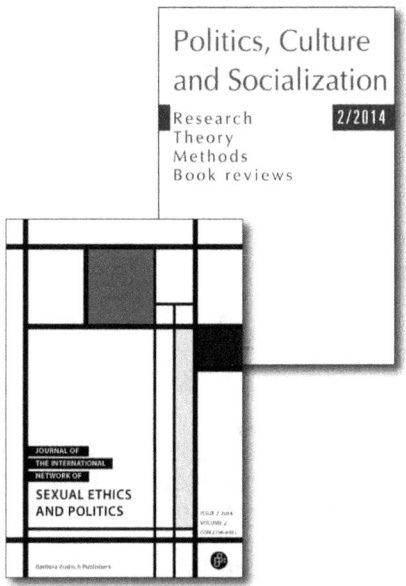

- Single article download
- Print + online
- Subscription
- Free content:
  ToCs
  editorials
  Book review
  open access content

Barbara Budrich Publishers
Stauffenbergstr. 7
51379 Leverkusen-Opladen

ph +49 (0)2171.344.594
fx +49 (0)2171.344.693
info@budrich-journals.com

Find our journals on www.budrich-journals.com

Schreiben, Publizieren, Präsentieren

budrich training
bietet Schulungen für Studierende und AkademikerInnen in den Schlüsselkompetenzen der wissenschaftlichen Kommunikation – auf Deutsch und auf Englisch.

Workshops, Vorträge, Seminare:
- Wissenschaftliches Schreiben
- Wissenschaftliches Publizieren
- Präsentieren und Moderieren

Wir bieten auch Einzelberatungen und Coachings.

budrich training – Schlüsselkompetenzen in der Wissenschaft

Wir freuen uns auf Ihre Anfrage:
budrich training
Stauffenbergstr. 7. D-51379 Leverkusen Opladen
Tel +49 (0)2171.344.594 • Fax +49 (0)2171.344.693 •
info@budrich.de

www.budrich-academic.de • www.budrich-training.de

GPSR Authorized Representative: Easy Access System Europe, Mustamäe tee 50, 10621 Tallinn, Estonia, gpsr.requests@easproject.com

www.ingramcontent.com/pod-product-compliance
Lightning Source LLC
Chambersburg PA
CBHW051541020426
42333CB00016B/2036